From the
Risale-i Nur Collection

THE
LETTERS

2

Said Nursi

TRUESTAR

Published by
Truestar (London) Ltd
PO Box 2881
London N3 UD

Printed and bound in Turkey
by Caglayan A.S.

British Library Cataloguing in Publication Data. A catalogue
record for this book is available from the British Library.

Contents

The
Twentieth
Letter

Aspects of the Divine Unity

In His Name, Glory be to Him.
There is nothing that does not glorify Him with praise.

In the Name of God the Merciful, the Compassionate

There is no god but God, One having no partner; His is the Kingdom and to Him belongs all praise; He alone gives life and makes to die; He is living and dies not; in His hand is all good and He is powerful over everything, and unto Him is the return.

This sentence affirming the Divine Unity, which it is very meritorious to repeat after the prescribed prayers at the beginning and the end of the day, and equal in worth to the Greatest Name of God, comprises eleven phrases. Each phrase carries a distinct message of good tidings for human beings. In each is displayed and manifested a different aspect of the Unity of Lordship in a degree equal to the manifestation of one of the Greatest Names, a ray of the magnificence of the Divine Singularity and a perfection of the Divine Oneness. Referring the reader to *The Words* for a full explanation of such sublime truth, I will here summarize it in the form of an introduction and two stations.

1

INTRODUCTION

Be certain of this, that the highest aim of creation and its most sublime result is *belief in God*. The most exalted rank of humanity is the *knowledge of God*. The most radiant happiness and sweetest bounty for *jinn* and mankind is the *love of God* contained within the knowledge of God; the purest joy for the human spirit and the sheerest delight for man's heart is the *spiritual ecstasy* contained within the love of God. Indeed, all true happiness, pure joy, sweet bounties and unclouded pleasure are undoubtedly contained within the *knowledge and love of God*. The one who knows and loves God is either potentially or actually able to receive endless happiness, bounties, enlightenment and mysteries. While the one who does not truly know and love Him is afflicted spiritually and materially by endless misery, pain and fear. Indeed, even if a man, powerless and miserable, and unprotected amid other purposeless human beings in a world filled with wretchedness, were made the ruler of the whole world, what is this really worth for him – everyone can understand how miserable and bewildered a condition man endures, if he does not recognize his Owner, discover his Master.

If, however, he discovers his Owner and recognizes his Master, then he will take refuge in His Mercy and rely on His Power, and that desolate world will turn, for him, into a place of rest and felicity and become a place of exchange for the Hereafter.

THE FIRST STATION

Each one of the eleven phrases in the sentence quoted above affirming the Divine Unity carries a message of happy tidings for believers. Each message offers a cure, and from each cure emanates a spiritual pleasure.

2

The first phrase: *There is no god but God*

This phrase provides for the human spirit, which is subject to innumerable needs and prey to the attacks of countless enemies, an inexhaustible source of help, it opens for it the door to a treasury of mercy that can secure all its needs. The spirit finds in it a point of support that shows and makes known to it its Master and Owner, its Creator and True Object of Worship, Who possesses an absolute power that will secure the spirit against the evil of all its enemies. In this way, this mighty phrase saves the heart from utter desolation and the spirit from grievous suffering, it is forever uplifting and the means of a continual felicity.

The second phrase: *(He is) One*

This phrase implies the following happy news, both healing and auspicious: the human spirit, which is connected to most species in the universe, and is overwhelmed in misery and confusion because of that connection, finds in the phrase, *(He is) One,* a refuge and saviour that will deliver it from all that confusion and misery.

This phrase means to man: 'God is One, so do not tire yourself out having recourse to other things; do not demean yourself and feel obliged before them; do not humiliate yourself before them for security; do not give trouble to yourself by following them, and do not tremble before them in fear; because the King of the universe is one, with Whom is the key to, and in Whose hand are the reins of, all things. Everything is resolved by His command. If therefore, you have found Him, this means that you have obtained whatever you wish for, and been liberated from an (otherwise) interminable indebtedness and innumerable fears.'

The third phrase: *He has no partner*

God is One in that He has no partner in His Lordship, in His

3

acts and in His creating, as also that He has no partner in His Divinity and Sovereignty.

A worldly monarch may in principle have no partner in his sovereignty, but in the execution of his sovereignty his officials act as his partners and/or as intermediaries between him and his people. Whereas, God, the Monarch of all times, has no need for partners or helpers in the execution of His Sovereignty, just as He has, in principle, no partner in His Sovereignty. Without His command and will, without His leave and power, not a single thing can interfere with another. Also, since He has no partner or helper, and there are no intermediaries between Him and His creatures, everyone can have recourse to Him directly at any time and in any place.

This phrase, therefore, provides for the human spirit this glad tiding: a man who has attained belief may, without hindrance, opposition or interference, in any state, for any desire, at any time and in any place, enter the Presence of the Majestic, the All-Gracious, the All-Powerful One of Perfection, Who is the Eternal Owner of the treasures of mercy and bliss, and may present before Him his needs. By finding His Mercy and relying upon His Power, he can attain perfect ease and happiness.

The fourth phrase: *His is the Kingdom*

His is the Kingdom of all the heavens and the earth. So you are owned by Him and working in His Kingdom. This phrase implies the following joyful and healing news:

'O man! Do not imagine that you own yourself, for you are unable to administer even your own affairs. You can neither maintain your spirit and body by providing for their needs and securing them against calamities, nor can you avoid exhaustion and ageing since you have no dominion over time or other erosive factors. Therefore, do not suffer pain and torment without reason. Somebody else, not you, owns everything. That Owner

4

is both All-Powerful and All-Compassionate; rely on His Power and do not accuse His Compassion. Renounce grief and anxiety, and accept relief. Be rid of your troubles and find serenity.'

This phrase also means: 'This world that you love, to which you are connected, and which you see in disorder and are unable to put right, is the property of an All-Powerful and Compassionate One. So hand over the property to its Owner, leave it to Him, mind your own duty and do not interfere with His acts. Do not be troubled by what you are unable to overcome, and be at ease. The Owner of this property has free disposal of it and administers it as He wishes. But He is All-Wise, always acts for a wise purpose, and also He is All-Compassionate. So, whenever you take fright, say like Ibrahim Haqqi, *Let's see what the Master does; whatever He does is always best*, and observe His acts with complete trust in Him.'

The fifth phrase: *To Him belongs all the praise*

Only God absolutely deserves praise and acclaim and only to Him is all indebtedness. His are all bounties and they come from His treasury. As for the treasury, it is infinite and inexhaustible. This phrase, therefore, implies this happy news:

'O man! Do not be anxious that one day, the bounties (you presently enjoy) will cease. Know that the treasury of Mercy is inexhaustible. Nor cry out with anxiety for the possible cessation of enjoyment, every enjoyment you are granted is the fruit of an infinite Mercy. Now, the tree of that Mercy is undying, for each exhausted fruit is replaced with a new one. Furthermore, by reflecting on what you enjoy, in an attitude of thanks and praise, since every enjoyment is in essence a favour from the Divine Mercy and, in so being, a hundred times more enjoyable than the enjoyment by itself, you will be able to increase it a hundredfold. If a glorious king presents you with an apple, the pleasure you take in being honoured by a royal favour will be superior to the material pleasure of a hundred, even a thousand, apples. Similarly, through the phrase, *To Him belongs all praise*, will be opened to you the door of a spiritual enjoyment a thousand times sweeter than that you enjoy by itself, since this phrase makes you consider the bestowal of bounty, which in turn leads you to recognize the Bestower and to reflect on His merciful favours which are pouring out continually.

The sixth phrase: *He alone gives life*

The One Who gives life and sustains it through provision is He. Also the Provider of the necessities of life is He, and the sublime aims of life and its important results are related to Him. This phrase, therefore calls out to mortal and helpless man and gives him this joyful tiding: 'O man! Do not bother to shoulder the heavy responsibilities of life; do not feel unease because the world is transient. Do not let the insignificant worldly fruits of life drive you to regret that you came to this world. Rather, the 'life mechanism' in 'the ship of your being' belongs to the One Ever-Living and Ever-Self-Subsistent One, so it is He Who provides for all of life's needs and expenditures. Further, there are innumerable aims in life directing it to many important results, nearly all of which are related to Him. You are just a 'helmsman' on that 'ship' of your being, so perform your duty properly. Obtain your wage and take the enjoyment that comes with doing so. Ponder how precious that 'ship' is and how valuable its benefits; and consider how generous and compassionate is the Owner of that 'ship'. So, rejoice and give thanks and perceive that if you perform your duty righteously, all the results that life yields will, in one respect, be recorded as your good deeds to secure an immortal life for you in eternity.'

The seventh phrase: *...and makes to die*

He discharges you from the duty of life, changes your abode

from this transient world and releases you from the burden of service. That is, he takes you from a transient life to an eternal one. This phrase, therefore, explicitly says to mortal *jinn* and man: 'Good news for you: death is not annihilation or going to non-existence, nor is it eternal separation or a chance event without an author. Rather, it is being discharged from service by the Author, Who is All-Wise and All-Compassionate; it is a change of abode. It is being dispatched to ever-lasting happiness, to your true home. It is the door to union with the Intermediate World, which is the place where you will meet with ninety-nine percent of your friends.'

The eighth phrase: *He is living and dies not*

The Undying Object of Worship and the Everlasting Beloved, One Who possesses a beauty, perfection and munificence wholly and utterly superior to the beauty, perfection and munificence to be observed in all creatures that arouse love, and one single manifestation of Whose Beauty is sufficient to replace all other beloveds, has an eternal life free from any trace of cessation or ephemerality and exempt from any flaw or defect. So, this phrase makes this joyful announcement to all conscious beings, including *jinn* and mankind, and to people of love:

'Here is good news for you! There is an Eternal Beloved Who will heal your wounds caused by countless separations from the ones to whom you give your heart. Since He exists and is undying, whatever may happen, do not worry about those others. Moreover, the beauty and good in them, the grace and perfection which cause you to love them, are but a dim, shadow-like manifestation of the Eternal Beauty of the Everlasting Beloved, which has passed through many veils. Do not grieve, therefore, at their disappearance, for they are 'mirrors' of some sort: through the changing of mirrors the reflection of that Beauty is renewed and becomes more radiant. When you find Him, you have found everything.

The ninth phrase: *In His hand is all good*

That is, He possesses all good, and only He guides you to do good. Also, He records on your behalf any good, righteous deed that you do. Thus, this phrase announces to *jinn* and mankind this happy news:

'O you helpless ones! When you move to the grave do not cry out in despair: "Alas! Everything we owned is destroyed and all our efforts have come to nought. We have left that wide, beautiful world and entered this narrow grave." Everything of yours is preserved: all your deeds were written down and every service you rendered was recorded. The One of Majesty, in Whose hand is all good and Who is able to do whatever is good, has summoned you in order to reward your service: He will keep you under the ground temporarily and then will bring you to His Presence. How fortunate you are that you completed your duty and service; your labour has ended, you are on the way to ease and mercy. Having gone through your period of toil, you are going to receive your wages.'

The All-Powerful One of Majesty, Who preserves seeds and grains, which are the records of the activities and the deposit-boxes of the services done in the last spring, and unfolds and publishes them the following spring in the most dazzling, abundant and benevolent manner, is undoubtedly preserving the results of your deeds also, in the same way, and will likewise reward your service in the most abundant manner.'

The tenth phrase: *He is powerful over everything*

That is, He is the One and Singular and He has power over everything. Nothing is difficult for Him. To create a whole spring is as easy for Him as to create a single flower, and He creates Paradise with as much ease as He creates the spring. The countless creatures that He continually brings into existence every day, every year, every century, bear witness with innumerable tongues to His limitless Power. Thus, this phrase, too, implies these glad tidings:

'O man! The service you offer and the worship you perform do not go for nothing. A world of reward, an abode of bliss, has been prepared for you. In place of this transitory world of yours, an everlasting Paradise is awaiting you. Have faith and confidence in the promise of the Majestic Creator, Whom you know and worship. It is inconceivable that He should break His promise. In no respect is there any deficiency at all in His Power. Impotence can never interfere in His works. As He creates your small garden, He can also create Paradise for you. And He created it and has promised it to you. Since He has promised, He shall certainly admit you to it.'

We plainly observe how every year on the earth He revives most speedily, yet with perfect order and ease, hundreds of thousands of species and groups of animals and plants. Such an All-Powerful One of Majesty is most certainly able to carry out His promise. Further, since He creates every year samples of Paradise, which He has promised through all His revealed books; since all His acts and functions are performed with truth and seriousness, and, as we witness in all His works, all perfections point to and testify to His infinite Perfection, with no flaw or defect at all in Him, and since the breaking of a promise, lying, falsehood and deception are the ugliest of qualities, then most decidedly will that All-Powerful One of Majesty, that All-Wise One of Perfection, that All-Compassionate One of Grace fulfil His promise. He will open the gate to eternal happiness and admit you, O people of faith, into Paradise, which was the original home of your forefather, Adam.

The eleventh phrase: *And unto Him is the return*

Human beings are sent to this world of trial and examination with important duties and business and to do some particular services. After they have completed their duties, they will return and meet once more with their All-Munificent Master, the Majestic Creator, Who sent them out in the first place. That is, they will leave this realm of transience, be delivered from the turbulence of cause-and-effect cycles and from the obscure veils of intermediaries, and will be honoured in the eternal abode in the Presence of their Compassionate Lord and meet with Him without veil before His Seat of Everlasting Kingdom. Everyone will find out directly who his creator is, the Worshipped One, Lord, Master and Owner. Thus, this phrase implies the following news, much happier than all the rest:

'O man! Do you know where you are going? To where you are being impelled? You are going to the sphere of Mercy, to the peaceful Presence of the All-Beautiful One of Majesty. A thousand years of happy life in this world cannot be compared to one hour of life in Paradise, and a thousand years of life in Paradise cannot be compared to one hour's vision of His Countenance of utmost beauty. The loveliness and beauty in all the creatures of this world, including those worldly loved ones by which you are so fascinated and stricken, are merely a kind shadow of a single manifestation of His Beauty and of the loveliness of His Names; and the whole of Paradise, with all its charm, is merely a manifestation of His Mercy, and all longing, love and attraction are merely a flash from the light of His Love. You are going into the Presence of the One Eternally Worshipped and Everlastingly Beloved, and are invited to Paradise, which is His eternal feasting place. Since this is so, enter the grave not with tears but with a smile.'

The same words also give this glad news:

'O man! Do not be apprehensive, imagining that you are going to extinction, non-existence, nothingness, darkness, oblivion and decay and dissolution. You are going not to extinction but to permanence. You are being impelled not to non-existence, but to eternal existence. You are entering not the world of darkness but the world of His Light. You are returning to your true Owner, to the Seat of the Eternal King.

'You will not drown in multiplicity, but you will take your rest in the sphere of unity. You are bound not for separation, but for union.'

***

THE SECOND STATION

(This station is a brief indication to prove the Divine Unity at the level of God's Greatest Name.)

The first phrase: *There is no god But God*

This phrase affirms God's Oneness in His Divinity and His being the Sole Object of Worship. The following is a very strong proof of the Divine Unity at this level.

A most orderly activity is apparent in the entire universe, especially on the surface of the earth. We also observe there a most wise creativity, and clearly see a most systematic unfolding. That is, everything is given the most proper shape and form. Furthermore, we witness a most affectionate, generous and merciful provision and bountifulness. This state, then, of necessity proves, or makes one feel, the necessary existence and unity of an Active, Creative, Opening and Shaping and Bestowing One of Majesty.

Indeed, all existents demonstrate, through their continual decay and renewal, that they are the manifestations of the sacred Names of an All-Powerful Maker, and the reflections of the lights of those Names; the works of that Maker's creative activity, and the inscriptions of the Pen of His Destiny and Power, and also they are mirrors reflecting the grace of His Perfection.

Just as the Owner of the universe proves this greatest truth and the most exalted degree of the Self-Affirmation of His Oneness through all the scriptures and holy books that He revealed, so too here, all the people of truth and the perfected members of mankind prove this same degree through their investigations and spiritual discoveries. Also, creation, through the witnessing of the miracles of artistry, wonders of power and treasuries of wealth that it displays, in spite of its helplessness and poverty, points to the same degree of the Self-Affirmation of the Divine Oneness.

Those who do not accept that Single One of Unity, therefore, must either accept innumerable deities, or, like the Sophists, deny both their own existence and that of the universe.

The second phrase: *(He is) One*

This phrase states the Oneness of God at the level of explicit manifestation of His Unity. The following is to prove this level decisively.

When we open our eyes to gaze upon the face of the universe, the first thing that holds our attention is the fact of a universal perfect order and a comprehensive, sensitive equilibrium. Everything exists within a precise order and a delicate balance and measure.

When we take a somewhat more careful, studious look, a continuous ordering and balancing catch our eye. Someone revitalizes this order continually and with perfect regularity and according to precise measures; everything is, as it were, a model to be dressed in a great many well-ordered and balanced forms.

When we study it with even greater attention, a wisdom and justice appear behind that ordering and balancing. There is a purpose for every event in the universe, and a benefit resulting from it. Still a greater attention makes it clear to us that a power is evident from behind a wholly wise activity that all we see, and that there is a comprehensive knowledge encompassing all functions of all things. All of which together reveals to the mind that behind all those veils of order and balance operates an All-Powerful and All-Knowing One, Who puts everything in order according to a most sensitive balance, and for a universal purpose and justice.

Furthermore, when we consider the beginning and end of all things, we observe, particularly in living creatures, that their seeds appear to contain as if in a programme all the parts and structures of those creatures. Their fruits are such that the meanings of those creatures are filtered and concentrated in them; their life-histories are recorded in them. It is as if the seeds are coded collections of the principles according to which they are created; and the fruits are a sort of index of the commands of their creation and growth. Then, when we look into the outer and inner faces of living creatures, the free disposal of an extremely wise power and the fashioning and ordering of an effective will are revealed to us: the power creates; the will designs and fashions. Thus, all the creatures display, on account of their beginning, the instructions of a Knowledge; on account of their end, the plan and declaration of a Maker; on account of their outer forms, an artistic, well-made 'garment' they were made to dress by One Who does whatever He wills, and on account of their inner forms, a well-ordered machinery of an All-Powerful One. All this manifests that no time and no place and no thing can be outside the grasp of the Power of the One Majestic Maker. Each thing and all things, together with all their functions, are organized and directed within the grasp of Power of an All-Powerful Possessor of Will. They are made beautiful with the ordering and grace of One All-Merciful, All-Compassionate, and embellished with the ornaments of One All-Affectionate, All-Bounteous. For the one who is alert and has the power of sight, the order and equilibrium, and acts of ordering and balancing that are clearly observed in the universe, demonstrate, in the degree of unity, One Who is Single, Unique, Sole, All-Powerful, Possessing of Will, All-Knowing and All-Wise.

Assuredly, there is a unity in everything, and unity points to One. For example, the world is illuminated by one lamp only, the sun; therefore, the Owner of the world is One as well. Also, all the living creatures on the earth are served with air, fire and water, each of which is one, simple. That being so, the One Who employs them and subjugates them to us is also One.

The third phrase: *He has no partner*

Since this phrase has been proved in a most brilliant fashion in the First Station of the *Twenty-Second Word*, we refer the reader to it.

The fourth phrase: *His is the Kingdom*

Every creature from the earth to the 'Throne of God', from the ground to the firmament, from the minutest particles to all heavenly bodies, and everything within eternity of the past and future, this world and the Hereafter, is owned by Him. His is the highest, the most comprehensive degree of ownership in the form of the greatest manifestation of Divine Unity. A very strong proof of this highest degree of God's Kingdom and the greatest station of Divine Unity in its most comprehensive manifestation occurred to me in the language of Arabic at a pleasant time and in pleasant circumstances. For the sake of that pleasant memory, we shall note down those same phrases and then explain their meanings:

His is the Kingdom because the macrocosm is like the microcosm; both are the works of His Power and the missives of His Destiny. He created the macrocosm and made it as a place of prostration, a place of worship; He gave existence to the microcosm and made it that which prostrates. His construction of the former made it His property, while His giving of existence to the latter made it His slave. His artistry in the former is manifested as a book; His fashioning and colouring in the latter shine through speech. His power in the former reveals His Majesty; His Mercy in the latter organizes His bounty. His majesty in the former bears witness that He is One; His bounty in the latter proclaims that He is Single. His stamp on the former is on all things, universal and particular, while His seal on the latter is both on the body and limbs.

The first section: *The macrocosm is like the microcosm; both are* *the works of His Power and missives of His Destiny.* That is, the macrocosm, which is called the universe and the microcosm, which is its miniature and is called man, display the proofs of God's Oneness written with the Pen of Divine Power and Destiny, both within man himself and in the outer world.

Man displays, though on a very small scale, the same well-ordered art observed in the universe. Just as the art observed in that vast sphere of the universe points to the Single Maker, so too, the microscopic art in man testifies to that Maker and demonstrates His Oneness. Also, just as man is a meaningful missive of the Lord, a well-composed ode of His Destiny, so too, the universe is another well-composed ode written by the same Pen of Destiny, only on a vast scale. Is it even conceivable, then, that anyone or anything else other than the Single One of Unity could have a hand in putting the stamp of uniqueness on people's faces, which, although the same in structure and appearance, have their distinguishing marks, and have a hand in setting the seal of Unity on the universe, all of whose creatures are in close co-operation, helping and supporting each other?

The second section: *He created the macrocosm and made it a place of prostration, a place of worship; He gave existence to the microcosm and made it that which prostrates.* That is, the All-Wise Maker created the macrocosm in such a novel, wonderful form, inscribing on it the signs of His Grandeur, such that He made it a huge mosque in which He created man as an intellectual being to read those signs, and with a disposition to bow before Him in worship and to prostrate himself in wonder at the miracles of His art and His wonderful, originative Power. Is it then, even conceivable that the true object of worship of those prostrating worshippers in this huge mosque could be other than that Single Maker of Unity?

The third section: *His construction of the former made it His property, while His giving existence to the latter made it His slave.* That is, the Majestic Master of Sovereignty made the macrocosm, and especially the earth, in such a form that it is like countless concentric spheres: every sphere is like an arable field, where age by age, season by season, century by century, He sows, reaps and harvests crops.

He unceasingly administers His property, causing it to work. He has made this world of particles, which is the largest sphere, into a field, where He sows and harvests with His Power and Wisdom the universe-full of crops and dispatches them from the manifest world to the other invisible one, from the sphere of Power to the sphere of Knowledge.

Next, the earth, which is a medium sphere, is another place of cultivation for Him, where season by season, He plants 'worlds', species, and reaps and harvests them. He sends its immaterial 'crops', the immaterial results of the lives of all creatures, to the other immaterial World of the Unseen.

A garden, too, which is a smaller sphere, He fills hundreds or thousands of times with power and empties with wisdom. And an animate creature, for example, a tree or a human being, that is an even smaller sphere, He causes it to yield crops a hundred times greater than itself. In short, that Majestic Master of Sovereignty makes all things, big or small, universal or particular, as a model and dresses them in ever-different ways in the weavings of His art, which are embellished with ever-new inscriptions, exhibiting the manifestations of His Names and the miracles of His Power through them. He has made everything in His Kingdom as a page on which He inscribes in hundreds of ways His meaningful missives, displays the signs of His Wisdom, and has them read by conscious beings. As He made the macrocosm as a cultivated property, He has also created man and endowed him with such structures and organs, senses and emotions, and especially with such a soul and implanted in him such desires, appetites, drives and demands that, in that vast property, He has made him an owned slave in need of the whole of that property.

Is it, therefore, conceivable that anybody or anything other than that Majestic Master of Sovereignty, Who has made everything, from the vast world of particles to a fly, as a cultivated property, Who has appointed man, despite his physical insignificance, as a superintendent, and inspector, a tiller, a merchant, a herald and a worshipper in that vast property and taken him as an honoured guest and beloved addressee of Himself, could have free disposal over that property, and be lord over that owned slave?

The fourth section: *His activity in the former is manifested as a book; His fashioning and colouring in the latter shine through speech.* That is, the Majestic Maker's art in the macrocosm is so meaningful that because it is manifested in the form of a book, thus making the universe is intelligible like a vast volume, the human intellect has obtained from it all true scientific knowledge and written all scientific treatises according to it. And that universal book of wisdom is based on truth to such a degree that it has been proclaimed in the form of the Wise Qur'an, which is itself a copy of that vast manifest book.

Moreover, just as His art in the universe is manifest, due to its perfection, in the form of a well-ordered book, so too, His colouring and the inscriptions of His Wisdom in man have opened the flower of speech. That is, that art is so meaningful, delicate and beautiful that it has caused the components of that animate machine to speak like a gramophone.

That art has also given man such a Divine colouring in his 'fairest of forms' that in his material, corporeal and solid head has opened the flower of speech and discourse, which is immaterial, incorporeal and yet organic. Further, it has equipped that power of speech and expression with developed 'tools' and elaborate abilities and faculties enabling it to evolve to the degree where man can become the addressee of the Eternal Sovereign. Thus, the Divine colouring in man's essential nature has

opened the flower of Divine speech. Is it conceivable that anything other than the Single One of Unity could have a hand in
the art in all creatures, which has taken the form of a book, and
in that colouring in man which has reached the degree of the
power of speech? God forbid!

The fifth section: *His Power in the former reveals His Majesty;
His Mercy in the latter organizes His bounty.* That is, the Power of
the Maker manifesting itself through grandeur and majesty,
creates the universe in the form of a palace so magnificent that
He adorns and illuminates it with the sun as its electric light,
with the moon as its lamp, and with the stars as its candles. He
also makes the earth a laden table, an arable field and garden,
and the mountains each a storehouse, a peg, a fortress, and so
on. Again, He provides all things, on a vast scale, in the form of
the necessities of that huge palace, thus demonstrating the majesty of His Lordship in a most dazzling manner.

Similarly, by bestowing on every living creature down to the
most minute animate beings, the different varieties of His bounties, He manifests His Mercy in the form of graciousness. As He
sustains them through His Bountifulness, He adorns them with
the manifestations of His Kindness and Generosity. Thus, while
He causes huge bodies like the sun to proclaim His Majesty
through His Names, All-Gracious, Great, reciting 'O Glorious
One, O Great One, O Mighty One', those tiny animate creatures, like flies and fish, proclaim His Mercy, reciting 'O Gracious One, O Compassionate One, O Generous One'. Is it conceivable that anyone or anything other than that Gracious One
of Majesty, that Majestic One of Grace could interfere in any
way in the creation of this macrocosm! God forbid!

The sixth section: *His Majesty in the former bears witness that
He is One; His bounty in the latter proclaims that He is Single.* That
is, just as the Majesty of Lordship, which is manifest in the universe as a whole, proves and demonstrates Divine Unity, so

too, the Bounty of Lordship, which bestows on each living creature its regular provision, proves and demonstrates Divine
Oneness.

Unity means that all the creatures belong to One and they
look to One and they are the creation of One. As for Oneness, it
is to express that most of the Names of the Creator are manifest
in every individual thing. For example, the reflection of the
light of the sun on the face of the earth as a whole may be seen
as analogous to Unity while the fact that the sun manifests itself
in each transparent object and drop of water with its light, heat
and seven colours in its light at the same time, may offer an
analogy to Oneness. In the same way, the manifestation of most
of the Divine Names in each thing, especially in each living creature, and above all, in each human being, points to Oneness.

Thus this section indicates that the Majesty of Lordship,
which has total disposal of the universe, makes that huge sun
as a servant, a lamp and a furnace for living creatures on the
earth; and makes the mighty earth a cradle, a mansion and
place of trade for them; and fire, a cook and friend; and clouds,
the water filters and means of nourishment; and mountains,
storehouses and treasuries; and the air, a fan for living creatures, for breathing in and out; and water, a 'nurse' to new-
comers to life, a distributor of sweet drink supplying animate
beings with the moisture necessary for existence. This Divine
Lordship demonstrates Divine Unity in a most clear manner.

Indeed, who other than that One Creator could subjugate the
sun to the service of the inhabitants of the earth? Who other than
that Single One of Unity could arrange the air and employ it as
'swift servant' on the earth entrusted with many duties? Again,
who other than that Single One of Unity could make fire a cook
and cause a tiny flame the size of a matchhead to consume
thousands of tons of things? And so on. Every single thing, every single element, every single heavenly body, points to the All-
Majestic One in the manifestation of the Majesty of Lordship.

Thus, just as Unity is apparent on the 'horizon' of Grace and Majesty, so too, Bounty and Benevolence proclaim Divine Oneness on the 'horizon' of Grace and Mercy. This is because, among the works of all-embracing Divine artistry of the highest degree, there are in living creatures, and especially in man, developed structures and organs that can recognize and appreciate, desire and accept, innumerable different sorts of bounties. In particular, man is enabled to absorb the reflections of all the Divine Names manifested in the whole universe. Like a point of focus, he displays all the Beautiful Names together through the mirror of his essential nature, and proclaims God's Oneness thereby.

The seventh section: *His stamp on the former is on all things, universal and particular, while His seal on the latter is both on the body and limbs.* That is, just as the Majestic Maker has a greatest stamp on the macrocosm as a whole, so too, He has put a stamp of Unity on each of its parts and species. Likewise, just as He has set a seal of Oneness on the face and body of man, who is the microcosm, so too, on each of his limbs is a seal of His Unity. In short, the All-Powerful One of Majesty has put on all things, universal or particular, from stars to particles, a stamp of Unity that bears witness to him; on each he has set a seal of Unity that points to Him.

The fifth phrase: *To Him belong all praise*

Since the perfections observed in all creatures which are the occasions of giving praise and paying tribute, are His, all praise, too, belongs to Him. Eulogy and acclaim, from whomever to whomever it has come and will come, from past eternity to future eternity, are all in reality addressed to Him. This is because bounty and beneficence, perfection and grace, which are the causes of giving praise, and everything which leads to praise, belong to Him. Indeed, as pointed out by the Qur'an, whatever all creatures are doing or seen to do, is, in reality, worship, glorification, prostration, supplication, and praise, which rise continuously to the Divine Presence. The following is an explanation of a comprehensive evidence to demonstrate this truth affirming God's Unity.

When we look at the universe, it appears to us in the form of a huge enclosed park, its roof gilded with lofty stars, its ground inhabited by ornamented creatures. When we see it thus, we see that the well-ordered, luminous heavenly bodies and purposeful and ornamented earthly creatures in this park are pronouncing all together, each in its particular tongue,'We are the miracles of the Power of an All-Powerful One of Majesty. We bear witness to the Unity of an All-Wise Creator, an All-Powerful Maker.'

Then, we look at the earth in the park of the universe and see it in the form of a garden in which hundreds of thousands of varieties of multi-coloured and beautifully ordered flowering plants have been laid out and through which hundreds of thousands of different species of animals have been scattered. All of those adorned plants and beautified animals proclaim through their well-ordered structures and well-proportioned forms, 'each of us is a miracle, a wonder of art created by a Single All-Wise Maker, and a herald, a witness to His Unity.'

When, afterwards, we look at the upper parts of the trees in that garden, we see fruits and flowers in various forms that have been made knowingly, wisely, generously and beautifully. These are all pronouncing with one tongue, 'We are miraculous gifts and wondrous bounties of an All-Merciful One of Grace and an All-Compassionate One of Perfection.'

Thus, the heavenly bodies and beings in the park of the universe, and the plants and bushes in the garden of the earth, and the flowers and fruits on its trees and vegetation, testify and proclaim with an infinitely resounding voice, 'our Creator and Fashioner, Who has granted us gifts, is powerful over all things.

Nothing is difficult for Him. Nothing is outside the sphere of His Power; in relation to that Power, particles and stars are equal; a universal is as simple as a particular; a particular is as valuable as a universal. The biggest is as easy as the smallest in relation to His Power; and the small is as full of artistry as the big, rather as far as artistry goes, the small is greater than the big.'

All the happenings of the past, which are wonders of His Power, bear witness that that Absolutely Powerful One is absolutely able to bring into effect and existence the wonders of the contingencies of the future. The One Who brought about yesterday will bring about tomorrow; that All-Powerful Being Who created the past will also create the future. The All-Wise Maker Who made this world, will also make the Hereafter. So, just as the true object of worship is that All-Powerful One of Majesty, the only one absolutely deserving of praise is again Him. Just as He is the exclusively Worshipped One, so too, praise and glory are peculiar to Him.

Is it conceivable that the All-Wise Maker Who has created the heavens and the earth could leave man to himself with no purpose, who is the most significant and most perfect fruit of the tree of creation, and hand him over to random cause and effect, thus reducing His profound Wisdom to futility? God forbid!

Again, is it conceivable that a being who is wise and knowledgeable, having planted a tree and grown it up with utmost care and for important purposes, would leave them either to the hands of thieves or to scatter and rot on the ground? Of course, it could not be that he would ignore them since a tree is given care and importance because of the fruits it bears.

If that is so, then the universe's conscious being and its most perfect fruit, result and aim is man. Is it then conceivable that the All-Wise Maker of that universe would give to others the praise and worship, thanks and love, which are the fruits of that conscious 'fruit' – man – and thus cause His evident Wisdom, His purpose for creating him, to be nullified, or His absolute Power to be stained with impotence, or His All-Encompassing Knowledge converted into ignorance? God forbid! A hundred thousand times!

Since conscious beings among whom man is the most distinguished, are the pivot of Divine aims in the creation of the palace of the universe, it is unquestionably evident that the thanks and worship which they show in response to the bounties they receive should not be directed to one other than the Maker of that palace. Further, one who is not able to create a whole spring, who is not able to create all fruits, even all of one kind – apples for instance – the stamp on which is the same, can by no means create a single apple to give someone to eat as a bounty and grace, and receive, in return, thanks for it, thus taking a share in the praise due to the One absolutely deserving of praise. Since this is so, it is again quite clear that the Creator of the universe and its Majestic Provider, Who sustains all creatures down to the most insignificant ones and makes Himself loved by conscious beings through the innumerable miracles of His art, will not abandon to nature and causes their thanks and worship, their praise and love, their recognition and gratitude, making His Absolute Wisdom denied and the Sovereignty of His Lordship nullified. So, thanks and praise belong exclusively to Him, and the reality of the universe proclaims unceasingly with the tongue of truth. 'To Him is the praise from every single being from past eternity to future eternity.'

The sixth phrase: *He alone gives life*

That is, the one who gives life is He alone and, since this is so, it is also He alone Who creates all things. This is because the spirit, light, essence, result and cream of the universe is life, so whoever gives life must also be the Creator of the entire universe. The One Who gives life is certainly One Who is Himself Ever-Living and Self-Subsistent. The following is to point out a most decisive proof of God's Unity at the level of His manifestation as the Ever-Living and Self-Subsistent One.

We see the magnificent armies of living creatures with their tents pitched on the surface of the earth. Out of the innumerable armies of the Ever-Living, Self-Subsistent One, every spring a new one emerges from the world of the Unseen freshly mobilized. This army comprises hundreds of thousands of diverse and different nations of vegetable and animal kinds. We see, much to our surprise, that although the uniform of each nation or tribe, as well as their provisions, instructions, discharge, period of service, are all different, a single Commander-in-Chief alone, through His infinite Power and Wisdom, boundless Knowledge and Will, His infinite Mercy and inexhaustible treasuries, and without forgetting a single individual, without confusing or delaying any of them, provides all their different needs, with perfect orderliness and precise balance at exactly the right time, and trains and demobilizes each according to their particular service and character.

Is it conceivable, then, that anyone else could interfere and have a share in this yearly mobilization, that is, in this yearly resurrection and precise administration, in this training and sustaining, other than the One Who has an all-encompassing knowledge to know that army with all its particulars, and One Who has absolute power to administer that army together with all its necessities? God forbid! A hundred thousand times!

It is a fact that human beings, because of their incapacity, feel compelled to equip a battalion in a single fashion, even if that battalion is composed of the soldiers from ten different tribes. But the Ever-Living, Self-Subsistent One provides each of hundreds of thousands of tribes within that magnificent army with their peculiar equipment necessary for their life. Moreover, He provides them with no trouble or difficulty, in a slight and easy manner, most wisely and in exact order. He causes that mighty army to pronounce with one tongue, 'He is the One Who brings to life', and causes that vast congregation

25

in the mosque of the universe to recite:

God! There is no god but He – the Living, the Self-Subsistent, Eternal. No slumber can seize Him nor sleep. His is what is in the heavens and what is on the earth. Who can intercede with Him except as He permits? He knows what is before them and what lies behind them, while they encompass nothing of His knowledge save that which He wills. His Throne embraces the heavens and the earth, and it tires Him not to uphold them both. He is the Most High, the Supreme .[1]

The seventh phrase: *He makes to die*

That is, just as it is He Who gives life, it is also He Who takes it. Indeed death is not just a destruction or extinction which might be attributed to nature and causes. Rather, just as a seed outwardly dies and rots under the ground while inwardly growing into a new, much more elaborate living plant form, so too, though it seems to be a disintegration and extinction, death is in reality, for man, the introduction or starting-point of eternal life. If this is so, it is certainly the Absolutely Powerful One Who creates death just as it is He Who grants and administers life. We point to a mighty proof of Divine Unity manifested in this phrase in the highest degree as follows:

By Divine Will, all existence moves in a continuous flow. The universe is in an incessant motion by the Command of its Lord. All creatures, by God's Leave, are unceasingly flowing in the stream of time; they are being dispatched from the World of the Unseen; they are being dressed in external (material) existence in the corporeal world and then poured into the other world in an orderly fashion. By the Command of the Lord, they continually come from the future, stop in passing at the present, pause for a breath, and are then poured into the past. This flowing of creatures is ordered and carried out with the wisest mercy and benevolence; so too their consistent movement is done

---

1. *al-Baqara*, 2.255.

by a most knowledgeable wisdom and orderliness, and the current of flow is managed within solicitude and equilibrium – everything is done from the highest to the lowest for purposes, benefits and aims. That is to say, an All-Powerful One of Majesty, an All-Wise of Perfection continually gives life to, and employs, the families of beings, from the individual within them to the worlds they form, and then He discharges them for a purpose: He makes them die and dispatches them to the other world. He transfers them from the sphere of Power to the sphere of Knowledge.

Is it conceivable then that one who does not have the power and ability to administer this universe in its totality, who does not have authority over all times, whose power is not sufficient to give life to diverse creatures and call them to death as single individuals, and who cannot create the spring as easily as if it were a single flower and attach it to the earth and then pluck it through death, could claim to create death and make living things die?

So, death of even the most insignificant living things, like its life, must necessarily take place according to the Law of an All-Majestic Being in Whose hand are all the truths of life and varieties of death, and by His Permission, Command, Power and Knowledge.

The eighth phrase: *He is Living and dies not*

That is, His life is perpetual and eternal, with no beginning or end. Death and non-existence cannot befall Him. Indeed, He Who has no beginning must, of course, have no end. He Who is Necessarily Existent, must, of course, be eternally enduring.

Indeed, how could non-existence befall a Life such that all existence, in all its varieties, is its shadow? Non-existence and perishing cannot touch a Life which requires and is required by a necessary existence. Also, cessation and extinction could in no way affect a Life through Whose manifestation all lives come into being, and on which all the permanent truths of the universe are dependent, and through which they subsist.

Indeed, a single manifestation of that Life gives uniformity to things that are subject to extinction and decrease in this world of multiplicity, and saves them from disintegration, thus making them gain a sort of permanence. That is, Life accords some sort of unity to multiplicity and gives to existent forms some form of permanence either through the life of a species or through their seed and offspring or in memories, and so on. Most certainly, therefore, ephemerality and transience could have nothing to do with such a Necessary Life, a single manifestation of Which is the cause of innumerable instances of life.

The transience and decrease of this universe is a decisive witness to this truth. That is, just as existents bear witness and point to the Life of the Ever-Living and Necessarily-Existent One through their own existence and lives,[2] so too, they testify and point to the permanence and eternity of that Life through their decay and death. Because the fact that beings are followed after their death by new ones shows that there is an Ever-Living One Who unceasingly renews the manifestation of life.

Bubbles at the surface of a flowing river sparkle in the sun and disappear. Those bubbles, coming troop after troop and then, having displayed the same sparkle, disappearing, point to the permanence of a high and enduring sun. In the same way, the alternation of life and death in those constantly moving existents bears witness to the permanence of an Ever-Living, Ever-Enduring One.

These beings are 'mirrors': as darkness is the mirror to light

---

2. In proving, before the Nimrod, God's Existence and Unity, and His absolute Sovereignty over the universe, The Prophet Abraham argues that God gives life and makes to die, and then mentions that He causes the sun to rise in the east and to set in the west *(The Qur'an,* 2.258). This is a progress and a transition from a particular meaning of giving life and death to a universal meaning, and therefore demonstrates the most illuminating and widest sphere of that proof. It is not, as asserted by some interpreters of the Qur'an, a transition of an implicit proof to an explicit one.

and the more intense the darkness the more brilliantly it displays the light, so do these beings act as mirrors to the Names and Attributes of God in many respects, by reason of the contrast of opposites.

For example, just as beings act as mirrors to the Power of the Maker through their impotence, and to His Riches through their poverty, so too, they act as mirrors to His Permanence through their transience. The earth and trees in particular, through their poverty in wintertime and their dazzling pomp and riches in springtime, reflect in a most clear fashion the Power and Mercy of One Absolutely Powerful and Absolutely Wealthy. It is as if all beings are supplicating in the language of their different ways of being, like Uways al-Qarani:

Our God! You are our Lord because we see that we are mere slaves; We are unable to train ourselves, so it is You Who train us. Also, You are the Creator because we are created beings, we are being made. Again, You are the Provider because we need provision and we are not able to provide for ourselves, so it is You Who make and provide for us. Further, You are the true Owner because we are owned: One other than ourselves is exerting free disposal over us, so it is You Who are the Owner.

You are the Mighty, having dignity and grandeur. When we look at ourselves, we see that a mightiness is manifested through us despite our poverty and helplessness. So, we are mirrors to Your Sublimity and Might. It is again You Who are the Absolutely Wealthy. We are poor but we are granted riches that we are unable to obtain by ourselves. So, You are the Wealthy, You are the Giver. You are also the Ever-Living, Ever-Permanent One because we are born and die and, in our coming to life and our dying, we see the manifestation of a perpetual Giver of Life. You are the Ever-Permanent One because we see Your continuation and permanence in our demise and transience. Again, none but You are the One Who answers us and grants us gifts because we, all creatures, are ever calling out and requesting, beseeching either through words or through the language of our ways of be-

ing, and our desires are satisfied, our aims achieved. So, it is You Who answer our pleas.

And so on.

Every creature, universal or particular is, like Uways al-Qarani, a mirror in the form that has the meaning of supplication, reflecting the Divine Power and Perfection through their helplessness, poverty and deficiency.

The ninth phrase: *In His hand is all good*

That is, all good things are in His hand, all good deeds are in His Book, all benevolence is in His Treasury. Because of this, he who desires good must seek it from Him, the one who wishes for what is best must entreat Him. In order to demonstrate the truth of this phrase in a convincing fashion, we shall point out the signs of an inclusive instance of innumerable evidences of Divine Knowledge, as follows:

The Maker Who creates and exerts authority in this universe as observed through all His acts in it, has an All-Encompassing Knowledge. That Knowledge is inherent to His Essence: for it is a thousand times inconceivable that the Knowledge of the Being Who has created these well-ordered beings should be separated from Him.

Just as this All-Encompassing Knowledge is indispensable to that Being, it is also essential to all things because of their being enveloped by It. As it is not possible for the objects on the face of the earth not to see the sun, it is a thousand times more impossible for the objects to be hidden from the light of the Knowledge of the Majestic, All-Knowing One. This is because they are in His Presence: everything is within the range of His Sight and He penetrates into all things.

If that solid sun, those unconscious X-rays, and whatever else that is a source of light, and also that helpless man, can see and penetrate everything that faces them, although they are contingent, defective and accidental, nothing at all, of course, can remain hidden from the light of that Eternal Knowledge, which is necessarily all-encompassing and essential. There are countless signs in the universe that point to this truth, as may be seen in the following examples:

All the instances of wisdom witnessed in all beings point to that Knowledge. Because He Who performs His work out of kindness and graciousness certainly does so knowingly. Also, all well-ordered creatures, each within a precise balance, and all balanced and measured forms, each in a perfect order, point to that All-Encompassing Knowledge. For to do any work in orderly fashion requires knowledge. Again, all graces and adornments show knowledge. The one who works artistically, according to a strict measure and balance, is of course relying on a powerful knowledge. Further, the precise proportions witnessed in all creatures, the shapes cut out in accordance with purpose and benefits, and the fruitful conditions and compositions giving one the impression that they have all been made according to the principles of Divine Decree and with the 'compasses' of Divine Determination, all demonstrate His All-Encompassing Knowledge.

Indeed, it is not possible save through an all-encompassing knowledge to give each thing a unique, yet well-ordered, form which is appropriate to, and has relevance for, its life and existence.

Besides, it is only through an all-encompassing knowledge that the needs of all living creatures are provided for in a suitable way, at the appropriate time, in unexpected places. Because only the One Who knows who is needy of what, when and where, can provide for all needs in a suitable way.

In addition, the appointed hour of death of all living creatures, unknown to the creatures themselves, is dependent on a law of determination and shows an all-encompassing knowledge. For, though it does not appear at first sight that an hour of death was appointed for all families of creatures and individuals, plants in particular, yet the hour was appointed for any family within defined limits of time. And it again demonstrates an all-encompassing knowledge that the seeds and issue of that family or individual are preserved so as to continue its duty or function and to be the means of transformation into new lives.

Also, it points to a comprehensive knowledge that each being is appropriately gratified by Mercy, which encompasses all beings. Because, for example, the One Who feeds the offspring of sentient creatures with milk and Who sustains the vegetation of the earth with the water and rain it needs, must of course know the infants and their needs, must see that vegetation and perceive how necessary the rain is to its survival.

Further, the care that is seen in the making of all creatures as well as the artistic design and skilful adornment of them demonstrates an all-encompassing knowledge. Because only through that knowledge is it possible to choose an orderly, adorned, artistic and purposeful state from among thousands of possible states.

Again, the perfect ease in the creation and origination of things points to a most perfect knowledge. Because, the ease and facility in an achievement is directly proportional to the degree of knowledge and skill: the more one knows something the more easily one accomplishes it. And indeed we do see how all things, each a miracle of art, is created with astonishing ease and facility, without trouble or confusion, in a short period of time, miraculously.

Like those mentioned in the examples above, there are thousands of true signs that the One Who has free disposal over the universe has an all-encompassing knowledge. He knows all things with their qualities and functions, and then He acts. Since the Owner of this universe has such knowledge, most certainly He sees human beings and their actions and He knows what reward and punishment they deserve. He deals and will deal with them according to the requirements of His Wisdom and Mercy.

So, O man, be sensible! Think carefully of just what kind of Being it is Who knows you and watches you; realize it and pull yourself together.

A possible objection: If you object that Knowledge alone is not sufficient for this wonderful composition of creatures, and that Will is also necessary, my answer would be thus:

All creatures point and bear witness to Divine All-Encompassing Knowledge; they also point to the universal Will of the Possessor of that Knowledge.

A universal Will is demonstrated in many ways: each creature, especially each sentient being, while hesitating among many possibilities, is given a most well-ordered particular identity through a single probability determined from among a great profusion of probabilities, and through a certain way leading to a result out of many fruitless ways. This well-ordered identity, measure and form are given according to a most sensitive scale and most subtle organization, cut out of the solid elements 'flowing' at random in endless possibilities and fruitless ways, and this necessarily and self-evidently demonstrates that they are the works of a universal Will. For choosing a single state from innumerable possible states can only happen by means of a designation, a preference, a purpose and a will, by specification, by a deliberate intention and desire. Specifying certainly requires one who specifies and preference requires one who prefers. And this one that specifies and prefers is Will.

For example, as the creation of a being like man, who is like a machine composed out of hundreds of different systems and components, is from a drop of water; and the creation of a bird, which has hundreds of different members, out of a simple egg;

and that of a tree, which is divided into hundreds of different parts, out of a simple seed, testify to Power and Knowledge, they also indicate in a necessary and decisive fashion the Universal Will of their Maker, with which He specifies every constituent member and part of each being and gives to each a different and particular shape.

In short, just as the resemblance and correspondence between, for example, the major parts of animal bodies in regard to their fundamentals and results, decisively indicate the Oneness of their Maker, so too, the distinction between their identities and faces demonstrates that their Maker of Unity has Will and absolute freedom in His acts: He does what He wishes to do, He does not do what He does not wish to do; He acts independently of the whole universe and has an absolute, universal Will. Since this is so, that is to say, since there are as many indications and testimonies to Divine Knowledge and Will as creatures or, rather, as functions of those creatures, it is tantamount to falsehood as great as the number of creatures and a lunacy of misguidance compounded to the number of those creatures' functions that some philosophers deny Divine Destiny, or that certain unorthodox and misguided people claim that Divine Knowledge does not comprehend all particulars, or that certain naturalists attribute the existence of some creatures to mere natural cause and effect. For one who denies the countless instances of true witnessing is telling a lie of infinite dimensions.

So, you can consider how mistaken and contrary to the truth it is to say intentionally of events, all of which take place through Divine Will, 'naturally', instead of 'if God wills it so.'

The tenth phrase: *He is powerful over everything*

That is, nothing is difficult for Him. He is able to clothe everything with existence most easily. It is so simple and easy for Him to make things that He has but to command them to be and they are.

If a very skilful artist only puts out his hand when he wants to make some work and everything operates to that end as obediently as a machine, we may say of him, in order to express his speed and skill, that he has command over his work to such a degree that his works of art seem to come into existence by a single touch, or a single command. So too, the verse, *His command when He wills a thing, is only to say to it 'be' and it is,*[3] declares that things are in absolute subjugation and obedience to the Power of the All-Powerful One of Majesty, and that His Power operates with utmost ease. We shall explain in five points, five of the countless mysteries contained in this comprehensive truth.

The first point: In respect of Divine Power the greatest thing is as easy as the smallest. The creation of a species with all of its members is as untroubling as the creation of a single individual. To create Paradise is as easy as to create the spring and the spring as easy as a flower. This mystery has been explained at the end of the *Tenth Word,* which is about Resurrection, and through the comparisons, namely Luminosity, Transparency, Reciprocity, Balance, Orderliness, Obedience and Abstraction, which are mentioned in the 'Second Aim' of the *Twenty-Ninth Word,* which is about the angels, the immortality of the spirit and Resurrection. It has been demonstrated in all these that in relation to Divine Power it is as easy to create stars as particles and innumerable individuals are as easy to create as a single individual.

The second point: We readily observe how in the creation of animals and vegetation, there is the highest degree of mastery and exquisite artistry with an infinite multiplicity and liberality; the greatest degree of distinction and differentiation within the utmost profusion and intermingling; and the artistry of the highest worth and the most splendid beauty of creation with the greatest abundance and profusion. Furthermore, although their creation requires a great machinery and much time, they

---

3. *Ya Sin,* 36.82.

are made with the utmost ease and speed as if suddenly and out of nothing.

This activity of Power, readily observed every season on the earth, proves irrefutably that, in relation to the Power that originates those acts, the greatest thing is as easy to create as the smallest and countless individuals are as easy to manage as a single individual.

The third point: Why it is equally easy for the Power of the All-Powerful Maker to create the highest universal as to create the smallest particular with the same value of art arises form these three sources:

First: the assistance coming from Divine Oneness

Second: the facility originating in Divine Unity

Third: the manifestation of Divine Uniqueness

The assistance coming from Divine Oneness: If all things are owned and commanded by one single being, then because of his oneness, he can concentrate the power of all things behind one single thing and he can manage all things as easily as a single thing. We shall explain this subtle point by way of comparison in order to make it more understandable.

The monarch of a country can, by virtue of being the single authority in the country, mobilize the moral strength of a whole army behind every single soldier, and because he can do this, a single soldier can capture another king and have command over him in the name of his monarch. That monarch, by reason of being the single sovereign, can also manage the whole army and all his officials as easily as he employs and administers a single soldier and a single official. It is as if, by virtue of his monopoly of all administrative powers, he could send all to the aid of each and each could thereafter rely on the strength of all. If, however, the rope of that unity of sovereignty were to break, and disunity of authority and disorder were to burst out, then each soldier would lose a limitless strength and fall from a position of great strength to that of a weak ordinary individual. And to administer them would cause as many difficulties as the number of the soldiers.

Similarly, – *God's is the highest comparison* – the Maker of the universe, because of His Oneness, concentrates upon one single thing the manifestation of the whole of His Names operating on all things together and thus creates it with infinite art, in a valuable form. By means of all things He gives assistance, when necessary, to a single thing and strengthens it. Again by virtue of Oneness He also creates, disposes and administers all things as if they were a single thing.

Thus, it is through the assistance of Divine Oneness that in the universe a certain quality of the highest degree in art and value is apparent within the utmost abundance and variety.

The facility originating in Divine Unity: If things are managed from one centre, by one hand, according to one law, then everything will be very easy, which otherwise would be most difficult. For example, if the essential equipment of all the soldiers of an army is manufactured in one centre, according to one law and at the command of a single commander-in-chief, it is as easy as equipping one soldier. Otherwise, the equipment of a single soldier will be as difficult as equipping a whole army. Also thousands of fruits are very easy to grow on a particular tree which depends on one law and one root. If, on the other hand, only one fruit was to be obtained from one tree, then that individual fruit would be as difficult to grow as a tree, and would entail the elements necessary for the life of a tree.

Thus, as can be seen in these two comparisons, – *God's is the highest comparison* – because the Maker of the universe is Single, One, He acts through Unity, and since He acts through Unity, all things are as easy for Him as a single thing. Moreover, He is able to make a single thing as valuable as all things together with regard to the art it contains. Further, He creates innumerable individuals in a very valuable form, and thus demonstrates His absolute liberality through the language of that visible, boundless abundance and limitless profusion, and He manifests His infinite generosity and creativity.

The manifestation of Divine uniqueness: That is, since the Majestic Maker is not physical or corporeal, time and place cannot restrict Him. Creation and space cannot interfere with His presence and witnessing. Means and mass cannot veil His acts. There is no fragmentation or division in what pertains to Him or to His acts. His acts do not impede one another; He performs innumerable acts as if they were one act. Because of this, He can contain a world in a single individual as He encapsulates a huge tree in its seed. He directs and disposes the whole creation as if it were a single individual.

We have explained in some other *Words* how this is possible.

Since the sun is, to some degree, unrestrictable on account of its luminosity, its image is reflected in every burnished and shining object. If hundreds, or even millions, of mirrors are held towards it, in each is found a complete, unrefracted image of it, without one preventing the other. If the capacity of the mirror was such, the sun would be able to demonstrate its effects in it in all its magnitude. It can enter thousands of places together with the ease of entering only one place. It is in this way – *God's is the highest comparison* – that the manifestation of the Majestic Maker of this universe is such, with all His Attributes, which are pure light, and with all His Names, which are luminous, that, on account of His Uniqueness – though He is not in any place – He is Ever-Present and All-Witnessing in every place, and He performs every act at the same time, in all places, without difficulty, without obstruction.

Thus, it is through these three means – the assistance coming from Divine Oneness; the facility originating in Divine Unity;

the manifestation of Divine uniqueness – that, when the whole creation is attributed to a single Creator, the creation and administration of all creatures can be understood to be as easy as that of a single creature, and each individual entity can be as valuable as all as regards to the value of its art. This truth is demonstrated by the fact that, within the endless abundance of creatures, there are innumerable subtleties of art in every individual. If, in contrast to this, creation is not directly attributed to a single Creator, then each creature becomes as difficult as all beings and the value of all creatures falls to that of a single creature.

It is because of this truth that the Sophists, who were the most extreme in the crudeness of their reasoning, realizing that the path of associating partners with God is infinitely more difficult to follow than the way of truth and affirming God's Unity, and because they already turned away from the way of truth, felt compelled to 'renounce their intellects' and deny the existence of everything.

The fourth point: The creation of Paradise is as easy as that of the spring in relation to the Power of the All-Powerful One Who administers the universe with acts that are readily observed. Likewise, a flower can be as delicate in art and beautiful in form and as valuable as a whole spring. This truth comes from three sources:

The first: The necessity of the Creator's Existence and His total detachment from creation.

The second: The complete otherness of His Essence and His Being unrestricted.

The third: His not being bound by space and His invisibility.

The first source: The fact that the necessity of the Creator's Existence and His total detachment from creation cause infinite ease and facility is an extremely profound mystery. We will facilitate understanding of it by means of the following allegory:

39

There are varying degrees of existence and the worlds of existence are all different. Since they are all different, a particle from one level of existence, which is deeply rooted in existence, is so great as to be able to contain a mountain from the level of existence which is less substantial than the other. For example, the faculty of memory, which is the size of a mustard seed in a head that is from the manifest corporeal world, can hold as much as a library from the world of meanings. A huge city is, through reflection, encompassed by a mirror the size of a fingernail from the external world. If, then, that memory and mirror had had consciousness and a creative power, they would have been able to be endlessly operative and bring about endless transformations in those worlds of meaning and reflection through the power of their minute existences in the external world. This means that the power of an existent entity is directly proportional to the firmness of its establishment in existence. Especially after existence has attained to complete firmness and stability, being detached from corporeality and unrestricted, then even only a partial manifestation of it will be able to direct many worlds of other less substantial levels of existence.

Thus – *God's is the highest comparison* – the Majestic Maker of this universe is Necessarily Existent. His Existence is substantial to His Essence and is eternal; its non-existence is inconceivable and its cessation impossible. It is the most firmly established, the most fundamental, the strongest and the most perfect of the levels of existence. In relation to His Existence, other levels of existence are like extremely pale shadows. His Necessary Existence of that degree is so deeply rooted and real, and the existence of all other beings, which are contingent, is so pale and insubstantial that many researchers of discernment, like Muhyi al-Din ibn al-'Arabi, have concluded that there is no existent save He, thus reducing other levels of existence to the level of the illusory or imaginal.

Thus, for the Power of the Necessarily-Existent Being, which is both necessary and substantially related to His Essence, the created, accidental, weak and relatively stable existence of contingent beings is infinitely easy and simple. To resurrect all the dead for the Great Mustering and then judge them is as easy for Him as to return even a single tree to life every spring to bring it into leaf and flower, and to cause it to yield fruit.

The second source: Why the complete otherness of His Essence and His unrestricted Being is the means of ease is this: Certainly, the Maker of the universe is not the same kind as the universe. His Essence resembles no other essence at all. Since this is so, no obstacle or restraint can impede Him or constrain His acts. He has complete and free control over everything. If the management of the universe and the events occurring in it were to be attributed to the universe itself, it would cause so many difficulties and so much confusion that it is inconceivable that any thing could exist at all and, if it could, there would be no order and harmony in the universe.

For example, it is inconceivable that the stones of a fine, vaulted dome fashioned and arranged themselves, or that an army battalion could be effectively commanded by soldiers themselves. Even if it were possible, everything would go into chaos. By contrast, if the arrangement of the stones is attributed to a craftsman who is not of the same kind as stones, and the command of the battalion to an officer, both the artistic arrangement and the command are easy. This is so because, whereas the stones and soldiers are obstacles to each other, the craftsman and the officer can deal with them from all sides, they can give orders without obstacle.

Thus – *God's is the highest comparison* – the sacred Essence of the Necessarily-Existent Being is not of the same kind as the essence of contingent beings. Rather, all the truths in the universe are rays from the Name, the Truth, one of the Beautiful Names of that Essence. Since His sacred Essence is necessarily existent and completely detached from materiality and different from all other essences, with no like or equivalent, then, most certainly, in relation to the Eternal Power of that All-Majestic Being, the in sustaining and administration of the whole universe is as easy as that of the spring, rather, as of a single tree. Also, the creation of the other world, of Paradise and Hell, and the raising of the dead on the Day of Judgement, is easy in the same way as the resurrection in springtime of a single tree that had died the previous autumn.

The third source: Why the indivisibility of His Essence and His not being bound by space are the means of ease is this: since the All-Powerful Maker is beyond place, He is equally present in every place through His Power. Also, since He is indivisible, He certainly has free disposal over everything through all His Names. Again, since He is present everywhere and administers everything, existent beings, means and masses cannot hinder Him in His acts; essentially, there is no need at all for them to do so. If we suppose that there were some need, then, like electric wires, the branches of trees, and veins in the human body, things would act as facilitating means for the arrival of life and the cause of promptness in actions, rather than restricting, obstructing and impeding. Everything is, in essence, in absolute obedience and submission to the Majestic All-Powerful One's Power.

In sum: the All-Powerful Maker creates everything in an appropriate form without trouble, swiftly and easily, without undergoing any process. He creates universals as easily as particulars, and particulars as artistically as universals.

Indeed, He Who creates universals and the heaven and the earth is most certainly the One Who creates the particulars and animate individuals that are contained therein. For those tiny particulars are the fruits, seeds and miniature specimens of universals.

We see that the particulars are each like a seed and tiny copy in relation to universals. This being so, He Who creates particulars must certainly be the Creator and Controller of the universal elements and the heavens and the earth so that, in accordance with the principles of His Wisdom and the balances of His Knowledge, He makes the particulars encapsulate the contents, the meanings, the samples of the universal, all-encompassing entities.

Indeed, with regard to wonder of artistry or marvellousness of creativity, particulars are not less than universals; flowers are not 'lower' than stars, nor are seeds 'inferior' to trees. Rather, the meaning of a tree inscribed in the seed by Divine Destiny is more wonderful than the actual, fully grown tree woven by Divine Power. Likewise, the creation of man is more wonderful than the creation of the universe. If a Qur'an of wisdom were inscribed on an atom in particles of some etheral substance, it would surpass in value a Qur'an of grandeur written in stars on the face of the heavens. So too, there are many particulars that are superior to universals with respect to the miraculousness of their art.

The fifth point: The infinite ease and utmost speed in the creation of beings gives to the people of guidance this firm conviction: in relation to the Power of the One Who creates beings, paradises are as easy to create as the spring, the spring as easy as gardens, and gardens as easy as flowers. Also, as the verse, *Your creation and your upraising are as but a single soul* [4] states, the resurrection of all human beings is as easy as making a single individual die and raising him to life again; and as stated explicitly in the verse, *It will have been only one cry, then behold, they are all arranged before us* [5], to raise to life all humankind for the last Great Mustering is as easy as calling together with the sound of a trumpet an army that has dispersed to rest.

Although this utmost speed and infinite ease are clear proofs

---

4. *Luqman,* 31.28.
5. *Ya Sin,* 36.53.

of the perfection of the Maker's Power, they have led the mis-guided to attribute the creation of things to things themselves. That is, since they see that some ordinary things come into existence very easily, they mistake their formation as self-formation. Consider how infinite stupidity that is! They make what proves the existence of an infinite power, the proof for its non-existence. They thereby open the door to boundless possibility, because, by doing this, they attribute to each particle of every creature the attributes of perfection, like infinite power and all-encompassing knowledge, which are essential attributes of only the Maker of the Universe.

The eleventh phrase: *And unto Him is the return*

That is, everything will return from the realm of transience to the abode of permanence, and will go to the 'Seat' of Eternal Sovereignty of the Ever-Enduring One. Everything will transfer from the world of multiple causes to the sphere of the Majestic One of Unity, where His Power is operative without the veil of the laws of cause and effect. Your place of recourse, therefore, is His Court, and your place of refuge, His Mercy.

Like those mentioned above, there are many more truths that this 'eleventh phrase' takes up. Among them, the truth concerned with eternal happiness and Paradise has been explained so clearly in the *Tenth* and *Twenty-Ninth Words* that no need remains for further explanation. Those two *Words* convince the reader that, just as the sun that sets will rise again the following morning, so life too, which is the 'immaterial sun' of this world, will rise so as to shine permanently in the morning of the Resurrection after it sets with the destruction of the world. Then, a certain portion of *jinn* and mankind will be rewarded with eternal bliss, while the other portion will be condemned to eternal torment.

Indeed, the All-Wise Maker of this universe, Who has boundless All-Encompassing Knowledge, limitless universal Will and infinite All-Enveloping Power, the All-Compassionate Creator of human beings, has promised in all His heavenly Scriptures and decrees Paradise and eternal happiness to the believing members of humankind. Since He has promised this, He will most certainly bring it about, because it is inconceivable for Him to break His promise. Breaking a promise is a most ugly fault, and arises either from ignorance or incompetence. But, because the One of Absolute Perfection is totally exempt and free from any fault, and ignorance and impotence are inconceivable for the Absolutely Powerful, the All-Knowing One, breaking a promise is inconceivable for Him.

Moreover, all the Prophets, saints, scholars of highest attainment, and the believers and, above all, the *Pride of the World*, that is, the Prophet Muhammad, upon him be peace and blessings, have continually requested and entreated the All-Compassionate and Generous One for the eternal bliss that He has promised. They have entreated it through all His Beautiful Names. For, to begin with, His Mercy and Compassion, His Justice and Wisdom, that is, His Names, Merciful and Compassionate, Just and Wise (as also most of His other Beautiful Names, like Lord and God and His Attributes like Lordship and Sovereignty), all require the Hereafter and eternal happiness, and testify to its reality. Furthermore, the Wise Qur'an, which is the greatest creed of God, demonstrates and teaches this truth in scores of its verses, with clear evidences and decisive proofs. Also, the one most beloved by God, who is the pride of mankind, that is, the Prophet Muhammad, upon him be peace and blessings, on the basis of countless dazzling miracles, taught this truth throughout his life, with all his strength, proclaimed and demonstrated and proved it.

O God, bestow blessings and peace and benedictions on him and on his family and on his Companions, to the number of the breaths of the people of Paradise in Paradise, and resurrect us and resur-

rect him who publishes this treatise, together with his friends, and his companion Said, and our parents and brothers and sisters, under his banner, and grant us his intercession, and enter us into Paradise in the company of his family and Companions, through Your Mercy, O Most Merciful of the Merciful. Amen. Amen.

Our Lord, take us not to task if we forget, or do wrong.

Our Lord, do not make our hearts to swerve after You have guided us; and give us the gift of Your Mercy from You; indeed, You are the Giver of Gifts.

My Lord, open up my breast and ease for me my task. Loosen a knot from my tongue so that people may understand my words.

And our Lord, turn towards us in forgiveness. Indeed, You are the Accepter of Repentance, the Compassionate.

Glory be to You! We have no knowledge save what You have taught us. Indeed, You are the All-Knowing, the All-Wise.

***

AN ADDENDUM
to the Tenth Phrase of the Twentieth Letter

In His Name, glory be to Him
There is nothing that does not glorify Him with praise.

In the Name of God, the Merciful, the Compassionate

For verily, in the remembrance of God are the hearts at rest.[6]

God has struck a parable: a man who is shared by many masters, each pulling him to himself.[7]

Question

You have argued in many places that there is infinite ease in Oneness and endless difficulties in multiplicity and associating partners with God. In consequence, believing in One God should be, for man, inevitably necessary, while accepting more than One God should be inconceivable. However, the difficulties and impossibilities that you point out seem also to be present with Oneness. For example, you say that if particles were not under the Command of the One God, then it would be necessary for each particle either to have an all-encompassing knowledge and absolute power, or have at its command innumerable conceptual operations. This is, of course, absolutely inconceivable. Even if they were under the Command of God, would it not still be necessary for them to have the same qualities so as to be able to accomplish their infinitely orderly duties?

Answer

Further to what has been already said on this point: If the creation of all creatures is attributed to a single Maker, it becomes as easy as the creation of a single thing, but if it is attributed to

---

6. *al-Ra'd*, 13.28.
7. *al-Zumar*, 39.29.

47

nature and multiple causes, a single fly becomes as difficult as the heavens, a flower as the spring, a fruit as a garden. We shall now put forward only three brief allegories to reassure the soul and the mind about this truth.

The first allegory: For example, a tiny transparent glistening speck cannot contain in itself a light even the size of a match-head; it can, in its own right, contain a light only the size of an insignificant particle, according to its own dimensions and mass. However, if that transparent speck is open to the manifestation of the sun, it will be able to comprehend that immense sun, its light (with all its colours) and heat; it will display a most comprehensive manifestation of the sun. That is, if that speck remains on its own, it will be able to function to the limit of its dimensions, namely of a particle. Whereas, if it is connected to the sun, turning to and being a mirror to it, it will be able to display in some measure examples of the sun's functioning.

Thus – *God's is the highest comparison* – if the existence of each being, each particle even, is attributed to nature, to causes or to itself, then each particle must, when the wonderful duties it performs are considered, either have an all-encompassing knowledge and absolute power or countless devices must be operative within it. If, on the other hand, the whole existence is attributed to a Single One of Unity, then each particle, through its connection to Him, becomes His officer. This connection makes it display some manifestation of Him, and through this connection and through being an object of His manifestation, it depends on His Infinite Knowledge and Power. Then, by virtue of that connection and dependence, it performs, through the Power of its Creator, functions and duties far beyond its own power.

The second allegory: Suppose there were two brothers, one brave but self-dependent, the other patriotic and devoted to his country. When a war broke out, the self-dependent one wanted to act independently of the state and, therefore, had to carry, as far as his strength allowed, his equipment and ammunition around his neck. In accordance with that individual strength, he could only engage one corporal of the enemy army in combat – to do more was beyond him.

The other brother did not depend on himself. He knew himself to be powerless on his own and accordingly enrolled in the army, thus forming a connection with the king. Through that connection, the whole army became a support for him, and owing to that support, he plunged into the war with the moral strength of the army behind him. So, when he encountered a field-marshal of the defeated army's king, he took him as a prisoner of war in the name of his own king. This is because while the first man was compelled to carry his equipment and sources of strength himself, and therefore was not able to perform but an extremely insignificant service, that second one did not have to carry his source of strength, rather, the army and the king carried it. Just as though he was connecting his receiver to existing telecommunication lines with a tiny wire, that man, through the connection he formed, connected himself to an infinite power.

Thus – *God's is the highest comparison* – if all creatures, all particles are attributed directly to the Single One of Unity and if they themselves are submitted to Him, then, through the power of that submission and through the strength of their Lord, by His command, even an ant can, and did, demolish Pharaoh's palace; a fly can, and did, dispatch Nimrod to Hell; a microbe can send an unjust tyrant off to his grave; a seed the size of a grain of wheat can become a workshop for the production of a huge pine tree; and a particle of air can enter into the formation of all flowers and fruits in an orderly fashion.

All that ease evidently arises from that submission and being an officer. If, by contrast, everything is left to itself and, in association of partners with God, the existence and operation of each creature is attributed to independent causes or to itself, then each creature can function only within the bounds of its own physical entity and to the measure of its own consciousness.

The third allegory: Suppose there were two friends who wished to write a geographical work, based on statistical data, on a country that they had never seen.

One of the two friends formed an intimate connection with the government of that country. He entered the national telecommunication centre and, with a piece of wire worth a few pence, connected his own telephone receiver to the state lines and was able to communicate with every place and receive information. Consequently, he put together a sound, well-composed work of geography based on statistical data.

As for the other, in order to write a sound work like his friend, either he would have to travel continuously for fifty years to see every place and obtain all the necessary information or, spending millions of pounds, he would have to set up as the government did a comprehensive telegraph and telephone system of his own.

In the same way – *God's is the highest comparison* – if countless things, creatures, are attributed to Single One of Unity, then through that connection each becomes an object through which the 'Eternal Sun' manifests Himself. This enables it to obtain a connection with the laws of His Wisdom, the principles of His Knowledge and the laws of His Power. Then, through Divine Strength and Power it rises to the rank of displaying a certain manifestation of the Lord by which it has an eye that sees all things, a face that looks to all places, and words that have weight in all matters. If that connection is cut off, since the universe is an organism all parts of which are related to one another, its relation to all other things will be severed, and it will then be nothing more than its own mass. In this case, it would have to possess absolute divinity so that it might perform the functions described above.

In short, in the way of unity and faith there is infinite ease in the degree of 'necessity', while in the way of associating partners with God there are difficulties impossible to surpass. For one being may arrange numerous things easily in a particular way so as to obtain a certain result. If this arrangement is left to the things themselves to obtain the same result, then it would be impossibly difficult. For example, as stated in the *Third Letter*, if the fine spectacle made by the planets in the sky under the 'command' of the sun, and the yearly and daily movements of the earth which are the cause of the alternation of seasons and of daytime and night, are ascribed to the One Eternal Sovereign, then it will be very easy and sufficient for Him to employ only one of His 'soldiers' such as the earth to achieve this splendid result. After it has received the order 'Move!', the earth will rise up with joy and whirl, like a Mawlawi dervish, and glorify the Names of its Lord, and the desired result will be obtained very easily and with perfect orderliness.

However, if the earth is denied this order to move and the affair is left to the heavenly bodies themselves, any reasonable person can easily judge what a disastrous chaos must result, even if millions of stars thousands of times larger than the earth set themselves in motion.

In conclusion: The Qur'an and the believers attribute numberless creatures to One Maker, and ascribe every affair directly to Him. Their way, therefore, is so easy to follow that every creature's existence and every event become necessary. By contrast, the rebellious polytheists, by ascribing a single thing to innumerable causes, follow a way so beset with difficulties as to be impossible. What is necessary for the coming into existence of a single creature in the explanation of the misguided is sufficient for the creation of the whole universe in the explanation of the believer in the Qur'an. The issuing of all things out of one is very much easier than the issuing of one thing out of innumerable things, just as an officer can command a thousand soldiers as easily as he can command a single soldier, while the command of a single soldier by a thousand officers would cause chaos since it would be as difficult as commanding a thousand soldiers separately.

This magnificent verse hurls this truth at those who associate partners with God:

> God has struck a parable: a man who is shared by many masters, each pulling him to himself; and a man who entirely belongs to one master. Can the two be equal in comparison? Praise be to God! Nay, but most of them do not know.[8]

> Glory be to You! We have no knowledge save what You have taught us. Indeed, You are the All-Knowing, the All-Wise.

> O God, bestow blessings and peace on our master, Muhammad, to the number of the particles of the universe, and on all his family and Companions. Amen. And all praise be to God, the Lord of all the worlds.

> O God! O Unique One! O Single One! O Besought-of-All! O He, than Whom there is no other god but Himself alone, Who has no partner! O He, Whose is the Sovereignty, the Kingdom and Whose is all praise! O He, Who gives life and makes to die! O He, in Whose hand is all good! O He, Who is Powerful over everything! O He, to Whom is the homecoming! For the sake of the mysteries contained in these phrases, join the publisher of this treatise, his friends, and his companion Said, with the perfected affirmers of God's Unity and the truthful, meticulous researchers and God-fearing believers. Amen.

> O God! For the sake of the mystery of Your Oneness, make the publisher of this book disseminate the mysteries of Your Unity and make his heart filled with the lights of faith and his tongue speak of the truths of the Qur'an. Amen. Amen. Amen.

***

---

8. al-Zumar, 39.29.

The Twenty-first Letter

Affection towards parents

In His Name, glory be to Him

There is nothing that does not glorify Him with praise.

In the Name of God, the Merciful, the Compassionate

Your Lord has decreed, that you worship none save Him, and to be good to parents. If one of them or both of them attain to old age with you, say not to them 'Fie' neither chide them, but speak unto them a gracious word. And lower unto them the wing of humility out of mercy and say, 'My Lord, have mercy on them both, as they did care for me when I was little.' Your Lord is best aware of what is in your minds. If you are righteous, verily He is All-Forgiving to those who are patient.[1]

O you, who are unaware of the filial responsibility towards parents, in whose house is one of his old parents, or helpless, invalid relative or brother-in-religion unable to make his living! Heed the verses quoted above and see how they insist in five different ways on the affection to be shown to parents!

Of course, paternal affection for children is one of the sublime realities of worldly life and, in turn, filial gratitude to them is a most urgent and heavy duty to be performed. Parents sacri-

---

1. *al-Isra'*, 17.23–5.

fice their lives lovingly for their children, and if this is so, what falls to a child who has not lost his humanity and become transformed into a monster of ingratitude, is to show sincere respect for them, to serve them willingly, and to try to gain their approval. With regard to filial respect and service, uncles and aunts are like parents.

Now, you, who are neglectful of your duties to your parents, know how terribly disgraceful and lacking in scruples it is to be bored with the existence of old parents and to desire and expect their death. Know this and come to your senses! You must understand what an unjustice it is that you desire the end of the lives of those who have sacrificed their lives for you.

O you, who are immersed in earning your livelihood! Know that your disabled relative whom you regard as unbearable in your house is, in fact, the means of blessing and abundance. Never complain that *you can scarcely make a living* (that your means of subsistence are strained), for were it not for the blessing and abundance bestowed on you, you would have to face even more difficulties in making your living. This is an undeniable reality, which I could prove to you except that I would like to keep this letter brief.

Believe me, I swear by God that this is an established reality to which even my satan and evil-commanding self have yielded. Indeed, as is witnessed by the whole of the existence, when the Generous, Majestic Creator, Who is infinitely merciful, compassionate, gracious and munificent, sends children to the world, He sends them together with their sustenance which He provides through the breasts of mothers abundantly. In the same way, He sends in the form of blessing and unseen, immaterial abundance, the sustenance of the old, who are like children and even more worthy and needy of compassion than children. He does not load their sustenance onto mean, greedy people.

The truth expressed in the verses, *Surely God is He Who is the*

All-Provider, the Possessor of Strength and the Steadfast[2] and *How many an animate creature that bears not its own provision, but God provides for it and you,*[3] is openly proclaimed by living creatures of all kinds through the tongue of their dispositions. So, not only the sustenance of old relatives, but also that of pets, like cats, which are created as friends to human beings and usually live on food from human beings, is, again, sent in the form of blessing. I have personally observed this:

Some years ago, my daily ration consisted of half a loaf of bread. Since the loaf was very small, I barely managed with it, until four cats became my everyday guests. No sooner did they begin sharing my bread, than the same ration was always enough for all of us.

I witnessed this so often that it convinced me that I benefited from the blessing coming through the cats. I openly declare that they were not a burden upon me, and that I was rather indebted to them, and not they to me.

O man, a human being is the most esteemed, noble and most worthy-of-respect among creatures; among human beings, the believers are the most perfect. Among the believers, the helpless, old people are those who are the most worthy and needy of respect and compassion. Among the old, the relatives deserve affection, love and service more than the others, and among the relatives, parents are the most truthful confidants and most intimate companions. Now, O man, if an animal becomes the means of blessing and abundance when it stays as a guest in a man's house, then you can conclude how invaluable a means of blessing and mercy parents are in a house and, additionally, as stated in the *hadith* — *But for the old bent double, calamities would be pouring down upon you* [4]— what an important means for the removal of calamities they are.

---

2. *al-Dhariyat*, 51.58.

3. *al-Ankabut*, 29.60.

4. al-Ajluni, *Kashf al-Khafa'*, 2.163.

If this is so, O man, come to your senses! If you have been assigned a long life, certainly, you too, will grow old, and if you do not show due regard for your parents, then, according to the rule, *one is rewarded or punished in accordance with the kind of one's action,* your children will not respect you either. Further, if you consider your afterlife seriously, it is a precious provision for your afterlife to gain the approval of your parents by serving them. If you love the worldly life, again you should please them so that you may lead a pleasant life. If, by contrast, you regard them as unbearable, if you break their easily-offended hearts, and if you desire their death, you will be the object of the Qur'anic threat, *he loses both the world and the world to come.* So, whoever wishes for the mercy of the All-Merciful must show mercy to those entrusted to him by God in his house.

I had a brother-in-religion called Mustafa Cavus. I noticed that he usually succeeded in both his worldly affairs and the matters related to the Hereafter. I did not know how he could do so. Then, I came to understand that he succeeded because he observed the rights of his parents strictly. So, whoever desires to be prosperous in both worlds should do as he did.

O God, bestow blessings and peace on him who declared, 'Paradise is beneath the feet of mothers', and on his family and Companions altogether.

We have no knowledge save what You have taught us; surely You are the All-Knowing, the All-Wise.

***

The
Twenty-second
Letter

Islamic brotherhood
Contentment and greed

In His name

There is nothing that does not glorify Him with praise.

(This letter has two chapters. The first one calls the believers to brotherhood and love of each other.)

THE FIRST CHAPTER

In the name of God, the Merciful, the Compassionate

Verily the believers are indeed brothers; so make peace between your brothers.[1]

Repel (evil) with that which is better; then he, between whom and you there is enmity, shall be as if he were a loyal friend.[2]

Those who restrain their rage and forgive people – verily God loves the good-doers.[3]

Dispute and discord among the believers, and partisanship, obstinacy and envy, which lead to rancour and enmity among

---

1. *al-Hujurat*, 49.10.
2. *al-Mu'minun*, 23.96.
3. *A. Imran*, 3.134.

them, are distasteful and vile, harmful and sinful, for personal, social and spiritual life, by the testimony of truth and wisdom, and from the viewpoint of the supreme humanity that is Islam. Also, they are poison for the life of mankind. Out of numerous aspects of this truth, we shall set forth only six.

The first aspect

That it is wrong from the viewpoint of truth:

O unjust man who nourishes rancour and enmity against a believer! Suppose that you were on a ship, or in a house, with ten people, one innocent, the others criminal. If someone were to try to make the ship sink, or to set the house on fire, because of that one criminal, you know how great an injustice he would be committing. You would cry out to the heavens against his injustice. Even if there were one innocent man and nine criminals aboard the ship, it would still be against all rules of justice to sink it.

In the same way, a believer may be compared to a house or a ship belonging to God, and he has, not nine, but as many as twenty innocent attributes such as faith, Islam and neighbourliness. If, then, you cherish rancour and enmity against him on account of one criminal attribute that is adverse to you, and you desire the sinking of that 'ship' or the burning of that 'house' created by God, then this would be a most atrocious crime.

The second aspect

That it is wrong also from the viewpoint of wisdom:

As is well-known, love and enmity are, like the light and darkness, opposites so they cannot be combined in a heart in their true nature.

If love is truly felt by a heart, by virtue of the predominance of the causes that produce it, then hostility in that heart will take on the form of pity. A believer should love and indeed

A

does love his brother and is pained by any evil he sees in him. He tries to improve him not with harshness but gentleness. Because of this, as warned in a Prophetic saying: *A believer should not be angry with another, nor refuse to speak with him, for more than three days.*[4]

If, by contrast, the causes that produce enmity predominate and accordingly, hostility truly invades a heart, then the love in that heart will become merely formal and take on the form of pretence and flattery.

O unfair man! See now how great an injustice is rancour and enmity towards a brother believer! If you were to regard worthless pebbles as more valuable than the Ka'ba and greater than Mount Uhud, it would be a repugnant absurdity. Likewise, while all the Islamic attributes like faith, which has the value of the Ka'ba, and Islam, having the splendour of Mount Uhud, demand love and concord between believers, it is a disgrace and folly of the same degree, and a great injustice, to nurture hostility towards a believer. To do so would mean preferring to faith and Islam certain shortcomings in him which arouse hostility, but which, in reality, are like the worthless pebbles compared to Mount Uhud or the Ka'ba.

Indeed, unity in faith requires the unity of hearts, and the oneness of creed demands the oneness of society. You cannot deny that if you are in the same squadron as someone, you will feel a friendly attachment to him; that a friendly relation will be formed between you and him due to your both being under the command of a single commander. You will also experience a brotherly relationship because of living in the same barracks. All these things considered, you should understand the extent to which you are attached to a believer by ties of unity between you as numerous as the Divine Names, bonds of accord and relations of brotherhood coming from the light and consciousness of faith.

---

4. Bukhari, *Adab*, 57; Muslim, *Birr*, 23; Abu Dawud, *Adab*, 47.

Both of you are the slaves of the same, One Creator, One Sovereign, One Object of Worship, One Provider... so there are a thousand ties of unity between you, to the number of His Names. Besides, your Prophet, your religion, your *qibla*, are one and the same, and the number of such ties amount to almost a hundred. In addition, your town is one, your country is one, your state is one; tens of things are one and the same for you. All of these ties require unity and oneness, union and concord, love and brotherhood, and they are, as immaterial chains, strong enough to link all the planets together. If, despite all this, you prefer those things, as frail and trivial as a spider's web, that cause dispute and discord, rancour and enmity and the bearing of grudges against a believer, then you must understand – unless your heart is dead and your intelligence extinguished – how great is your disregard for those ties of unity, how grave the slight you give to those causes of love, how serious your transgression against those relationships of brotherhood!

The third aspect

According to the Qur'anic decree, *No soul laden bears the load of another*,[5] which expresses absolute justice, to nurture rancour and enmity against a believer is like condemning all the innocent attributes found in him on account of one criminal attribute, and is therefore a very great injustice. If you go further to include in your enmity all the relatives of the believer with whom you are angered because of a single evil attribute of his, then you will be the object of the Qur'anic reproach, *Verily man is much given to wrongdoing*.[6] While truth and the law and wisdom of Islam warn you against this much greater act of injustice, how can you imagine yourself right and still say, 'I am in the right'?

In the view of truth, the forms of evil which arouse enmity

5. *al-An'am*, 6.164.
6. *Ibrahim*, 14.34.

are in themselves evil and dense like earth; others are not necessarily touched or moved by them. If it should happen that another person does, after seeing those forms of evil, imitate them, that is a different matter – it is more from his inclination to those forms of evil than the effective powers of evil that he is led to do evil. By contrast, good actions and qualities spring from love and arouse love, they are luminous as love is; it is in their nature to be infectious and so to be transmitted. It is for this reason that they say it as a proverb, *The friend of a friend is a friend;* as also it is on everybody's tongue that *Many eyes are loved for the sake of one eye.*

So, O unjust man! If this is the case from the viewpoint of truth, you will understand now, if you are able to see the truth, how great an offence to truth it is to harbour enmity towards a brother in religion who is innocent and worthy of love or towards his relatives because you happen to have taken a dislike to him.

The fourth aspect

That it is wrong from the viewpoint of personal life.

Consider the following four principles which are the basis of this fourth aspect:

The first principle

When you know your way to be right and your opinions to be true, you may be justified if you say, *My way is right and better,* but you do not have the right to say, *Only my way is right.* As stated in the wise saying, *The eye of contentment is too dim to perceive faults; whereas the eye of anger exhibits all vice,* your unjust view and distorted opinion cannot judge between the ways and should not condemn the way of another as wrong.

The second principle

It is incumbent upon you that all that you say should be true, but you do not have the right to claim to say the whole of what is true. If you do so, the person you address may be irritated by your advice and react unfavourably – especially where the intention is not quite sincere.

The third principle

If you wish to nurse the anger of hostility, then direct it against the feeling of enmity in your heart and try to remove that. Also, be an enemy to your evil-commanding self and its fancies and try to reform it, for it is more harmful to you than all else. Do not nurse anger and hostility against believers to please that injurious self. If you cannot rid yourself of enmity, then there are numerous unbelievers and heretics to nurse your anger and hostility against. As the attribute of love deserves the response of love, so too, is enmity fit to receive enmity as its response. If you wish to defeat your enemy, then respond to his evil with good. For if you respond with evil, enmity will increase; even though he may be outwardly defeated, he will nurture rancour in his heart and enmity will persist. If, by contrast, you respond to him with good, he will repent and become a friend to you.

As expressed in the couplet,

If you treat the noble nobly, he will be yours,
But if you treat the ignoble nobly, he will revolt.

it is the nature of a believer to be noble and he will be subjected to you by noble treatment. However, should there be among the believers a man apparently ignoble, he is yet noble with respect to his belief. It often happens that if you repeatedly tell a man 'you are good', he will become good; and if you insistently tell a good man 'you are bad', he will become bad. Therefore, heed the following sacred principles established by the Qur'an, for happiness and salvation are to be found in them:

If they come across vanity, they pass by with dignity.[7]

---

7. al-Furqan, 25.72.

If you pardon and overlook and if you forgive, surely God is All-Forgiving, All-Compassionate.[8]

The fourth principle

One who indulges rancour and enmity wrongs and transgresses against his own soul, his brother believer, and the Divine Compassion. He condemns his soul to painful torment on account of his rancour and enmity. He inflicts anguish upon himself whenever he sees his enemy obtain some blessings or advantage, and he suffers pain on account of his fear of him. If his enmity arises from envy, this is the most severe form of torment. For envy, first of all, consumes and destroys the envious, and does not harm the one envied; even if it does so, it does so only a little.

The cure for envy: Let the envious individual ponder the fate of those things that arouse his envy. Then he will conclude that the physical beauty, strength, worldly rank, and wealth enjoyed by his rival are transient. Their benefit is slight, but the trouble they cause is great. If the things arousing his envy are merits possessed by his rival with respect to the Hereafter, they cannot be an object of envy. But if one does envy another on account of them, then he is either himself a hypocrite, wishing to use up the rewards to be paid in the Hereafter while yet in this world, or he imagines the one whom he envies to be a hypocrite, thus being unjust towards him.

If the envious person rejoices at the misfortunes that the envied one suffers and is grieved by the bounties he receives, it means he is offended by the good done to the other by Destiny and Divine Compassion, and is, indirectly, criticizing Destiny and objecting to Compassion. Whoever criticizes Destiny is striking his head against an anvil on which it will break, and whoever objects to Compassion will himself be deprived of it.

How can justice and sound conscience accept that the re-

---

8. *al-Taghabun*, 64.14.

sponse to something unworthy of even a day's enmity should be a year's rancour and enmity? Besides, you cannot condemn your brother believer by attributing solely to him the evil you have experienced at his hands because:

Firstly, Destiny has a certain part in allowing that evil to be, to which you should respond with quiet acceptance.

Secondly, the share of Satan and the evil-commanding self should also be taken into consideration. In this case, you will rather pity your brother than become his enemy, for having been overwhelmed by his carnal self.

Thirdly, God may have punished you through your brother for a defect in your own soul of which you are unaware or of which you do not wish to be aware.

As for the remaining small share, if you respond to it with tolerance, forgiveness and magnanimity, a way to conquer your enemy most swiftly and safely, then you will be saved from wrongdoing and harm. Otherwise, if, like someone drunken or crazed merchant who buys fragments of ice and glass at the price of diamonds, you respond to worthless, transient and insignificant affairs of this world with violent, persistent hostility and permanent rancour, as if you would remain in the world forever with your enemy, it would be excessive wrongdoing, drunkenness and a kind of lunacy.

If then, you care for yourself, do not allow enmity and desire for revenge, which are so harmful to inner life, to enter your heart. If they have already entered, do not listen to what they command. Hear what truth-seeing Hafiz of Shiraz says:

The world is not a commodity worth contending for.

The world is worthless because it is transient. If this is true of the huge world, then you can grasp how insignificant are the petty affairs of the world! Hafiz also says:

The tranquillity of both worlds lies in two things: Magnanimity towards friends, wise management of enemies.

If you say, 'I have no choice, there is enmity in my nature. Moreover, these things angered me, so I cannot overlook them,' my answer will be this:

If, in resisting the force of the evil impulse in yourself and the tendency to behave badly, you refrain from carrying out your intention, and (in doing so) become conscious of your own defect, there is no harm. This is because awareness of your own defect and admission of the wrong in having such an evil impulse, are a means and form of repentance and seeking God's forgiveness which will deliver you from the evil consequences of that evil impulse. That is indeed why I wrote this part of this Letter – so as to urge you to seek forgiveness, to distinguish right from wrong, and to prevent enmity from being presented as right.

A case worthy of notice: I once witnessed that, as a result of partisan bias, a pious scholar of religion went so far in condemnation of another pious scholar whose political opinions he did not share as to imply that he was an apostate. On the other hand, he praised with respect a hypocrite who was of the same opinion as himself. I was appalled at such evil results of political partisanship and concluded, *I seek refuge in God from Satan and politics.* From that time on I withdrew from politics.

The fifth aspect

Obstinacy and partisanship are very harmful for social life.

Question

A tradition says: *Difference among my community is a mercy (for them).*[9] Difference requires partisanship. Even though partisanship is a social disease, it relieves the oppressed common people from the oppressive elite, for if the elite of a town or village join together, they tyrannize the ordinary people. If there are parties, the oppressed may take refuge with one of them and thus save themselves.

---

9. al-Munawi, *Faydh al-Qadir,* 1.210.

It is also from the confrontation of opinions and the disagreement of minds that truth comes to light in its full measure. Do you agree with this argument?

Answer

The difference meant in the tradition is a positive difference. That is, it is a difference whereby each side strives to promote and propagate its own argument, not seeking to destroy and nullify that of the other, but rather to improve and reform it. As for negative difference which aims at the destruction of the other side because of partisan bias and hostility, this is rejected by the Prophet, upon him be peace and blessings. Those who are at each other's throats cannot act positively (towards each other).

To the second part of the question we would answer that if partisanship is in the name of truth, it may well become a refuge for those seeking their rights. But the current partisanship, which is biased and self-centred, is only a refuge for the unjust and a focus of support for them. For, if a devil comes to a man engaged in biased partisanship and backs him, that man will call down God's blessings on that devil. But if a man of angelic character joins the opposite side, then he will – God forbid! – go so far as to invoke curses on him.

To the third point in the argument we would say: If confrontation of opinions is in the name of truth, it is only a difference of means; in reality, it is an agreement, a unity, with respect to aim and basic purpose. Such difference can make manifest all the different aspects of truth and so serves justice and truth. However, it is not 'gleams of truth', but rather flames of dissension which will emerge from a confrontation between biased, partisan opinions based upon egotism and fame-seeking, a confrontation which takes place for the sake of a tyrannical, evil-commanding self. For, it is unity of purpose that must be the goal, whereas opposing views of this kind can never find a point of convergence anywhere on earth. Since they do not differ in the name of truth, they split into absolute extremes and give rise to divisions that are irreconcilable.

In short, if one's conduct is not based on the exalted principles, *loving for the sake of God, disliking for the sake of God, judging for the sake of God,* dispute and discord will result. If one does not take due account of these principles, attempts to do justice will result in injustice.

An event which should provide a lesson: Imam 'Ali, may God be pleased with him, once threw an unbeliever to the ground. Just as he drew his sword to kill him, the unbeliever spat at him. 'Ali released the man without killing him. The unbeliever asked: 'Why did you not kill me?' 'Ali answered: 'I was going to kill you for the sake of God. But when you spat at me, I became angered and the purity of my intention was clouded by the inclinations of my soul. It is for this reason that I did not kill you.' The unbeliever replied: 'I spat at you so that you would become angered and kill me instantly. If your religion is so pure and disinterested, then it must be truth.'

An incident worthy of notice: When once a judge showed signs of anger while cutting off the hand of a thief, the just ruler who happened to observe him dismissed him from office. For, if he had cut off the thief's hand in the name of the Sacred Divine Law, he would have felt pity for the man and cut it off without showing either mercy or anger. Since the inclinations of his soul had some share in his deed, he was unable to perform the execution with justice.

A regrettable social condition and a perilous disease paralyzing the life of society, fit to be wept over by the heart of Islam: It is a requirement of harmonious social life, recognized and practised by even the most primitive peoples, that internal enmities should be forgotten and abandoned when foreign enemies appear and attack. What then ails those who claim to be serving the Muslim community that, at a time when countless enemies are ever ready to attack, one after the other, they, by failing to forget petty hostilities, prepare the ground for the assaults of enemies? This is a corruption, a kind of barbarity and treachery committed against the community of Islam.

A story with an important lesson: The Hasanan, a tribe of Bedouin, had two clans that were at war with each other. Although more than fifty had been killed on each side, whenever another tribe such as the Sibkan or Haydaran appeared against them, these two hostile clans would forget their enmity and fight together, shoulder to shoulder, until they repelled the attacking tribe, without recalling their internal animosities.

O people of faith! Do you not know how many 'tribes' and enemies are ready to attack the 'tribe' of believers? There are more than a hundred, like a series of concentric circles. When the believers should be taking up defensive positions, each supporting the other and giving him a helping hand, is it at all fitting for people of faith that, by insisting on biased partisanship and hostile rancour, they facilitate the assault of the enemy and open the gates for them to penetrate the fold of Islam? There are as many as seventy circles of hostile forces, ranging from the misguided, the atheists and the people of false belief, to the vicissitudes of worldly life, each meaning you harm, and regarding you with anger and hatred. Your firm weapon, shield and citadel is Islamic brotherhood. So be aware of how far it contradicts conscience and the interests of brotherhood to shake this citadel of brotherhood on account of petty enmities and other pretexts, and come to your senses!

It is reported in some Prophetic traditions that extremely harmful and terrible persons such as *Sufyan* and the *Dajjal* will come to lead the heretics and hypocrites at the end of time and exploit the worldly ambitions and dissensions among the Muslims and mankind, so that, with only a small force, they will reduce humanity to anarchy and the vast world of Islam to slavery.

O people of faith! If you do not desire to fall into slavery and humiliation, come to your senses and take refuge against oppressors who would exploit your differences, in the citadel of *the believers are naught else than brothers.* Otherwise, you will be able neither to preserve your lives nor to defend your rights. It is evident that if two champions are fighting with each other, even a child can beat them. If two mountains are balanced in the scales, even a small stone can disturb their equilibrium, causing one to rise, and the other to fall. Thus, people of faith, your strength will be reduced to nothing as a result of your passions and hostile partisanship, so that you can be defeated by the slightest forces. If you have any commitment to a collective life of social harmony and solidarity, then make the exalted principle of *The believers are together like a well-founded building, one part of which supports the other*[10] your guiding principle in life! Then you will be delivered from humiliation in this world and wretchedness in the other.

The sixth aspect

Spiritual life and correctness of worship are spoilt by enmity and rancour, because the purity of intention that is the means of salvation is spoilt. For a biased partisan wishes for superiority over his enemy in the good deeds he performs and becomes unable to act purely for the sake of God. Also he prefers, in his judgement and dealings, the one who takes his side, so he cannot be just. Thus the purity of intention and justice that are the basis of all good deeds are lost because of enmity.

This aspect could be elaborated further, but we keep it short here in order to reserve space for other matters.

---

10. Bukhari, *Salat*, 88; Muslim, *Birr*, 65; Tirmidhi, *Birr*, 18.

THE SECOND CHAPTER

In the name of God, the Merciful, the Compassionate

Surely God it is Who is the All-Provider, the Possessor of Strength, the Steadfast.[11]

How many a creature that bears not its own provision, but God provides for it and you! He is the All-Hearer, the All-Knower.[12]

O people of faith! You will have understood by now how harmful enmity is. Understand also, that greed is another great disease, as harmful for the life of Islam as enmity. It brings about disappointment, sickness and humiliation, as well as deprivation and misery. The humiliation and misery of the Jews, who have leapt at this world more avidly than any other people, are a decisive proof of this truth.[13]

Greed demonstrates its evil consequences throughout the world of animate beings, both at the level of species and of particular individuals. Seeking one's provision while putting one's trust in God is, by contrast, a means to tranquillity and demonstrates everywhere its good effects. For example, fruit trees and plants, which are a species of living beings and accordingly need provision, stand still where they are, 'contentedly, putting their trust in God, showing no impatience'. That is why their provision hastens to them of itself and why they reproduce more vigorously than animals. The animals, by contrast, are able to attain their provision only insufficiently and at the cost

---

11. *al-Dhariyat*, 51.58.

12. *al-Ankabut*, 29.60.

13. The Qur'an says concerning the Jews: *'Ignominy shall be their portion wherever they are, unless they (seize) a rope from God or a rope from people'* (A. Imran, 3.112). This means that when the Jews restore themselves in obedience to God's commandments or are backed by some powers, as it is the case today, they can achieve some progress; otherwise ignominy shall always be their portion. So, however better they seem today when compared to their long history of ignominy, still they live in constant fear and insecurity, and are not certain about their future. (Tr.)

of great effort since they pursue it with impatience. In the animal kingdom only the young, who 'demonstrate their trust in God through their weakness and impotence', receive in full measure their rightful and delicious provision from the treasury of the Divine Compassion, while wild beasts that leap greedily at their provision are able to obtain an 'illicit' and coarse food at the cost of great effort. These examples show that greed is the cause of deprivation, while trust in God and contentment are the means to Divine Mercy.

Within the human kingdom, the Jews who, more than any other people have clung greedily to the world and been passionately attached to the worldly life, have been able to secure with great effort only some usurious and, accordingly, illicit wealth of little benefit, over which they exercise stewardship, but in return they have become exposed to international blows of humiliation and misery, death and insult. This too, shows that greed is a source of humiliation and loss. There are so many instances of a greedy man being exposed to loss that *the greedy are subjected to disappointment and loss* has become a proverb and a universally accepted truth. That being the case, if you love wealth, seek it not with impatience but with contentment, so that you may earn it abundantly.

The contented and the greedy can be likened to the two men who enter the audience hall of a great personage. One of them thinks: 'It is enough that he should admit me so that I can escape from the cold outside. Even if he seats me in the lowest position, it will be a favour to me.'

The second, in his arrogance, hopes for the highest position, as if he had some right to it and as if everyone were obliged to respect him. He enters with greed and, fixing his gaze upon the highest position, attempts to advance toward it. But the owner of the audience hall turns him back and seats him in a lower position. Instead of thanking the owner, the man is angered against him in his heart and criticizes him. The owner of the hall is annoyed with him.

The first man enters most humbly and shows his willingness to be seated even in the lowest position. His modesty pleases the owner of the hall and he invites him to sit in a higher position. This increases his gratitude.

Now this world is like an audience hall of the Most Merciful One. The surface of the earth is like a banquet laid out by Divine Compassion. The different degrees of provision and grades of bounty correspond to the seating positions in the audience hall.

Even in the most particular of affairs, everyone can experience the evil effects of greed. For example, everyone will have noticed how, when two beggars ask something of him, he is offended by the one who importunes greedily, and is inclined therefore to refuse his request; whereas he will give to the other, peaceable one out of pity. Or to give another example, if you are unable to sleep at night and wish to go to sleep at once, you may succeed if you remain indifferent to it. But if you desire with impatience to get to sleep immediately, you may lose your sleep completely.

Yet another example is this, that if you await impatiently the arrival of someone for some important purpose, continually complaining that 'he has still not come', ultimately you will lose patience and get up and leave. But a minute later the person will come and your purpose then remains frustrated.

The reason for all this is as follows:

In order to produce a loaf of bread, you must cultivate the field, harvest the crop, take the grain to a mill and bake the loaf in an oven. In the same way, in the arrangement of all things there is a certain deliberation decreed by Divine Wisdom. If, because of impatience, one does not act in compliance with this deliberation and neglects to follow all the steps in the arrangement determined for all things, one will either overleap or omit some step, and so fail to achieve the desired result.

O brothers, dizzied by preoccupation with your livelihood, and stupefied by your greed for this world! When greed is so harmful and injurious, how is it that you do all kinds of humiliating deeds for its sake; that you accept all kinds of wealth without distinguishing between what is allowed and forbidden by your religion and sacrifice much of the Hereafter. In order to satisfy your greed, you have even abandoned the payment of *zakat*, which is one of the most important pillars of Islam and a means of being blessed with increase and fertility and of repelling misfortunes. The one who does not pay *zakat* is bound to lose the amount of wealth equal to the amount that he had to pay as *zakat;* either he will spend it on useless things or it will be taken from him by some misfortune.

In a veracious dream which I had during the fifth year of the First World War, I was asked the following question:

What is the reason for this hunger, this financial loss and bodily trial that now afflict the Muslims?

I replied in the dream:

'From the wealth He grants to us, God Almighty demands from us, as *zakat*, either a tenth or a fortieth[14] so that we may benefit from the grateful prayers of the poor and avoid being the target of their rancour and envy. But we have not paid the *zakat* because of our avarice, so God Almighty has taken from us the accumulated amount of the *zakat*, thirty out of forty or three-fourth where a fortieth was owed, and eight out of ten or four-fifth, where a tenth was owed.

'He wanted us, as *fasting,* to endure, for no more than one month each year, a hunger that has as many as seventy beneficial purposes. But we took pity on ourselves and did not endure that short and beneficial hunger. As a punishment, God

---

14. A tenth of wealth such as corn which every year yields a new crop; a fortieth of whatever yields a financial surplus in the course of the year, or of the pasturing animals (such as sheep or goats) numbering at least forty.

Almighty compelled us to fast for five years, with a hunger that combines almost seventy kinds of afflictions.

'God also required of us, out of each twenty-four hours, one hour to be assigned to a form of Divine training, pleasing and lofty, illuminating and beneficial. But in our laziness we did not perform five prayers a day and wasted that one hour along with the rest of the hours of the day. God Almighty, in return, chastened us by making us undergo a form of training and physical exertion for five years.' I then awoke and, pondering over it, realized that a very important truth was contained in the dream. As was clearly pointed out in the *Twenty-fifth Word*, where the principles of modern civilization are compared to the commandments of the Qur'an, all immorality and disturbances in human social life proceed from two sources, from these two attitudes:

> *The first: Once my stomach is full, what do I care if others die of hunger?*

> *The second: You work and I will eat.*

What perpetuates these two attitudes is the prevalence of usury on the one hand and the abandonment of *zakat* on the other. The only remedy for these two awful diseases can only be provided through implementing *zakat* as a universal principle and duty and banning usury. *Zakat* is a most essential pillar not only for individuals and particular communities, but for the whole of mankind to live a happy life. Mankind usually comprise two classes; the elite and the commonalty. Only the obligation of *zakat* can arouse compassion and generosity in the elite towards the commonalty and respect and obedience in the commonalty towards the elite. In the absence of *zakat*, what will come to the commonalty from the elite is oppression and cruelty and what will rise from the commonalty towards the elite is rancour and rebellion. That will give rise to a constant struggle and a constant opposition between the two classes of mankind,

74

resulting finally in the confrontation of labour and capital, such as happened in Russia at the beginning of the century.

O people of nobility and fairness! O people of munificence and liberality! If acts of liberality are not performed in the name of *zakat*, they bring no use; they may even cause three harmful results. For, if you do not give in the name of God, you are actually making a poor man indebted to you, imprisoning him in some feeling of obligation. Thereby you deprive yourself of his prayer which would be acceptable in the sight of God. Also by not giving in the name of God, you are imagining yourself to be the real owner of the wealth which God has bestowed on you to distribute among His servants, and thus committing an act of ingratitude for the bounties you have received from God. If, by contrast, you give in the name of *zakat*, you will be rewarded for having given for the sake of God Almighty and you will have offered thanks for the bounties received. What is more, the needy person will not feel obliged to flatter you or fawn upon you, so his self-respect will not be injured and his prayer on behalf of you will be accepted.

See, then, how great is the difference between on the one hand, giving as much as or more than the amount one would give in *zakat*, only to earn, in return, the harm of ostentation, fame and the imposition of obligation, and on the other hand, performing the same good deed in the name of *zakat*, and thereby fulfilling a religious duty, and gaining a reward, the virtue of sincerity, and the acceptable prayers of the poor.

Glory be to You, we have no knowledge save that which You have taught us. Surely You are the All-Knowing, the All-Wise.

O God, bestow blessings and peace on our master Muhammad, who said: 'The believers stand together like a firm building, one part of which supports the other', and who also said: 'Contentment is a treasure that will never be exhausted'; and on his family and his Companions. And all praise be to God, the Lord of the Worlds.

ADDENDUM

Concerning backbiting

In His Name. There is nothing that does not glorify Him with praise.

The Qur'anic verse, *Would any of you like to eat the flesh of his dead brother?*[15] which induces in the heart an aversion to backbiting in six miraculous ways, shows how disgusting a thing backbiting is in the view of the Qur'an, and therefore leaves no room for further explanation on the subject. Indeed, there is no need, nor any possibility, for further explanation where the Qur'an has made so decisive a proclamation.

The Qur'anic verse quoted above reprimands the backbiter with six degrees of reprimand and restrains him from this sin with six degrees of severity. When the verse is read as addressed to those actually engaged in backbiting, its meaning is as follows:

The *hamza* at the beginning of the sentence in its original Arabic is interrogative. This sense of interrogation penetrates all the words of the verse like water, so that each word carries an interrogative accent.

Thus, the first word asks, following the *hamza*, 'Do you have no intelligence, with which you ask and answer, and can discriminate between good and bad, so that you fail to perceive how abominable this thing is?'

The second word, *like*, asks, 'Is it that your heart, with which you love or hate, is so spoiled that you love a most repugnant thing like backbiting?'

Third, the phrase, *any of you*, asks, 'What has happened to your sense of the nature and responsibility of society and civili-

---

15. *al-Hujurat*, 49.12.

76

zation that you dare to accept something so poisonous to social life?'

Fourth, the phrase, *to eat the flesh,* asks, 'What has happened to your sense of humanity that you are tearing your friend to pieces with your teeth like a wild animal?'

Fifth, the phrase, *of his brother,* asks, 'Do you have no human tenderness, no sense of kinship, that you sink your teeth into some innocent person to whom you are tied by numerous links of brotherhood? Do you have no intelligence that you bite into your own limbs with your teeth, in such a senseless fashion?'

Sixth, the word, *dead,* asks, 'Where is your conscience? Is your nature so corrupt that you commit so disgusting an act as eating the flesh of your dead brother who is deserving of much respect?'

According, then, to the total meaning of the verse and the indications of each of its words, slander and backbiting are repugnant to the intelligence, and the heart, to humanity and conscience, to human nature and religious and societal brotherhood. You see, then, that the verse condemns backbiting in six degrees in a very concise and most precise manner and restrains men from it in six miraculous ways.

Backbiting is a shameful weapon and most commonly used by people of enmity, envy and obstinacy; no self-respecting, honourable man will ever demean himself by resorting to such a vile weapon. Some celebrated person once said:

I hold myself in so great esteem as not to punish (my enemy) with
backbiting,
For backbiting is the weapon of the weak and the low.

Backbiting consists in speaking about an absent person in a way that would repel and annoy him if he were to be present and hear. If the words uttered are true, that is backbiting; if they are not, this is both backbiting and slander and, therefore, a doubly loathsome sin.

Backbiting can be permissible in a very few, particular circumstances:

First: A wronged man can present a formal complaint to some officer, so that with his help, a wrong may be righted and justice restored.

Second: If a man contemplating co-operation with another comes to hold counsel with you, and you say to him, disinterestedly and purely for the sake of his benefit, and in order to counsel him properly, without any further motive, 'Do not co-operate with him; it will be to your disadvantage.'

Third: If a man says only by way of factual description, not to expose to disgrace or notoriety, 'That crippled, foolish man went to such and such a place.'

Fourth: If the man being criticized is an open and unashamed sinner; that is, far from being ashamed of it, he takes pride in the sins he commits; if he takes pleasure in his wrongdoing and commits sins openly.

In these particular cases, backbiting may be permissible, provided it is done disinterestedly and purely for the sake of truth and in the collective interest. Otherwise, backbiting is like a fire that consumes good deeds in the manner of a flame eating up wood.

If one has engaged in backbiting or listened to it willingly, one should seek God's forgiveness, saying, 'O God, forgive me and the one whom I backbited', and when he meets the person about whom he spoke ill, he should say to him: 'Forgive me!'

***

The
Twenty-third
Letter

Answers to questions on different matters
Patience and a fine point concerning the end of
the story of Joseph

In His Name, glory be to Him
There is nothing that does not glorify Him with praise.

Upon you be peace and the mercy of God and His blessing forever,
to the number of the seconds and minutes of your life and the par-
ticles in your body.

My dear, persevering, truthful, sincere and capable brother,

Differences of time and place cannot form an obstacle to friendly conversations of brothers-in-truth like us. Even if they are as
far apart from each other as east and west, even if one is in the
past and the other in the future, one in the world and the other
in the Hereafter, they may still be considered to be together and
have a conversation. Those, in particular, who perform the
same duty are accounted the same as each other. I imagine you
every morning to be with me, and assign half or a third of my
spiritual reward to you (may God accept it!). I include you, besides 'Abd al-Majid and 'Abd al-Rahman, in my prayer and I
hope that you are receiving your share.

I have felt, feeling with you, some sorrow on account of the troubles you are having in your worldly affairs. Yet, since this is an impermanent world, and since some good lies behind the troubles it brings to us all, it occurred to me for your sake that they, too, would come to an end. *There can be no real life save the life of the Hereafter.* Having thought that, I recited: *Surely, God is with the patient,* and then, *Surely we belong to God, and to Him we are returning.* In that, I found, thinking with you, some consolation.

If God loves a slave of His, He causes him to see the world ugly and renounce it. I hope that you are among such beloved slaves of God. Let it not sadden you that the obstacles to publishing *the Words* become multiplied. I am hopeful that when the portions you have already published receive God's mercy, they will flourish in great abundance, in the manner of seeds growing into a multitude of flowers.

You have put a number of questions to me. Most of the *Words* and *Letters* used to be beautiful since, my brother, they came to me suddenly and unwilled. If, therefore, I am to answer your questions, relying, as the Old Said did, on the strength of my knowledge, they will be dim and imperfect. Inspiration has been at a stop for some time, and my memory has weakened. Nevertheless, in order not to leave your questions unanswered, I will attempt brief answers to them:

Your first question

What is the best kind of petitionary prayer *(du'a)* of a believer for another?

Answer

It is one in accordance with the conditions of its acceptability. A prayer is more or less acceptable in consideration of certain conditions being met.

For example, when one prays to God for something, he should first cleanse himself by asking for forgiveness from God, and then call God's blessing on the Prophet Muhammad as an intercessor before and after the prayer. For calling God's blessing on the Prophet is an acceptable prayer and the prayer said between two acceptable prayers is usually acceptable also. In addition, such a prayer should be said in the absence of the believer for whom it is said and be the kind of the prayers mentioned in the Qur'an and *Hadith*. For example, one should prefer comprehensive prayers such as: *O God, I ask forgiveness of You, for me and him, and soundness in religion, in this world and in the Hereafter! Our Lord, grant us in the world good, and in the Hereafter good, and guard us against the chastisement of the Fire!*

One should pray with sincerity, from the heart and with a religious seriousness and solemn reverence. Also, one should do so after the five daily prayers *(salat)* and, particularly, after the dawn prayer and in blessed times such as Friday – especially during the hour when prayer is absolutely accepted – the three months of additional prayer before Ramadan, during Ramadan itself, and, most particularly, the Night of Power. Further, one should make one's petition in the mosque. God is expected, through His Mercy, to accept a petition made in observance of such conditions, and He accepts it so that either it is answered in this world or the one in whose name it is made will hopefully benefit from it in the Hereafter. For this reason, if one does not obtain the result for which he prayed, he should not think that the prayer has not been accepted, rather, he should consider that it has received a better acceptance.

Your second question

It has become a preferred tradition to say of a Companion of the Prophet, *May God be pleased with him.* Is it proper to say this after the names of others?

Answer

It is proper. For the phrase, *May God be pleased with him,* is, unlike the phrase, *Upon him be peace and blessings,* which is particular to God's noble Messenger, upon him be peace and blessings, not particular to the Companions exclusively. Rather it should be said of the persons who, like the founders of the four schools of Islamic conduct *(madhhab 'amali),* and 'Abd al-Qadir al-Jilani, Imam Rabbani and Imam Ghazali, were able to attain to the rank of being approved by God through succession to the prophetic mission, which is the greatest rank of sainthood. Nevertheless, according to the common usage of religious scholars, we tend to say of a Companion *May God be pleased with him,* and *May God have mercy upon him* of one who belonged to the two succeeding generations after the Companions; while those who followed them are mentioned with the phrase *May God forgive him,* and people of sainthood with the phrase *May God sanctify him.*

Your third question

Who is higher in virtue – the greatest of the jurists or the greatest of the saints who inspired or founded the sound *tariqas?*

Answer

Not all of the jurists who had the qualifications to derive judgements from the Qur'an and *Sunnah,* but the jurists who founded the Islamic schools of conduct, namely Abu Hanifa, Malik, Shafi'i and Ahmad ibn Hanbal, are higher in virtue than even the greatest of the saints. Although some extraordinary saints, like 'Abd al-Qadir al-Jilani, given the title of 'pole of the age', have superiority in some particular virtues, those Imams of the Islamic schools of conduct are superior to the leading saints of the *tariqas.* The four Imams mentioned are regarded as superior to all except the Prophet's Companions and the Mahdi.

Your fourth question

What is meant by, *Surely God is with the patient?* [1]

---

1. *al-Baqara,* 2.153.

Answer

God has established, as a requirement of His Name, the All-Wise, an order, a definite procedure, like the steps of a ladder, for things to come into existence. An impatient person does not act with deliberation, either he overleaps and falls, or omits some step and cannot reach his goal. It is for this reason that avarice is a cause of deprivation, and patience is, by contrast, a key to the solution of problems. That is why the saying, *Greed is subject to disappointment and loss, but patience is a means of relief,* has become a proverb.

God Almighty helps the patient and makes them successful. There are three kinds of patience:

The first kind consists in resisting the temptations of the carnal self and refraining from sins. This is 'fear of God' and makes the patient person the referent of the Divine declaration, *Surely God is with the God-fearing.*[2]

The second kind of patience consists in enduring misfortunes. This is reliance on, and complete submission to, God, and brings to the patient the honour of being referred to in the Divine proclamations, *Surely God loves those who rely on Him,*[3] and *God loves the patient.*[4]

Impatience implies complaining of God; it amounts to criticism of His acts, accusation of His Mercy and disapproval of His Wisdom. Indeed, a weak, helpless man wails over his misfortunes, but he should complain to Him, not of Him, just as the Prophet Yakub (Jacob) did who said: *I make complaint of my anguish and sorrow unto God.*[5] That is, he should make complaint of his misfortunes to God. It is futile, and even harmful, to encourage the weak to self-pity by uttering sighs, as if in complaint about God, like, 'What did I do that this has befallen me?'

---

2. *al-Baqara*, 2.194.
3. *A. Imran*, 3.159.
4. *A. Imran*, 3.146.
5. *Yusuf*, 12.86.

The third kind of patience is insistence on worshipping God. This elevates the patient to the rank of being a perfect slave of, and being beloved by, God, which is the greatest of spiritual ranks.

Your fifth question

The average age of puberty, when a person is obliged to perform his religious duties, is accepted as about fifteen. That being the case, how did God's Mesenger worship before his Prophethood?

Answer

He worshipped according to the surviving principles of Abraham's religion which still survived in the Arabian peninsula, albeit in an indistinct fashion. He worshipped not because he was obliged to, but in a supererogatory way. This subject demands a full explanation, but let this short observation suffice for the time being.

Your sixth question

What is the Divine purpose for raising him as a Prophet when he was forty, which is regarded as the age of maturity, and why did his blessed life end at the age of sixty-three?

Answer

There are many purposes, one of which is as follows:

Prophethood is a very great and heavy duty. Only through the perfection of intellectual faculties and full development of spiritual potentialities can this duty be performed, and the age of this development and perfection is forty. Besides, since youth is the time when a man is excited to carnal desires, and boils up with worldly ambitions, it is not fit for Prophethood, a duty which is holy and divine, and is purely related to the Hereafter. However noble and sincere a man may be before forty, fame-seekers might regard him as pursuing fame and glory, and he cannot free himself easily from the accusations of such people (however false). However, since a man is nearer to the grave than the world after forty, he is more likely to be free of such accusations in his acts related to the Hereafter. Also, people may free themselves from groundless suspicions about him.

As for the reasons why he lived to sixty-three years, here is only one of many:

Believers are religiously obliged to love and respect God's Messenger to the utmost degree, and to commend every manner of his, without feeling any dislike for any aspect of him. For this reason, God did not allow him to live the troublesome and usually humiliating period of old age, and sent him to the 'highest abode' when he was sixty-three, the average life-span of the members of his community, thus making him the example also in this respect.

Your seventh question

Is *The best of the young among you are those like the old among you, and the worst of the old among you are those like the young among you,* a prophetic saying? If so, what is meant by it?

Answer

I have also heard it referred to as a prophetic saying. What is meant by it is this: The best of the young is he who, like an old man, thinks of death and, without being captivated by fancies of youth, strives for his next life. As for the worst of the old, he is that old man who, trying to imitate the young in worldly aspirations in heedlessness of Divine commandments, obeys, like a youth, the temptations of his carnal self.

The correct form of the second part of your framed inscription is as follows – I hung it on the wall as a warning-notice and I look at it every morning and evening to take a lesson:

If you want a friend, God is sufficient. Indeed, if He is a friend to you, so is everything.

If you want companions, the Qur'an is sufficient. You may imagine yourself to be in the company of the Prophets and angels mentioned in the Qur'an, study their experiences and are intimate with them.

If you want wealth, contentment is sufficient. Indeed, the one with contentment becomes thrifty, and the one who is thrifty gets blessed abundance in his wealth.

If you want to feel enmity, your evil-commanding self is sufficient as an enemy. One who is self-conceited obtains griefs but one who is not haughty obtains care and peace.

If you want counsel, death is sufficient. The one who thinks of death, gets rid of love of the world and strives for his next life.

I am adding to your seven, an eighth, which is as follows:

A few days ago, a memorizer of the Qur'an recited a certain portion of the *Surah Yusuf,* down to the verse, *Make me die submissive (unto You), and join me with the righteous* .[6]

Suddenly a subtle point occurred to me: Everything related to the Qur'an and faith is, no matter how insignificant it may seem, in fact, of great significance. Anything that contributes to eternal happiness is not insignificant, so, we should not regard it as unworthy of explanation. Being the first to study such matters and appreciative of Qur'anic subtle points, Ibrahim Hulusi will, of a certainty, desire to hear this point. Then, listen to it:

This is the finest, most subtle point of the finest Qur'anic story: The verse, *Make me die submissive (unto You), and join me with the righteous,* which marks the end of the story of Yusuf, upon him be peace, – the finest story in the Qur'an – is expressive of a glad tiding in a vivid and miraculous fashion. It is as follows:

The pleasure received from a joyful happy story results in a

---

6. *Yusuf,* 12.101.

deep sorrow because of the final news of separation or death. This is really so, or arouses more sorrow, when we get the news of separation or death at a time when the character of the story has just found ease and happiness. However, the verse quoted above, even if it contemplates the death of the Prophet Yusuf (Joseph) at the happiest point of his life when he became the *Aziz* (grand-vizier or chancellor) of Egypt and re-united with his parents and brothers, it gives it in a different way and declares: In order to be the object of a far greater happiness, the Prophet Yusuf prayed God for his death and, through death, he received that happiness. This means that a more attractive and pleasure-giving bliss than the greatest happiness of the world is awaiting us at the other side of the grave. It is because of this that a truth-seeing person like the Prophet Yusuf, in order to find that bliss, asked for death, which is apparently very painful, when he was enjoying the greatest happiness of the world.

Look, then, at the eloquent way the Wise Qur'an reports to us the end of the story of the Prophet Yusuf, and see how it adds, instead of giving pain and regret, to the joy and happiness of the listener. Further, it guides us to the fact that we should strive for the other side of the grave, where are found real happiness and pleasure. It also demonstrates the exalted truthfulness of the Prophet Yusuf and announces that even the most joyful and brightest condition of the worldly life cannot captivate him, rather it leads him to ask for death and the other life.

Only the Everlasting is everlasting.
Said Nursi

***

The Twenty-fourth Letter

Why Divine Mercy allows death and misfortunes
Prayer, and the Ascension of the Prophet

In the name of God, the Merciful, the Compassionate
God does whatever He wills and decrees whatever He wishes.

Question

How can we reconcile the tender care, the beneficial management and loving-kindness required by such of the Greatest
Names of God as the All-Compassionate, the All-Wise and the
All-Loving, with decay in the world, with death, separations,
misfortunes and troubles, which can be so terrible and frightening? Even if we can bear with the death of human beings since
it is a door to eternal happiness for a believer, why is it that the
delicate plants and flowers, and the animals, which cling to life
and continuance, are made to perish and to suffer many transformations, trials and separations before they perish? How can
Divine Compassion and Wisdom allow this, and what is the Divine purpose for it?

Answer

Through Five Symbols that demonstrate the motive and necessary cause for, and Five Signs which show the purposes and
benefits behind, the decay and death of living creatures, we will
try to catch a glimpse of this profound and sublime truth.

The first station

The First Station consists of Five Symbols.

The first symbol

As expounded in the Conclusion of the *Twenty-sixth Word*, a skilful clothes designer employs an ordinary man as a model to make a jewelled and artistically fashioned garment in return for wages. In order to display his skill and artistic ability, he gives a shape to the garment on that man and so makes him sit and stand. I wonder, then, if the man will have a right to object to the designer, saying, 'Why do you continually change the shape of this garment, which makes me look good, and give me trouble by making me sit and stand?' In the same way, the Majestic Creator takes each species of creatures as a model and, in order to display the manifestations of His Names and the perfection of His art, causes everything, especially the living creatures, to put on a garment of existence bejewelled with senses, and embellishes it with the Pen of Destiny and Decree. He gives, in return, to each being, as wages particular to it, a certain perfection and pleasure and bounteous gifts. That being the case, has anything the right to object to the Majestic Maker, the Owner of the Kingdom, Who has free disposal of everything in His Kingdom in whatever way He wills, saying, 'You are giving me trouble and disturbing me!'? God forbid!

The creatures can make no claim to any rights against the Necessarily-Existent Being; rather, if they have a 'right', it is to fulfil the duty of thanksgiving for the level of existence that God has conferred on them. For all the levels of existence conferred are actual, concrete realities dependent on a necessary cause, whereas the levels not conferred are only possibilities. A possibility does not have an actual, external existence, and there are possibilities of infinite number for a thing to have existence. Besides, there is no necessary cause whereby something infinitely possible should attain existence. For example, minerals cannot complain, saying, 'Why were we not created as plants?' For there were possibilities of infinite number for them to have any level of existence, whether inferior or superior. So, what they must do is to thank their Creator for the mineral existence with which they were favoured. Nor do the plants and animals have a right to complain to God why they were not granted a level of existence superior to theirs; rather, they must thank God, the plants for being favoured with existence and life; the animals for being granted a precious ore of spirit as well as life and existence. As for you, O man of complaint! You were not left non-existent; you were favoured with the garment of existence and experienced the pleasures of life. Further, you were made neither an inanimate object nor a plant nor an animal. You enjoy a healthful human existence. O man of belief, you were additionally favoured, without being left in misguidance, with the blessing of Islam. And so on.

It is, then, an ingratitude to complain about God – when you should be grateful to Him for the level of existence He bestowed on you as a pure blessing – that He did not favour you with still greater blessings to which you aspire passionately, though wrongly, since they are of the order of possibilities and so non-existent.

Suppose a man elevated to a very high position – say, one made to climb a minaret as far as its pinnacle, and favoured with a particular blessing at each step – were to complain that he had not been elevated still higher: would not even the most foolish people see that this is an attitude of great ingratitude and injustice on the part of that man?

O man of complaints, if you act in a greedy way, heedless of contentment and thrift, know for a certainty that contentment is a profitable thanksgiving, while greed is an ingratitude causing loss. Thrift shows a beneficial respect for bounties received, whereas extravagance means to make light of bounties in a harmful and shameless way. If, then, you are a sensible man, try to be content with, and show consent to, what you have. If you are suffering poverty impossible to endure, turn to the All-Patient One, and try to acquire a becoming patience, and do so without uttering complaints.

If you want, in any case, to have someone to find fault with, it is your carnal self, so complain to God Almighty about that.

The second symbol

One of the Divine purposes for the Majestic Creator's continuous renewal and re-creation of beings through the awesome activities of His Lordship is, as was explained fully in the Third Matter of the *Eighteenth Letter*, as follows:

Every creature is active because it has the yearning for, and takes pleasure in, activity. Further, in every activity lies a kind of pleasure; it may even be that activity itself is a pleasure. Pleasure points to a perfection, indeed, is itself a kind of perfection. Since, then, activity points to perfection, pleasure and beauty, and again since the Necessarily-Existent Being, Who is the Perfect One of Majesty, has all kinds of perfection in His Being, Attributes and Acts, then He will certainly feel, in a manner fitting to His Necessary Existence and Holiness, that is, in accordance with His essential independence of the whole of the creation, and with His absolute Perfection and being free from deficiencies and any sort of likeness to any creatures, infinite sacred affection and infinite sacred love. This sacred affection and love are the cause of an infinite sacred enthusiasm, which is the origin of an infinite, sacred joy, in turn the source of infinite sacred pleasure. God, the All-Merciful, the All-Compassionate, because of this pleasure as well as of His Compassion, feels infinite sacred gladness and infinite sacred pride for His creatures' realization of their full potentials and attainment of their relative perfections through their deeds by His Power. It is thus this sacred gladness and sacred pride that require the incessant, infinite whirl of creation which, in turn, demands an incessant changing, renewal and transformation in the universe. Finally, this incessant changing, renewal and transformation call for decay, death and separation.

Once in the past, the motives and causes set forth by human philosophies for the creation and life of beings seemed very insignificant to me. I inferred from this why such philosophies would inevitably result in the absurdity which leads prominent figures in philosophy either to the misguidance of naturalism or sophistry, or even to the denial of the Will and Knowledge of the Maker or to regard the Creator as self-compelled (to do what He does).

Just at that point, the Divine Compassion came to my aid with the Divine Name, the All-Wise, and showed me the comprehensive purposes for the creation of beings. Each creature is a Divine missive, such that all conscious beings study it. I remained content for one year with discovering this purpose, but later began to seek for some other great purposes. First, the wonder of Divine Art in beings became manifest to me and, afterwards, another great purpose showed itself: namely, the greatest of the purposes for the life and creation of beings are related to the Maker. I perceived that they present to Himself, in the manner of a mirror reflecting His Beauty and Perfection, the perfection of His art, the embellishment of His Names, the jewels of His Wisdom and the gifts of His Compassion. After a long while, I noticed the miracles of God's Power and the functions of His Lordship in a very rapid change and renewal brought about through the amazing acts of His creativity. After that, not content with all those purposes, I thought that there should be another still greater purpose for the life of creatures, and the motives and purposes which have already been partly explained in the foregoing *Symbol* and which will come below became obvious to me. I knew for certainty that the actions of Divine Power in the universe and the incessant flux of things are so meaningful that, through that flux, the All-Wise Maker causes all the kinds of beings to speak. It is as if the individual actice creatures in heavens and on the earth, and their actions are the words of the speeches of those kinds of beings, and each movement is an act of speech. That is, all creatures glorify God through their movements, including their birth and death.

The third symbol

Things do not go into absolute non-existence, rather they are transferred from the sphere of Power to the sphere of Knowledge, from the visible, material world, the world of changing and mortality, to the World of the Unseen, which is the world of light and permanence.

The beauty and perfection in things belong, in reality, to the Divine Names, being the manifestations of those Names. Since those Names are permanent with their never-ending manifestations, their inscriptions will almost certainly be renewed, freshened and become more and more beautiful. Not going into absolute non-existence, only their relative forms of existence change, with their real nature and identity, which are the source of beauty and the object of enlightenment and perfection, remaining permanently.

The inanimate beings owe their beauty to the Divine Names, so the admiration and love felt for them, belong to those Names, and their changing (since they are mirrors reflecting Divine Names) does not detract from the Names. As for the animate beings, the death of those without intelligence is not complete annihilation; rather, through death, they are freed from the corporeal body and the turbulence of life, and transfer the fruits of their duty to their permanent spirit, which, depending on a Divine Name, attains some kind of happiness peculiar to itself. The death of intelligent beings is a journey, through the All-Wise Maker's stations of the Intermediate World of the grave and the worlds of ideas and spirits, which are more beautiful and illumined than this world, to the World of Permanence where eternal happiness and material and spiritual perfections are obtained.

In short: Since the Majestic Maker exists and is permanent with His Attributes and Names, the inscriptions and manifestations of those Names are constantly renewed in spiritual permanence; they are not subject to absolute non-existence.

As is well-known, man is, on account of his humanity, connected to most of the creatures. He derives pleasure from their happiness and grieves about their misfortunes. He rejoices especially over the happiness of animate beings, particularly over that of human beings and most particularly of the men of perfection whom he approves and loves, and shares their griefs. Moreover, like an affectionate mother, he may go so far as to sacrifice his own rest and happiness for their welfare. Thus, every believer may, according to the degree of his belief and through the light of the Qur'an and belief, be happy with the happiness and permanence of creatures, and their being saved from nothingness and their being valuable missives of the Lord, and thereby he may acquire so comprehensive a light as to fill the entire world. Everybody benefits from this light according to his capacity. But a man of misguidance who regards death as absolute annihilation, falls to despair and depression, and suffers pessimism due to the misfortunes and death of all creatures; he is obsessed, because of his unbelief, by fear of going to absolute non-existence, and suffers hellish torment even before he goes to Hell.

The fourth symbol

As I have stated in several places in my books, just as there are many departments of a king's government representing his functions as the supreme ruler, supreme judge, supreme commander and the supreme head of the religious office etc., so too, the Names of God Almighty have innumerable kinds of manifestation. The variety and difference of creatures result from the variety of those manifestations. Since every possessor of perfection and grace tends to see and show his perfection and grace, the various Names of God, too, would like, because permanent, to manifest themselves on behalf of the Most Sacred Being. That is, they desire to behold their inscriptions; they want to see and show the reflections of their perfection and grace in the mirrors of their inscriptions, and therefore they tend to renew or rewrite in a most meaningful way, moment by moment, the great book of the universe and the various missives of creatures, or to write thousands of different letters on a single page and present it for the viewing of the Most Holy Being, as well as for the viewing of conscious beings to read and ponder. Look at the following stanza of truth, which expresses this point:

> The sheets of the book of the universe are of innumerable kinds,
> Its individual letters and words are also countless.
> 'Written' in the 'printing house' of the Guarded Tablet of Truth,
> Each creature in the universe is a meaningful word.

Consider the lines of the books of the universe, for they are missives to you from the Highest Abode.

The fifth symbol

This consists of two points.

The first point: Since God exists, everything exists. Since everything is connected to God, each single thing is connected to everything. For each thing has, through its connection to God, a connection to everything because of God's Unity. And through this connection, each thing can be an object of the infinite light of existence. Decays and separations cannot impede this reality, so one can receive an infinite light of existence by living even for a moment in consciousness of this connection. If, on the other hand, this connection cannot be established or is ignored, one becomes the object of infinite separation and non-existence, for one will then experience endless despair and depression because of the decay and death of each creature to which one feels a connection. If one were to live, in this state, even for a million years, he would not be able to taste the true pleasure of a moment's life lived in connection to God. It is for this reason that men of truth have concluded: *a moment of life enlightened through connection to God is preferable to a million years of life devoid of such light.* It is for the same reason that men of truth have drawn the conclusion that receiving the light of existence is only possible through recognition of the Necessarily-Existent Being.

In view of the one who recognizes God, the universe is, in the light of existence, filled with angels and other beings of spirituality and consciousness. But the one who does not recognize God sees the universe as a vast, dark, and desolate place where beings are waiting for death and separations. It is indeed so: consider the fact that each fruit on a tree has a connection to all the other fruits on that tree and thereby has as many kinds of secondary existence as the number of the other fruits, and that when it is picked, it is in fact separated from all the other fruits and enveloped by a darkness of non-existence. It is for this reason that, due to the connection to the Power of the One Eternally-Besought, for each being or thing everything has an actual existence; otherwise there are as many types of non-existence as the number of things.

Thus, through the telescope of this Symbol, consider how comprehensive is the light of faith and how frightful is the darkness of misguidance. What we call faith is, in fact, the essence of the sublime truth explained in this Symbol. Where there is no faith, everything means non-existence for an unbeliever, just as nothing exists for a person without senses.

The second point : There are three facets of the world and things:

Its first facet turns to the Divine Names. Being the mirrors of those Names, this facet does not experience any decay and separation but is continually refreshed and renewed.

96

Its second facet turns to the Hereafter – the world of permanence. Being like a field sown with the seeds of the Hereafter to grow into permanent trees with permanent fruits, this facet of the world is in the service of the World of Permanence; it causes transient things to acquire permanence. It is again not decay and death, but life and permanence, which are manifested in this facet too.

Its third facet turns to us who are transient beings. People of desires and fancies love this facet of the world, which is, on the other hand, the market-place of sensible conscious persons and the stage of trial for the duty-bound. This facet is apparently the object of decay and death. However, there are, in its inward dimension, the manifestations of life and permanence to heal the sorrows coming from death, decay and separations.

In conclusion: Those streams of beings, that flux of creatures, are moving objects and ever-changing and renewed mirrors to renew and make more bright the lights of existence and creation of the Necessarily-Existent Being.

The second station

This station consists of an introduction and five indications. The introduction comprises two topics.

First topic: In order to observe the functions and acts of God's Lordship as if through a telescope, however little and dim it may be, a comparison will be written in each of the following five indications. These comparisons are incapable of expressing, or being a measure for, the truth of the acts and functions of God's Lordship; they are permissible only so far as they serve to enable the reader to understand what is meant by them. Similarly, the expressions in the foregoing Symbols as well as those which will come in the following comparison, being unfit for the acts and functions of the Sacred Being, belong to the inevitable shortcomings in attempting such comparisons.

For example, the colloquial meanings of pleasure and joy and gladness are far from expressing the sacred functions; they are used only to serve as an aid to reflection, as a means of meditation. Such comparisons may also serve, by enabling the reader to catch a glimpse of a comprehensive law of Divine Lordship, to prove the truth of the law in the functions of Lordship. By saying that, for example, a flower passes away but leaves behind thousands of instances of its existence, we point to a mighty law of Divine Lordship which is prevalent in all plants and flowers of spring as, indeed, in all the creatures in the universe.

In fact, the Compassionate Creator changes the robe of the earth every year by the same law as that by which He changes the feathered garment of a bird. It is again by the same law that He changes the appearance of the world every century, and He will also change, with the same law, the form and shape of the universe on the Last Day.

By the same law by which He disposes particles, He causes the earth to rotate and revolve like a Mawlawi dervish turning in ecstasy. He disposes, again by the same law, all the spheres and causes the solar system to move.

He renews your garden and vineyard every year and refreshes them every season by the same law by which He decomposes or repairs the cells in your body or renews them. Again, it is by the same law that He renews the face of the earth every season, arraying it in a new garment.

The All-Powerful Maker revives every spring that tree in front of us and the whole of the earth by the same law of Wisdom by which He revives an insect, and again by the same law, He will revive the creatures on the Day of Judgement. The Qur'an points to this truth in the declaration, *Your creation and resurrection are as but a single soul.*[1]

---

1. *Luqman*, 31.28.

Like those mentioned, there are many other laws of Divine Lordship that are prevalent in everything from particles to the whole of the universe. Reflect on the might and comprehensiveness and unity of those laws in the acts of Divine Lordship, then, see how, being both comprehensive and unitary and manifestations of knowledge and will, they establish decisively the Knowledge and Will of God as well as His Unity.

Most of the comparisons and allegories in most of the *Words* point to the existence of Divine Laws by showing a single manifestation of each. By demonstrating the existence of a law through comparison or allegory, the thesis is proved as decisively as if through a logical proof. This means that most of the comparisons or allegories or parables in the *Words* can be regarded as decisive proofs.

Second topic: As argued in the 'Tenth Truth' of the *Tenth Word,* there are in each flower and fruit on a tree as many instances of wisdom and purposes as the number of those flowers and fruits. Those instances of wisdom are of three kinds: The first kind are related to the Creator Himself, demonstrating the inscriptions of His Names.

The second kind relate to conscious beings, functioning as valuable, meaningful messages for them.

The third kind are related to the fruits or flowers themselves, their life and maintenance, besides their benefits for mankind.

While I was once pondering over multiple purposes of such kinds for the existence of every creature, the following thoughts came to me in Arabic in a way that forms the main themes of the five indications to come, concerning the universal purposes:

All that is before our eyes consists in objects in a flux, mirrors moving and acting so that the manifestations of the light of His creation, glory be to Him, may be renewed. This renewal takes place through the incessant changing of individual beings of relative existence, that is, all those objects receiving Divine manifesta-

tions are replaced by new ones, but after

firstly, their subtle meaning and metaphysical identities have gained permanence;

secondly, they have left behind truths pertaining to the Unseen World and forms recorded on the ideal tablets;

thirdly, they have produced other-worldly fruits and everlasting scenes;

fourthly, they have proclaimed glorifications of the Lord and manifested the requirements of His Names;

and fifthly, they are replaced in order that the functions of the Glorious One and the objects of His Knowledge may be displayed.

As pointed out in those five paragraphs containing the main themes of the five indications to follow, there are in each creature, especially the living ones, five different kinds of wisdom and purposes. O mortal man! If you desire that the truth you possess as a little seed may grow into a permanent tree (with the fruits of purposes which will be explained in the five indications to come), try to acquire the true faith. Otherwise, besides being deprived of those fruits, you will be pressed into that seed and rot away together with it.

The first indication

All those objects receiving Divine manifestations are replaced by new ones, but after, firstly, their subtle meaning and metaphysical identities have gained permanence;

That is, when a being dies, it goes, in appearance, to non-existence, but the meaning it has expressed is kept permanently; its form, its nature and metaphysical identity, are all preserved in the World of Ideas and on the copies of this world – the guarded tablets – and in the memories, which are samples of the guarded tablets. Thus, it gains, in exchange for an apparent, material existence, hundreds of other types of existence, immaterial and related to knowledge.

For example, in order to print a page of a book in a printing machine, the types are first arranged and after the page is printed, the types are removed. This page is later multiplied to the number of the edition, thus gaining permanence in thousands of forms and, with its meaning, in thousands of memories, although the types are no longer there. In just the same way, the Pen of Divine Destiny determines a shape, a form and a period for the meanings in Divine Knowledge and, in the case of vegetation for example, Divine Power gives them external, material existence in spring. After their forms and identities are transferred to the register of the Unseen World, Divine Wisdom requires that they should be replaced with the new ones to come in the next spring so that they, too, can exhibit their meanings.

The second indication

> ... secondly, they have left behind truths pertaining to the Unseen World and forms recorded on the ideal tablets;

That is, when each thing, especially each living thing, whether of particular or universal nature, dies, besides bringing forth many truths pertaining to the Unseen World, leaves on the ideal tablets in the registers of the World of Ideas all the forms it has taken on during its life. These forms serve as words or sentences to make up its life-history consisting of the Divinely destined events of its life, and the spirit beings reflect on them.

A flower, for example, dies, but, besides depositing in hundreds of its seeds the essentials of its existence, it leaves thousands of its forms in little guarded tablets of the Unseen World and in thousands of memories – the miniatures of the guarded tablets. It goes only after it has shown to conscious beings how it has glorified the Lord and how it has manifested the inscriptions of His Names through the forms it has taken on during its life. Likewise, being a flower in the global pot, spring, too, decays and, in appearance, goes to non-existence. But, in exchange for itself, it leaves behind as many truths pertaining to the Unseen World as the number of its seeds, as many ideal identities as the number of its flowers, and as many instances of wisdom as the creatures contained in it. Also, it makes room for the next spring so that it, too, may come and fulfil its function. In short, spring is stripped of a garment of apparent existence in exchange for a thousand garments of immaterial existence.

The third indication

...thirdly, they have produced other-worldly fruits and everlasting scenes.

That is, the world is a factory or an arable field where the products proper for the market of the Hereafter are obtained. As proved in several of *The Words,* just as the deeds of the *jinn* and mankind are being transferred to the market of the Hereafter, so too, the other creatures of the world perform many functions for the sake of the Hereafter and thereby produce many kinds of 'crops'. It may even be said that the earth, this Divine ship, which, through its revolution around the sun at a very great speed, draws the periphery of the Place of Mustering, makes this movement so that its inhabitants may reap the harvest of their work in the Hereafter. It is actually so, because, for example, the people of Paradise will desire to narrate to each other worldly experiences and take great pleasure in watching them as though on a cinema screen. That being the case, as indicated in the Qur'anic verse, *(they recline) face to face on couches raised,*[2] they will talk about the events of their worldly life and the images of those events will be present as ever-lasting scenes.

The world, thus, functions as a factory where, in order that those everlasting scenes may be formed, beautiful creatures appear one after the other and then disappear. In today's civilized world, for example, strange and spectacular things and events are filmed and thus given a kind of permanence for future generations. Similarly, the All-Wise Maker of the creatures records,

---

2. *al-Hijr,* 15.47.

as a requirement of His Names, the All-Wise, the All-Compassionate and the All-Loving, the outcomes of the functions fulfilled by the worldly creatures for the sake of the Hereafter and gives them permanence as ever-lasting scenes of the Eternal World.

The fourth indication

fourthly, they have proclaimed glorifications of the Lord and manifested the requirements of his Names;

That is, the creatures glorify God in many different ways through the stages of their life. As they glorify the All-Wise Maker to the number of the members of their bodies, they also display, through their life and existence, the requirements or functions of Divine Names, i.e. compassion required by the Name, the All-Compassionate, provision by the Name the All-Provider, favour by the Name the All-Favouring, and so on. A man eats delicious fruits and those fruits decompose, and apparently die away, in his stomach. But, besides the taste they produce in the mouth, they give some kind of pleasure to all the cells of the body coming from the activity of appropriating them and become the means of many purposeful functions such as the nourishment of the body and the maintenance of life. As sustenance, they themselves are promoted from the level of plant life to that of human life. It is just in the same way that when the creatures are concealed behind the veil of death, they entrust to the Names themselves the works and inscriptions of many Divine Names, thus obtaining permanence. I wonder, then, whether it is reasonable to lament over the death of a creature that has gained, through death, thousands of kinds of permanent existence in return for a transient one. One should think that (Divine) Compassion, Wisdom and Love have required it to be so; the preference of the reverse would mean to refuse thousands of benefits to avoid a single discomfort; such avoidance would result in thousands of kinds of harm. To conclude, the Names, the All-Compassionate, the All-Wise and the All-Loving, do not contradict death and decay, rather they necessitate them.

The fifth indication

and fifthly, they are replaced in order that the functions of the Glorious One and the objects of His Knowledge may be displayed.

That is, the creatures, particularly the living ones, shed their apparent existence after they have left behind many permanent things.

As explained in the Second Symbol, the Necessarily-Existent Being feels, on account of the functions of His Lordship and in accordance with His Holiness and His absolute independence of all created things, infinite love and affection, and limitless pride, so to speak, endless sacred delight and pleasure, and boundless Divine cheer that, through the amazing activity required by those functions, the creatures are set moving in continuous changes and transformations from the visible, material world to the World of the Unseen. Being in a continuous flux and restless movement, required by the functions of God's Lordship, the creatures impress the people of misguidance with wails of death and separation, whereas they impress people of guidance with voices of Divine remembrance and glorification. For this reason, each creature leaves, before departure from the world, numerous meanings, qualities and states by means of which the permanent functions of the Necessarily-Existent Being may be manifested. That creature also leaves, through the forms and states it has undergone throughout its life, an expanded existence which represents its external, material existence in the spheres of Divine Knowledge like the Manifest Record, the Manifest Book and the Guarded Tablet. As a result, each mortal creature strips off a single existence but, in return, gains a thousand kinds of permanent existence.

Consider another example: Some raw materials are put in a factory. They burn away there but, consequently, many valuable chemical substances are precipitated in the factory's stills. Also, the factory works with the thermal energy produced as a result of this process and manufactures the desired product. The combustion of raw materials thus results in many new things of greater value coming into existence. If this is so, is it at all reasonable to complain about the consumption of those raw materials, to wail that the manufacturer has shown no mercy to those lovely materials? It is in just the same way that – *God's is the highest comparison* – the All-Wise, All-Compassionate and All-Loving Creator, as a requirement of His Compassion, Wisdom and Love, sets the factory of the universe in motion to employ each mortal existent as a seed to grow into many kinds of permanent existence, making it the object of His functions of glory, the means for His purposes of Lordship, the ink for the Pen of His Destiny, and a shuttle for the textiles of His Power, in short, for these and many other sublime purposes unknown to us, He keeps the universe in constant operation. He sets particles in restless motion, the elements and plants in a continuous flux, the animals in an endless procession and the planets in a ceaseless revolution, thus making the universe speak and write expressively of His signs. He has made, on account of His Lordship, air, light, water and soil each an imperial medium for the operation of, successively, His commands and decrees, His Knowledge and Wisdom, His bounties and Mercy and of His preservation and revival, using them for the life of earthly creatures.

Know for certain that the bright, sublime truth pointed out in the foregoing Five Symbols and Five Indications can be discerned only through the light of the Qur'an and acquired through the power of faith. Otherwise, that eternal truth will be replaced by a dense, dreadful darkness. It is because of this that for the people of misguidance, the world is only a place of death and separations and where everything goes to absolute non-existence. The universe means for them, a kind of hell and everything in it is enveloped, after a twinkle of existence, by an overall non-existence. Both the past and the future are, for them, engulfed by layers of the darkness of non existence; only in the twinkle of the present can a tragic life of existence be found. But, for the people of guidance all time is, thanks to the Qur'an and the light of faith, illumined by the light of existence, by means of which they gain eternal happiness.

In conclusion: I pronounce in the manner of the poet, Niyazi Misri:

When my soul is annihilated in God
And the cage of my body breaks into pieces;
When my tongue is reduced to silence,
I call: O Truth, O Existent One, O Ever-Living, O Worshipped One
O All-Wise, O All-Loving, O All-Compassionate, O Desired One!

And I shout:

There is no deity but God, the Sovereign, the Evident Truth; Mu-
hammad is the Messenger of God, true to what he promised and
the Trustworthy.

Also, I believe and prove,

The raising of the dead is true, Paradise is true, Hell is true and
the eternal bliss is true, and God is surely Compassionate and
Wise and Loving; and surely Compassion, Wisdom and Love en-
compass all things and their functions.

[Those who have entered Paradise] say, 'Praise be to God, Who has
guided us to this. We could not truly have been led aright if God
had not guided us. Verily the Messengers of our Lord did bring the
truth.

Glory be to You, we have no knowledge save what You have taught
us; surely You are the All-Knowing, the All-Wise.

Our Lord! take us not to task if we forget, or make mistake. O God, bestow blessings on our master Muhammad in a way to please You and to perform his due, and on his family and Companions, and bestow peace also! Amen! And all praise be to the Lord of the Worlds.

Glory be to Him Who has made the garden of His earth a place where the works of His Art are exhibited, His creatures are assembled, His Power and Wisdom are manifested, His Mercy blooms, the seeds of His Paradise are sown, created beings appear and then disappear, existent things stream in and out, and creatures come and go according to a fixed measure. Adorned animals, embellished birds, fruitful trees, flowering plants are all the miracles of His Knowledge, wonders of His Art, gifts of His Munificence, proofs of His Grace, evidences of His Oneness, subtleties of His Wisdom and witnesses of His Compassion. Flowers smile because of fruits; birds sing because of the morning breeze; raindrops trill on the cheeks of flowers.

The finery displayed by fruits in these gardens and the compassion of all mothers, animal or human, for their young, all come from the recognition of the All-Loving, and the love of the All-Merciful, and the compassion of the All-Affectionate, and the affection of the All-Bounteous, toward the jinn, mankind, spirit, animals and angels, in short, toward all created beings.

***

THE FIRST ADDENDUM
to theTwenty-fourth Letter

In His Name

There is nothing that does not glorify Him with praise.

In the Name of God, the Merciful, the Compassionate

Say (O Muhammad): 'My Lord would not concern Himself with you but for your prayer'.[3]

Reflect on the following five points concerning the verse just quoted:

The first point

Prayer is a great mystery of servanthood to God, the very essence of it. As I have mentioned in several sections of my books, there are three kinds of prayer.

The first kind of prayer is that which is made by the tongue of innate disposition. All seeds and seed-stones pray to the All-Wise Creator through their disposition, their nature, to grow and flourish into an elaborate plant or a huge tree, so that they may make fully manifest the inscriptions of His Names.

The existence of all the circumstances necessary for a particular effect to come about is also a prayer through natural disposition, a plea that that effect be realized. That is, the arrangement of necessary circumstances may be likened to a tongue of disposition praying to the All-Powerful and Majestic One to create the desired effect. For example, water, heat, soil and light come together for a seed to grow into a tree to the effect that they pray God, 'O Creator, make this seed grow into a tree!' It is inconceivable that those unconscious, inanimate, individual material existences, like water, soil, heat and light, could of

---

3. *al-Furqan,* 25.77.

themselves create a tree, which is, in essence, a miracle of Divine Power, so the assemblage of causes that lead to a certain result is a sort of prayer done by the tongue of disposition.

The second kind of prayer is that which is made with the tongue of natural neediness. All living beings pray to the All-Compassionate Creator through their neediness, to satisfy their needs, which they are unable to meet by themselves. For we see that God always sends them, just on time, the provision that is impossible for themselves to supply. In this sense, their neediness is a kind of prayer.

In short, what reaches the Court of God from the whole universe is a kind of prayer. Causes are petitions to God to create the desired result.

The third kind of prayer is that which is made by conscious living beings for their special needs to be satisfied. This kind of prayer falls into two categories.

The first category consists of the supplications made in desperation or in connection with natural needs or by the tongue of disposition or with sincerity and pure intention. Most of such supplications are accepted. The great majority of scientific discoveries and technological innovations (regarded as a means of pride by supporters of modern civilization) are the results of the petitions made in the tongue of needs and potential or natural capacity; they are therefore normally acceptable unless some obstacle intervenes.

The second category consists of those prayers that we say every day. These also are of two types: one is active and by disposition, and the other verbal and from the heart. To plough the earth, for example, is an active prayer and means to knock at the door of the treasury of God's Mercy and Munificence, not to beg provision from the earth.

Omitting the details of other kinds, we will explain some mysteries of the verbal prayer in the following point.

The second point

Prayer has a very great effect; it yields a result in most, even in all, cases, especially when what is asked for is expressed in a universal form. It may even be argued that one of the reasons for the creation of the universe is prayer. That is, since the Creator knew before the creation of the Prophet Muhammad, upon him be peace and blessings, that the Prophet would desire in the future, on behalf of mankind, or indeed of the whole creation, eternal happiness, and that he would desire to be favoured with the manifestations of the Divine Names, He accepted the future prayers of Muhammad and created the universe. If, then, prayer is so significant and comprehensive, is it conceivable that the prayers uttered consistently for fourteen centuries by hundreds of millions of Muslims and innumerable blessed ones among mankind, by the *jinn*, by the angels and other spiritual beings, for the Prophet Muhammad to receive the greatest Divine Mercy, to gain eternal happiness and to achieve all his aims, is it conceivable that those prayers should not be accepted?

Since the prayers made on behalf of the Prophet Muhammad, upon him be peace and blessings, have such permanence, comprehensiveness and universality that they have reached the level of the prayers done in the tongue of potential and natural needs, then the Prophet Muhammad has acquired, by virtue of those prayers, in addition to his Prophethood and personal merits, such a great rank that if the whole of mankind were to unite their intelligence into a single one, they could not comprehend it.

So, O Muslim, consider how great an intercessor you may have on the Day of Judgement. In order to deserve his intercession, follow his *Sunnah!*

Question

If he is the Beloved of God, how or why does he need so many prayers on his behalf?

Answer

That blessed person, upon him be peace and blessings, concerns himself with the happiness of his whole *ummah* both individually and collectively, and he is anxious about whatever may befall them. Although he has, for himself, infinite degrees of eternal happiness and levels of perfection, yet he wishes ardently for the happiness in all times and degrees of each member of his nation and is grieved about each of their misfortunes, and so he needs and most certainly deserves countless blessings and prayers.

Question

Why is it that sometimes we pray for things sure to happen – like the prayer made when the sun or moon is eclipsed and sometimes for things which cannot possibly happen?

Answer

As explained elsewhere, prayer is a kind of worship. A servant proclaims through prayer his helplessness and poverty before God. The apparent purposes for prayer are rather causes for doing the worship of prayer. The reward for worship is principally given in the Hereafter. If the intended worldly aims are not achieved through prayer, one should not say, 'My prayer has not been accepted', rather one should say, 'The time for prayer is not yet over'.

Besides, is it conceivable that the people of belief will not be given the eternal happiness for which they ask continually with great zeal and utmost sincerity, that the absolutely Benevolent and Compassionate One, to Whose infinite Mercy all the universe testifies, will not accept their prayer to establish the World of Eternal Happiness?

The third point

The voluntary verbal prayer is accepted in two ways: either

what is requested is given to the one who prays or his prayer is returned with a better reward.

For example, someone prays for a son but God Almighty grants him a daughter like the Virgin Mary. In that case, we should not say, 'His prayer has not been accepted', rather we should say, 'His prayer has been accepted in a better way'.

Likewise, another one prays for worldly happiness but his prayer is returned with eternal happiness. In this case, we should rather say, 'His prayer has been accepted in a more beneficial way', than say, 'His prayer has not been accepted', and so on.

Since God Almighty is All-Wise, we beg from Him, and He returns our request in accordance with His Wisdom. A patient, for instance, may ask for honey, and the doctor gives him quinine sulphate for his fever. In this case, the patient should not criticize the doctor, saying, 'He has not heeded my request': the doctor diagnosed the illness very well and did what was better for the patient.

The fourth point

The most beautiful and pleasurable, and the quickest result of prayer is that the one who prays knows that there is One, Who has Absolute Power over everything, Who hears him, has pity on him, and provides a remedy for his pains. He is not alone in this guesthouse of the world, rather there is an All-Munificent One Who looks after him and provides him with companionship. He imagines himself to be in the actual presence of a Being Who is able to satisfy all his needs and overcome all his enemies, and, feeling relief as if a heavy burden were removed from him, he says, 'All praise be to the Lord of the Worlds'.

The fifth point

Prayer is the very essence of being a slave of God and an indicator of sincere belief. The one who prays demonstrates, through prayer, that there is One Who rules over the whole universe and is aware of all his affairs down to the most insignificant ones, and Who hears him and enables him to achieve his aims. Since he witnesses that that Being does everything down to the smallest, he hopes that He will fulfil his expectations. Consider, then, the comprehensiveness of the conception of Divine Unity formed by prayer, and the pleasure and purity of the light of belief it exhibits. Then, ponder the meaning of the verse, Say: *'My Lord would not concern Himself with you but for your prayer'*, and heed the Divine decree, *'Your Lord said, 'Pray to me and I will answer you'* [4].

If He did not want to give, He would not give the desire to want.

Glory be to You! We have no knowledge save what You have taught us. Surely You are the All-Knowing, the All-Wise.

O God, grant blessings to our master Muhammad from past eternity to future eternity, to the number of what is contained in God's Knowledge, and to his family and Companions, and grant them peace. Also, grant us peace and make us and our religion safe from every danger! All praise be to God, the Lord of the Worlds.

***

---

4. *al-Mu'min*, 40.60.

THE SECOND ADDENDUM
to the Twenty-fourth Letter

(This addendum is about the Prophet Muhammad's *Ascension*)

In His Name

There is nothing that does not glorify Him with praise.

In the Name of God, the Merciful, the Compassionate.

And verily He saw him yet another time by the Lote-Tree of the Utmost Boundary, nigh which is the Garden of Abode when there shrouded the Lote-Tree that which shrouded; the eye swerved not, nor swept astray. Indeed, he saw one of the greatest signs of His Lord.

(We will explain in five points the truths mentioned
in the *Mi'rajiya*[5] section of *Mawlud Nabawi*[6].)

The first point

Suleyman Calabi, the writer of *Mawlud Nabawi*, tells in verse a love story concerning the *Buraq*[7], which was brought out of Paradise. Suleyman Calabi is a saintly man and is surely relying on a definite tradition, so he may, through this, in verse story, be describing a truth, which is as follows:

The inhabitants of the Permanent World are deeply interested in the light of the Holy Messenger of God. For, it is through the light he brought that Paradise will be cheered and mankind and the *jinn* gain true happiness. Were it not for that light, eternal happiness would not be established and Paradise would not

---

5. *Mi'rajiya* is the section where the miraculous journey of Muhammad to God's Presence through all the material and spiritual worlds is recounted. (Tr.)

6. *Mawlud Nabawi*, written by Sulayman Calabi, is a long poem depicting some significant events in the life of the Prophet Muhammad, upon him be peace and blessings. (Tr.)

7. The 'Mount', which carried the Prophet Muhammad for his Ascension. (Tr.)

be cheered by mankind and the *jinn*, who have the capacity to make use of each species in Paradise. As explained in the Fourth Branch of the *Twenty-fourth Word*, like the nightingale, which announces its legendary love for the rose, each species of animals has a nightingale-like singer to announce its love of the plants for which animals have so great need.

These singers sing the praises of the plants that convey to them their food from the treasury of Divine Mercy. In just the same way, as the Archangel Gabriel serves the Prophet Muhammad, upon him be peace and blessings, on behalf of all the angels with perfect love and thereby demonstrates why angels showed devotion and submission to the Prophet Adam, since Muhammad, upon him be peace and blessings, is the ultimate cause for the creation of the worlds and the means of eternal happiness and the Beloved of the Lord of the Worlds, so too, the interest in, and attachment to, the Prophet Muhammad felt by the people, and even the animals, of Paradise, are expressed through the love of the *Buraq* for him.

The second point

We read also in the *Mi'rajiya* that Almighty God expressed His sacred love for His holy Messenger in the expression, *I have fallen in love with you!* Although this expression seems, in its colloquial meaning, not to be in conformity with the holiness of the Necessarily-Existent Being and His essential independence of the created, it must also have a reality which is as follows:

The Necessarily-Existent Being has infinite grace, beauty and perfection; the grace, beauty and perfection shared by all parts of the universe are signs and indicators of His Grace, Beauty and Perfection. Thus, as anyone who has some degree of beauty and perfection loves his beauty and perfection, so does the One of Majesty love His Beauty and Perfection as much as deserved by Him. He also loves the radiances of His Grace and Beauty, which are His Names. As He Loves His Names, He also loves His art, which shows the beauty of His Names, and His creatures which are the mirrors reflecting His Beauty and Perfection. Since He loves those that reflect His Beauty and Perfection, He also loves the beauties of His creatures which indicate the beauty and perfection of His Names. Those five forms of love are indicated by the Qur'an in some of its verses.

So, since the Holy Messenger of God, upon him be peace and blessings, is the most perfect and most distinguished member of the whole creation;

since he appreciates the Divine Art and exhibits it through an exuberant recitation and glorification of God's Names;

since he disclosed through the language of the Qur'an the treasuries of beauty and perfection possessed by the Divine Names;

since he demonstrated decisively and forcefully through the language of the Qur'an how the creational and the operational laws of the universe testify to the perfection of its Maker;

since he functions, through his universal servanthood and worship, as a mirror to Divine administration and sustaining of the universe;

since he is, through his comprehensive nature, a perfect object of the manifestation of Divine Names;

then it is self-evident that the All-Gracious and Beautiful One of Majesty loves, on account of His Love of His own Grace and Beauty, the Prophet Muhammad, who is the most perfect mirror of that Grace and Beauty.

And He loves, an account of His love of His own Names, the Prophet Muhammad, upon him be peace and blessings, who is the most brightest mirror of those Names, and He also loves those who resemble the Prophet Muhammad in faith and conduct in proportion to the degree of their resemblance.

And He Loves, because of His love of His own art, the Prophet Muhammad, who exhibits that art in the whole universe in a most expressive way and through so vigorous a recitation and glorification of God's Names as to enrapture all the inhabitants of heavens, the earth and its seas, and He also loves those who follow him.

And He loves, because of His love of His creatures, the living beings, the most perfect of the creatures, and the conscious beings, the most perfect of the living beings, and the human beings, the best of the conscious beings, and most of all, the Prophet Muhammad, who is, unanimously, the most perfect of human beings.

And He loves an account of His love of the laudable virtues of His creatures, the Prophet Muhammad, who is, unanimously, the highest in laudable virtues, and He also loves those who resemble Him according to the degree of their resemblance. In short, like His Compassion, the Love of God Almighty, too, has encompassed the universe.

In conclusion, since in each of the foregoing five aspects attracting Divine Love, the Prophet Muhammad is of the highest rank among countless beloved ones, he deserves the title of 'the Beloved of God'.

Thus, it is this highest rank of being beloved which Suleyman Calabi described through the Divine expression, *I have fallen in love with you.* This expression serves as an 'observatory' through which the truth explained should be contemplated. Anyway, if this expression still causes some association of ideas incompatible with the Essence of Divine Lordship, we should, instead of it, use the expression, 'I have been pleased with you'.

The third point

The events described in the *Mi'rajiya* do not seem, in their literal meaning, to be compatible with the pure sacred truths. Those events and dialogues should, rather than literally, be taken as a means of contemplation and indicators of certain sublime, pro-

117

found truths; they serve to remind us of certain truths of faith and to point to certain meanings difficult to express explicitly. Therefore, we cannot extract those truths from those dialogues; rather, we can obtain, through our heart or soul, a pleasure of faith and a spiritual joy. For, as Almighty God has no like in His Essence and Attributes, so He has no equal in the Essence and functions of His Lordship; as His Attributes are not like those of the creatures, neither is His Love similar to that of contingent beings.

In short, such descriptions in the *Mi'rajiya* as those mentioned above are of a figurative nature; they are there to remind us that the Necessarily-Existent Being has some functional attributes like *Love* but in accordance with His Necessary Existence and Holiness, and with His absolute Perfection and essential independence of the created.

The fourth point

Question

It is also related in the *Mi'rajiya* that the Prophet Muhammad, upon him be peace and blessings, saw God Almighty from behind seventy thousand veils. This expresses a spatial distance, whereas the Necessarily-Existent Being is free from being bounded by space and time and is nearer to everything than itself. So, what is meant by that aspersion?

Answer

You can find the answer in detail in the *Twenty-first Word*; what follows may suffice here for some understanding of the matter:

God Almighty is the nearest to us while we are infinitely far from Him. Consider that even if we are quite a long way from the sun, the sun itself is very near to us through the mirror in our hand; it is even nearer to us than ourselves through its reflection in our eyes, and manifests itself in every transparent thing with its light and heat. If the sun were an animate, conscious being, it would communicate its messages to us through our mirror. Likewise, while keeping in mind God's having no like or equal, God, the Eternal Sun, is nearer to everything than itself, for His Existence is necessary and He is free from being bounded by space; nothing can veil Him. Nevertheless, everything is infinitely far from Him.

The fact that while we are infinitely far away from God, God is, as stated in the Qur'anic verse, *We are nearer to him than his neck vein*,[8] no distance to us, explains how God's Messenger covered almost an infinite distance in his *Mi'raj* (Ascension) and came back in an instant. The Ascension of God's Messenger is, in one respect, his journey of spiritual elevation in the way of God and the title or final rank of his sainthood.

Just as the people of sainthood attain to the rank of certainty of experiencing the truths of faith, within a period from forty days to forty years, so too, the Holy Messenger of God, upon him be peace and blessings, who is the king of saintly people, attained, through his Ascension which he accomplished as the greatest wonder of his sainthood not only through his heart and spirit but also through his body and outer and inner senses and faculties, the highest rank of experiencing the truths of faith within a period as short as forty minutes. He reached, by way of the Ascension, the Divine Throne of Majesty, witnessed with the certainty of vision the truths of belief in God and the Hereafter to the point of being so near to God as 'two bows' length and, entering Paradise, experienced the eternal happiness. Through the Ascension, he opened up a broad way for those qualified among his nation to follow in their spiritual journey toward the rank of sainthood.

The fifth point

The recitation of *Mawlud Nabawi* and *Mi'rajiya* is a beautiful and

---

8. *Qaf*, 50.16.

119

beneficial Islamic tradition. It has been a pleasurable and lovely means of social gatherings in the social life of Muslims. Further, it is an agreeable course for the remembrance of the truths of faith. It is also an effective means to show, and quicken thoughts and feelings to, the lights of belief and the love of God and the Prophet. May God Almighty allow such traditions to last until eternity and have mercy on those who, like Suleyman Effendi, write *Mawlud*, and admit them into the *Jannat al-Firdaws*, the highest abode in Paradise! *Amen!*

Conclusion

Since the Creator of this universe has created a perfect and distinguished individual among every species and made it the pride and means of perfection of that species, He would, most certainly, create, through the manifestation of His Greatest Names, a most distinguished and perfect individual in the universe. As there is a Greatest Name among His Names, there will also be, among His creatures, a most perfect individual upon whom He will concentrate all the perfections existing in the universe, and He will observe Himself through that individual.

That perfect individual will self-evidently be among living beings for living beings are the most perfect of the species in the universe. Then he will be among conscious beings for among living beings conscious beings are the most perfect. Next, that matchless individual will be a human being for only human beings have an aptitude for infinite progress. Finally, that being will most certainly be the Prophet Muhammad, upon him be peace and blessings, for history has not matched him since the beginning. For that being has, for fourteen centuries, held under his spiritual rule half of the globe and one-fifth of mankind, and become a teacher in all kinds of truth to all men of perfection.

As unanimously agreed by friends and foes alike, he possesses all sorts of laudable virtues in the highest degree. From the very beginning of his mission he challenged alone the whole world. Again, that distinguished being will most certainly be the Prophet Muhammad, who, besides all those qualities mentioned above, brought the Qur'an of Miraculous Expression, which has been constantly recited everyday for fourteen centuries by hundreds of millions of people. He is both the seed and fruit of that tree of creation. *Upon him and his family and Companions be blessings and peace to the number of the species of existence and the creatures in existence.*

So, understand how pleasant, joyful, good, pride-enhancing and light-diffusing a religious ceremony it is for believers who regard that being as their master, leader and intercessor, to hear, through *Mawlud* and *Mi'rajiya* the beginning and end of his spiritual evolution and learn the spiritual meaning of the important events of his life.

O God! For the sake of Your Holy Beloved, upon him be peace and blessings, and Your Greatest Name, allow and enable the hearts of those who publish this treatise and of their friends to receive the lights of belief and enable them to use their pens to multiply the treatises concerning the mysteries of the Qur'an; and enable them to follow the right path without any deviation! Amen!

Glory be to You! We have no knowledge save what You have taught us; surely You are the All-Knowing, the All-Wise.

Only the Everlasting is everlasting.
Said Nursi

***

The
Twenty-sixth
Letter

The Qur'an's argument against Satan and his party
Negative nationalism and various matters of belief

(This letter has four topics in little relation to each other.)

THE FIRST TOPIC

In His Name, glory be to Him
There is nothing that does not glorify Him with praise.

In the Name of God, the Merciful, the Compassionate

If a provocation from Satan should provoke you, seek refuge in God, verily He is the All-Hearing, the All-Knowing.[1]

The Qur'an's argument against Satan and his party

The first topic comprises a rational discussion with Satan to refute a deceptive argument of his; in the discussion he is finally silenced and overcome, along with the people of transgression.

It was eleven years ago that, one day in the blessed month of Ramadan, I was listening to recitation of the Qur'an in the Bayazid Mosque in Istanbul. Suddenly I felt as if someone not visible to me in person was saying to me: 'You regard the Qur'an as highly exalted and radiant. Study it for once in an objective

---

1. The Qur'an, *al-A'raf*, 7.200.

manner and see whether it is so radiant and exalted!'

I was taken in for a brief moment and in that moment fancied that the Qur'an is the work of a human being. I began to feel that the lights of the Qur'an gradually became obscured just as the mosque is left in darkness as the lights are turned off. I then perceived that the one who was talking to me was Satan, who desired to imperil me. I sought help from the Qur'an and straightaway I felt a light in my heart, which encouraged me to argue against Satan. I said to him:

– O Satan! Objective reasoning means impartial judgement or not taking sides, but the objective reasoning which you and your disciples suggest is, in fact, taking the part of those in opposition to the Qur'an; not impartiality but an attitude of temporary unbelief. This is really so because to suppose the Qur'an the work of a human being and to build an argument on this supposition is to side with unbelief or falsehood.

Satan retorted:

– Then, accept it as neither the Word of God nor the work of a human being!

I answered:

– That is not justifiable either, for, if some item of property is disputed between two parties, it is deposited in the hands of a trusted third party, provided that the two parties are in reasonable proximity to each other. However, if the parties are quite far apart, the property is left, until the dispute is settled, in the possession of the one who already holds it – the matter is not left undecided.

To follow the analogy through, if the Qur'an may be regarded as a priceless piece of property, there is an infinite distance between its present owner – God – and its claimant – man – so the matter cannot be left undecided as there cannot be, in this case, a third party into whose custody it may be entrusted. That being so, it should be left in the 'hands' of God. Second, the number of people who have accepted it as the Word of God over fourteen centuries amounts to billions, so it falls upon those in opposition to it to prove, if they can, that it is the work of a human being, not upon the Muslims to prove it to be the Word of God. If its opponents are able to refute all the proofs that the Qur'an is the Word of God, only then can it justifiably be argued whether it is the Word of God or the work of a human being. Otherwise, not!

Therefore, O Satan! Who would dare to pull out that brilliant Qur'an from the Greatest Throne of God onto which it is fixed with thousands of 'nails' of decisive proofs? Despite you, O Satan, the people of truth and justice deal with the issue by just reasoning and strengthen their belief in the Qur'an even through the least of those decisive proofs. As for those who are taken in by you and your disciples, it is very difficult for them to get out of the darkness of unbelief into the light of belief since it requires a proof as strong as all the 'nails' with which the Qur'an is fixed to the Greatest Throne of God, once it has been cast to the ground by supposing that it to be the work of a human being. It is because of this that many people are deceived by you into that false pretence of 'objective' reasoning and ultimately lose their faith.

Satan insisted:

– The Qur'an resembles the word of a human being in that it follows the style of human speech or conversation. If it were the Word of God, it should be extraordinary in all its aspects. As God's artistry cannot be likened to what is human, His Word likewise should not resemble human speech!

I replied:

– Our Prophet, upon him be peace and blessings, was a human being; except for his miracles and states of Prophethood, all his acts and attitudes originated in his humanity. Like all other human beings, he was subject to and dependent upon, the creational and operational laws of God; he suffered from cold, felt pains and so on. He was not extraordinary in all his acts and attitudes, and set an example to mankind through his conduct. If he had been extraordinary in his conduct and attitudes, he could not have been an absolute guide in every aspect of life and the mercy for all the worlds through all his states. In the same way, the Wise Qur'an is a leader to conscious beings, a director to mankind and the *jinn*, a guide to men of perfection, and an instructor to truth-seeking people. For that reason, it needs to be in the style of human speech and conversation: for mankind and the *jinn* take out of it their supplications, they learn from it their prayers, they converse about their affairs in its terms and they derive from it the principles of good conduct. In short, every believer adopts it as the authorized recourse or reference on all his affairs. If, by contrast, it had been like the Word of God which the Prophet Moses heard on Mount Sinai, no one could have borne to hear it, let alone adopt it as a recourse. One of the five greatest Messengers of God, namely the Prophet Moses, upon him be peace, was able to hear only a few pieces of that Word and asked: 'Is this Your speech?' God answered: 'I have the power of all tongues and languages.'

Satan continued:

– Many persons give voice in the name of religion to almost the same subjects as those in the Qur'an. So, is it not possible for a human being to produce the like of the Qur'an?

I answered him through the light of the Qur'an:

– *First of all*, a religious man voices the truth for the love of religion and in the name of God's commandments; he never lies against God. He would never venture so far as to imitate God and speak on his own for fear of the Qur'anic threat, *Whoever is greater in wrongdoing than the one who lies against God!* [2]

Second, it is by no means possible for a man to succeed in do-

---

2. *al-Zumar*, 39.32.

ing such a thing for a man can only imitate another one of nearly the same level. Only those of the same species can take each
other's form; only those of nearly the same level can pretend to
each other's level. However, it is very difficult, even in this
case, for them to deceive people for long as their pretensions
and false display will certainly give them away sooner or later
in the sight of perceptive people.

If, on the other hand, the counterfeiter is greatly inferior in
rank to the one he tries to imitate, if, for example, an ordinary
man were to pretend to the knowledge of Avicenna or a shep-
herd were to make himself appear to be a king, he would most
certainly do nothing other than lay himself open to ridicule.

Is it at all possible that a firefly could make itself appear as a
star to observers for a thousand years? Can a fly make itself appear as a peacock for a year? Also, is it at all conceivable that an
ordinary private could pretend to be a famous marshal and occupy his chair for a long time without giving himself away?
Likewise, is it possible for a slandering, lying man of unbelief to
sustain for a lifetime, before the discerning, a false display of
the loyalty, truthfulness and conviction of a most pious man? If
all these 'ifs' are indeed inconceivable and if they are all unac-
ceptable to any intelligent man, then to suppose the Qur'an to
be the work of a human being, would mean regarding that Manifest Book, which has been like a star of truths or a sun of perfections radiating the lights of truths in the sky of the Muslim
world for centuries, as – God forbid! – a collection of falsehoods
invented by – God forbid! – a counterfeiter! It would also mean
that those who were in his company for twenty-three years and
followed him for fourteen centuries were not aware of his real
identity and, although he was – God forbid! – like a firefly,
knew and believed him to be a radiant, star-like source of
truths! This is the most inconceivable of suppositions and you,
O Satan, cannot deceive any sensible man into such an inconceivable supposition even if you were a hundred times more

advanced in your devilish craft! What you can manage, however, is to deceive people into looking at the Qur'an and the Prophet from a very great distance and see those star-like objects as fireflies.

Thirdly, to suppose the Qur'an to be the work of a human being would also mean that a most bright, true and comprehensive criterion of the human world, miraculous of exposition and which brings well-being to that world, is – God forbid! – the product of an illiterate individual, whose – God forbid! – pretence and counterfeiting always appeared to even great intellects and exalted geniuses as earnestness, sincerity and purity of intention! It is surely the most inconceivable of allegations. Further, to accept it would mean regarding as reality so inconceivable a supposition as that a most illustrious and virtuous being who, throughout his life, displayed and preached conviction, truthfulness, trustworthiness, sincerity, earnestness and uprightness in all his states, his words and his actions, and who brought up many truthful persons was – God forbid! – a mean and most discreditable rascal, wholly insincere and the foremost in unbelief. That is so great a delirium that even Satan would be ashamed to conceive it.

There is not a third alternative in this matter because, if the Qur'an is supposed as the work of a human being, it must be something so far debased as if it had fallen the distance from heaven to earth, and it would change from being a collection of truths into a source of superstitions. And the rank of the one who brought that wonderful decree – the Qur'an – would likewise be degraded from being a source of perfections to – God forbid – the greatest cheat; that must follow if he is – God forbid! – not a Messenger of God. For the one who lies in the name of God is the meanest of people. It follows such a supposition is as inconceivable as always seeing a fly as, and imagining it to have the qualities of, a peacock. Only an intoxicated man, moreover insane from birth, could regard such suppositions as possible.

Fourth, the Qur'an directs the Muslim community which includes, among its members (and this has been witnessed for fourteen centuries past) the greatest and most magnificent division of the children of Adam; the Qur'an holds that community in such an order and under such a discipline as to enable them to conquer both worlds – this one and the next – and has equipped them both materially and spiritually, and instructed and educated them in all rational, moral and spiritual matters according to the intellectual capacity of each of their individuals. It has also purified them and employed each member of their bodies and each of their senses and faculties in its most proper place. As for the Prophet Muhammad, upon him be peace and blessings, who brought the Qur'an from God, he also brought to mankind the laws of God examplified by his attitudes and actions throughout his life: he instructed mankind through his actions the laws of God throughout his life, instructed mankind through his sincere practice of the principles of truth, and showed and established through his sincere and reasonable sayings the ways of true guidance and well-being, and he is, as testified by his whole life and good conduct, the most knowledgeable of God and the most fearful of His punishment. He also established his splendid rule of perfection over half of the globe and one-fifth of mankind: he truly became, through world-famous manners and world-admired actions as a Prophet, statesman, commander, spiritual and intellectual guide, father, husband, friend, and so on, the pride not only of mankind but also of the whole creation. Such being the case, to suppose the Qur'an as the work of a human being would mean that it is – God forbid! – the worthless fabrication of – God forbid! – a dishonest liar who did not recognize God and felt no fear of Him! This is, again, the most inconceivable of suppositions and therefore, O Satan, you cannot deceive into such a supposition any sensible and 'sound-hearted' man, even if you were a hundred times more powerful in your devilish tricks!

Satan retorted:

– How can I fail to deceive! I have actually deceived the majority of mankind including the foremost in rational thought and led them to deny both the Qur'an and Muhammad!

I responded:

– *First:* When looked at from a great distance, the biggest thing can look as small as a tiny particle; a star can be considered as a candle.

Second: When considered in a superficial way, vulnerable to distraction and illusion, an inconceivable thing can appear conceivable.

Once, an old man was scanning the horizon in order to catch sight of the new crescent of Ramadan. A white hair from his eyelash which had curved over his eyes came into his line of vision: deceived by that illusion, he announced: 'I have seen the moon!' However inconceivable it is that a white hair could be regarded as the crescent, this inconceivability became actual in the eyes of the old man who was deceived by an illusion while searching for the crescent in the sky.

Third: Denial is different from non-confirmation. Non-confirmation is a kind of indifference and lack of judgement. For this reason, many inconceivable things may exist unintentionally in non-confirmation. As to denial, it is a judgement and means the confirmation of non-existence. A man usually gets to denial through reasoning. A devil like you, O Satan, deprives him of sound judgement and deceives him into denial. So, O Satan, through such devilish devices as heedlessness, deviation, sophistry, obstinacy, demagogy, arrogant superiority and conceit, seduction and custom which cause many to see falsehood as truth and the inconceivable as conceivable, you have deceived lots of unfortunate people (human in appearance but it is questionable whether they are so in essence,) into unbelief which, in fact, requires the acceptance of many inconceivable things.

Fourth: The Qur'an, besides the merits of it mentioned above, is a book of pure truths and matchless value; it has become a guide to the saints, scholars of truth and purity who are like stars in the sky of the human world; it continually invites the people of every age and race and those seeking perfection, to truth and love of the truth, truthfulness and loyalty, trustworthiness and reliability; and, through the truths of the pillars of belief and the principles of the fundamentals of Islam, the Qur'an secures happiness in both worlds. As for the preacher of the Qur'an, the Prophet Muhammad, upon him be peace and blessings, is, as testified by the religion and law of Islam which he preached, and demonstrated by his unanimously acknowledged piety and sincere worship manifested throughout his whole life, and as required by his laudable virtues, and as confirmed by all the men of truth and perfections, a most trustworthy being, the foremost and firmest in belief and conviction. That being the case, to suppose the Qur'an to be the work of a human being would mean that the Qur'an is – God forbid! – a collection of fallacies and lies, and the Prophet is – God forbid! – an unreliable, unbelieving liar without fear of God. This supposition is the most dangerous kind of unbelief and the most abominable of deviations and wrongdoing, which even devils and sophists would be ashamed to conceive.

In short: It was mentioned in the Eighteenth Sign of the *Nineteenth Letter* that those who have only the power of hearing to appreciate the miraculousness of the Qur'an acknowledge the Qur'an not to be of the same kind and degree as all the other books they have heard. The Qur'an is, therefore, either inferior to them all or superior. No one in the world, even if he be a devil, can claim that the Qur'an is inferior to other books, so it should necessarily be accepted that the Qur'an is superior to them all, and that it is, thereby, a miracle. That being the case, based on the two decisive proofs called 'dichotomy' and 'reductio ad absurdum', we openly declare:

O Satan! and O you disciples of Satan! The Qur'an is either the Word of God manifested through the Highest Throne of God and His Highest Name, or – God forbid! – the fabrication of an unbeliever who does not recognize and fear God. Even you, o Satan, cannot claim the truth of the second alternative; you were not, and will not, be able to voice such an allegation. If this is so, then the Qur'an is, of necessity and undoubtedly, the Word of the Creator of the universe, since, as explained and proved above, there is not a third alternative in this matter.

Likewise, Muhammad, upon him be peace and blessings, is either a Messenger of God, and the most perfect of the Messengers and superior to all other creatures, or he must be regarded as – God forbid![3] – a man of unbelief and of the lowest nature since he lied against God without recognition of Him and of His punishment. This is, O Satan, an allegation which has been, and will be, made by neither the philosophers of Europe nor the hypocrites of Asia, in whom you place great trust. Since there is no one in the world who will heed and accept such an allegation, even the most corrupt of those philosophers and most unscrupulous of the hypocrites are bound to admit that Muhammad was a very wise man and of exemplary good conduct.

Finally, since there are again only two alternatives in this matter and, as in the case of the Qur'an, of which the second is inconceivable, and acceptable to no one, then Muhammad, upon him be peace and blessings, is, self-evidently and of necessity, the Messenger of God, and the most perfect of the Messengers, and superior to all other creatures, even if you, O Satan, and your party are averse.

Upon him be blessings and peace to the number of angels, human beings and the jinn!

---

3. Since the Qur'an mentions such a supposition in order to refute the unbelief and bad language of unbelievers, I felt justified in mentioning it, though fearfully and with aversion, only as a most impossible supposition to show how groundless and false are the assertions of the misguided.

A second, insignificant objection of Satan's

While reciting the verses of the *Surah Qaf*,

> *Not a word he utters, but by him is an observer ready. And the agony of death comes in truth; that is what you were shunning! And the trumpet is blown; that is the Day of the Threat. And every soul comes, along with it a driver and a witness. 'You were heedless of this. Now We have removed from you your covering, and so your sight today is piercing.' And his comrade says, 'Cast, you twain, into Hell each rebel ingrate!'*[4]

Satan said:

'You find the eloquence of the Qur'an primarily in the fluency of its style and the intelligibility of its expression. Yet, where is the fluency and coherence in those verses [mentioned above] considering the great gaps between them: it jumps from the throes of death to the destruction of the world, and from the blowing of the Trumpet to the end of the Reckoning and therefrom to throwing the sinful into Hell?'

Answer

One of the most fundamental elements of the miraculousness of the Qur'an is its eloquence and precision. There are so many instances of that miraculous precision in the Wise Qur'an that observant critics have been filled with wonder and admiration. For example, some eloquent people have prostrated themselves before the verse,

> *And it was said: 'O earth! Swallow your water and, O sky! abate!' And the water was made to subside. And the commandment was fulfilled, and the Ark settled in Al-Judi, and it was said: 'Away with the people of the evildoers!'*[5]

which tells of the might of so great an event as the Flood so precisely and miraculously within a few short sentences.

---

4. *Qaf*, 50.18-24.
5. *Hud*, 11.44.

Also, in the following few short verses,

Thamud denied in their rebellious pride when the most wretched of them uprose; then the Messenger of God said to them, 'The She-Camel of God; let her drink!' But they denied him, and hamstrung her, so their Lord doomed them for their sin, and levelled them. He fears not the issue thereof.[6]

the Qur'an recounts the story of the people of Thamud, including what finally befell them, precisely and clearly, and in a way that does not detract from comprehensibility.

In the same way, in the verse,

And Dhul Nun – when he went forth in anger and was convinced that We would not straiten him: then he called out in the layers of darkness, 'There is no god but You. Glory be to You! I have been a wrong-doer.'[7]

there is much that is not said between *We would not straiten him* and *he called out in the layers of darkness*. Those few words re-tell the story of the Prophet Yunus (Jonah) with its chief points in such a way as not to diminish comprehensibilty or mar the eloquence, leaving what is not stated directly to the understanding of the person addressed.

Also, in the *Surah* Joseph, seven or eight sentences are omitted between *'so send me forth'* and *'Joseph! O you truthful one!,* which come at the end of verse 45 and at the beginning of verse 46 respectively. This also does not affect comprehensibilty, nor does it mar the eloquence of the Qur'an.

There are many other instances of miraculous precision in the Qur'an like those mentioned above. As for the verses in question from *Surah Qaf,* the precise description they make is still more beautiful and miraculous. They point to the future of unbelievers which is so long that each day of it is equal to fifty

---

6. *al-Shams,* 91.11-15.

7. *al-Anbiya',* 21.87.

thousand earthly years, and draw attention to the fearful events which will befall them through the dreadful upheavals of that future. They bring before the mind of the reader (or the listener) the whole span of those upheavals, and bring that long time readily before the eyes like a lightning stroke, and, compressed into a single page, present before us. They leave as understood the unmentioned events and thus achieve and manifest a sublime fluency.

When the Qur'an is recited, give you ear to it and pay heed, that you may obtain mercy.[8]

Now, O Satan, speak if you still have another objection!

Satan replied:

'I am not the one to oppose those truths. But there are many foolish people who follow me, and many satans in human form, who assist me. Among philosophers are many as conceited as Pharaoh who learn from me the matters which contribute to their pride and selfishness. They will prevent the publication of your *Words*, so I will never yield to you.'

Glory be to You! We have no knowledge save what You have taught us. Truly You are the All-Knowing, the All-Wise.

***

---

8. *al-A'raf*, 7.204.

THE SECOND TOPIC

In the Name of God, the Merciful, the Compassionate

O mankind, We have created you male and female, and have made you peoples and tribes, that you may know each other...[9]

that is, so that you may know social relationships and help one another, not so that you may feel antipathy and show enmity to each other.

This topic consists of seven matters.

The first matter

I feel compelled to write about 'nationalism' in order to serve the Glorious Qur'an and put up a stronghold against unfair attacks, not in the style of the New Said, who would like to withdraw from the social life, but in the style of Old Said, who had a connection with Islamic social life, since the exalted truth expressed in the verse mentioned above is related to social life.

The second matter

To explain the principle of *knowing one another and helping each other* declared by the verse, I say:

An army is divided into army corps, an army corps into regiments, a regiment into battalions, a battalion into squadrons or companies and a company into squads, so that the duties of each soldier and the relationships between the members of the whole army may be established, and the army may perform a general task under the principle of mutual assistance, and that the nation may be guarded against the assaults of enemies. The division of an army into different parts is not for the purpose that the parts should compete with each other or feel enmity against each other, or that they should oppose each other. It is just in the same way that the Muslim nation is like a large army,

---

9. *al-Hujurat,* 49.13.

divided into peoples and tribes. But they have numerous common factors and values which require their unity: for example, their Creator is one, their Provider is one, their Prophet is one, their Book is one, their country is one, the direction or the centre toward which they turn in worship is one, and so on to thousands other factors of unity!

Since, then, all these common factors or values require unity and mutual love, the division into peoples and tribes is for mutual acquaintance and assistance, not for mutual dislike and enmity.

The third matter

Nationalism or ethnic differences have been given great momentum in this century. It is particularly the intriguing chiefmakers of Europe who excite nationalist feelings among Muslim communities in order to divide them up and swallow them up one by one.

Nationalism gives some satisfaction albeit it encourages self-pride, and it produces a power albeit sometimes improper. For this reason, it is not proper to advise those engaged in social life to give up the idea of nationalism. But there are two kinds of nationalism: one negative, ominous, harmful, which is fed through swallowing up others and sustained through enmity against others. This kind of nationalism is the cause of mutual antagonism and discord, so it is disapproved and rejected by both and Qur'an the Prophet, as in the *hadith, Islam has forbidden the national (tribal) zealotry of the Age of Ignorance.* [10]

The Qur'an is explicit on the point as in the verse:

When those who disbelieve set in their hearts zealotry, the tribalism of the Age of Ignorance, then God sent down His peace and reassurance upon His Messenger and the believers, and fastened to them the word of self-restraint and God-fearing to which they have

---

10. For different versions, see, Bukhari, *Ahkam*, 4; Tirmidhi, *Jihad*, 28.

better right and of which they are worthy; and God has knowledge of everything.[11]

The sacred and positive Islamic nationalism does not leave room for the need of any negative partisan nationalism. I wonder what nation in the world has a population of more than one billion so as to enable any nationalist to have as many brothers, eternal brothers, as the number of the Muslims.

The negative partisan variety of nationalism has caused much harm during history both to the principle of Islamic unity and to the Islamic peoples. For example, the Umayyads gave some preference to 'Arab nationalities in their government and thereby both offended other Muslims and themselves suffered many misfortunes. Also, the European nations went too far in nationalism in this century, whence the long-standing ominous enmity between the French and German peoples and the dreadful destruction of the World War – which showed how harmful to mankind negative nationalism is. And, in our history, as in the Kingdom of Babylon destroyed through the division of the tribes which constituted the kingdom, many groups or societies were formed, at the beginning of the second constitutional period of the Ottoman State, by minorities, particularly by the Greeks and Armenians. What befell the Ottoman State thereafter and the lot of those who were swallowed by foreigners illustrate the harm of negative nationalism.

The national or tribal conflict between Muslim peoples or communities is so great a misfortune that it is like exposure to the biting of a snake in order to avoid the biting of a fly. At a time when the Western powers resembling huge dragons lie in wait for an opportunity to attack us in order to satisfy their insatiable greed, it is very harmful even to our national integrity to nourish hostility and take sides, because of national differences, against our citizens in the eastern cities and co-religionists

11. *al-Fath,* 48.26.

among our southern neighbours. There is not a justifiable excuse to feel enmity against our co-religionists in the south, from where the light of the Qur'an and the radiance of Islam came to us; besides, the national conflict between Muslim peoples means to help the Western enemies.

Enmity against our southern co-religionists may result in enmity towards the Qur'an and Islam, which in fact, means a treachery to both the worldly life and hereafter of all the citizens. To destroy the cornerstones of the two worlds – this and the next – under the pretext of serving the social life through nationalism or patriotism is stupidity, not nationalism or patriotism.

The fourth matter

The other kind of nationalism is that which is positive and, arising from the intrinsic requirements of social life, brings about mutual assistance and solidarity, produces a beneficial power and causes the Islamic brotherhood to be stronger.

This kind of nationalism should serve Islam and build a stronghold to protect it; it should not take the place of Islam. For the brotherhood desired and established by Islam is manifold and counts in both the Intermediate and Eternal Worlds. It is because of this that, however strong a nationalist brotherhood is, it can be only as strong as a single aspect of the Islamic brotherhood, so to substitute it for the Islamic brotherhood is as foolish an act as replacing the diamonds in a citadel with some stones from that citadel.

So, children of that country who are followers of the Qur'an! You have carried, not for six hundred years but for a thousand years, since the time of the 'Abbasids, the flag of the Wise Qur'an, over the three continents and challenged all the world. You have made your national feelings and solidarity a stronghold to protect Islam, and, repelling the dreadful assaults of the whole world, you have been included in the meaning of the verse,

> God will bring a people He loves, and who love Him, humble to-. wards believers, stern towards unbelievers, striving in the way of God, and fearing not the reproach of any reproachers.[12]

You should now be afraid of, and refrain from, being led by the deceitful instigations of Europe and Westernized hypocrites, being included in the meaning of the first part of the verse mentioned above,

> O you who believe! Whosoever of you turns from his religion...

A reality worthy of note: The Turks are more in number in the world Muslim population than any other people, and all of the Turkish people, wherever they are in the world, are Muslims. They are not, unlike other peoples, divided into two groups, as Muslims and non-Muslims. Although the smallest communities are even divided into two groups, all of the Turkish peoples are Muslims and some Turkish communities, like the Hungarians, who did not accept Islam, have lost their Turkish identity.

O Turkish brother! You should, more than anyone else, be careful! Your nationality is blended with Islam, being inseparable from it. If you separate them, you will be lost! All your past accomplishments form a pride for you and an honourable record of your services to Islam. As it is impossible for any power on earth to remove this record, do not, yourself, remove it from your heart!..

The fifth matter

The awakening peoples of Asia follow the idea of nationalism in blind imitation of Europe and sacrifice many sacred things for its sake. However, just like a suit which, though of the same kind of cloth, is not fit for every body, or just as an old prayer leader is not made to wear clothes suitable for dancing the tan-

---

12. *al-Ma'ida.* 5.24.

go, so should each people aspire to an authentic style: if Europe is like a market-place or barracks, Asia is like an arable field or a mosque. A businessman may go to dance but a farmer not. The conditions of barracks are not the same as those of a mosque.

Also, the appearance of the majority of the Prophets in Asia while the philosophers usually emerge in Europe is a sign from the eternal Destiny that the vitality and progress of Asian peoples is possible through religion and spirituality. Philosophy and science should support religion; they should not be substituted for it.

Second, indifference to religion, after false comparison of Islam with Christianity, is a grave mistake. It should, instead, be carefully noted that Europe is devoted to its religion, that some Western leaders like Wilson, Lloyd George and Venizelos are as fanatically devoted to their religion as a priest.

Third, the comparison of Islam with Christianity is a false one, since Europe progressed when it reformed its religion. Besides, religion caused internal wars in Europe for three hundred years and became a means in the hands of despotic rulers and priests to crush the poor and common people and intellectuals. But in Islam, as witnessed by history, religious devotion caused an internal war only once, and whenever Muslims have followed Islam earnestly, as in the case of the Islamic state of Andalusia, that greatest teacher of Renaissance Europe, they realized much greater progress than their contemporaries. Whenever they, by contrast, have been indifferent to religion, they have declined and fallen to a miserable state.

Further, with its numerous principles of compassion such as the obligation of giving the prescribed alms *(zakat)* and the prohibition of interest, Islam protects the poor and common people, and it regards – through its many warnings like *Will you not exercise your reason? Will they not contemplate and reflect? Do they not ponder?* – intellect and science as proofs for its truths, and protects men of sciences and encourages them to further and further researches. It is thus the citadel of the poor and of the scientists. For this reason, it can never be justifiable to regret being a Muslim.

The difference between Islam and other religions including Christianity lies in the following fact:

Islam is founded upon pure monotheism, denying any intermediary or intermediate causal creative or formative effect in the universe. Whereas, Christianity admits, on account of ascribing to God a son or begetting, influences of this sort, it allows saints and elders certain partnership in the manifestation of God's sovereignty over the creation, and this aspect of their way is included in the meaning of the verse:

> *They have taken as lords beside God their rabbis and their monks and the Messiah son of Mary, when they were commanded to serve but One God. There is no god but He, be He glorified from their associating partners with Him.*[13]

Because the Christians who rise to the highest of worldly posts can remain Christians, they even become, like Wilson, the late American president, bigoted Christians and still preserve their egotism. But Muslims who hold high office should renounce egotism and pride in order to be good Muslims, since Islam is based on pure monotheism. For this reason, those who are not able to preserve their piety either become indifferent to religion or even lose their faith.

The sixth matter

To those who go to extremes in negative nationalism and separatism, I say:

First, the surface of the earth, primarily including our country, has been the stage for many changes and emigrations, and once the centre of the Islamic administration was formed in this

---

13. *al-Tawba*, 9.31.

country, many of the other peoples, like moths to a light, flocked to it to settle. Since those people have intermingled, it is impossible to determine their national origins except by reading the Supreme Guarded Tablet. That being so, it is meaningless and harmful to build a society and our attitudes on nationalism. That is also why one of the leaders of those who support racial separation, indeed one who avowed great indifference to religion, had to acknowledge: 'If a people are of the same religion and speak the same language, they constitute a nation.' In order to determine national identity, the factors to take into consideration are language, religion and a (geographical) land. The existence of all these three elements together at the same time means the strength of the national structure; however, the lack of any one factor does not exclude the possibility of a strong national identity and sentiment.

Second, of hundreds of benefits which the sacred Islamic nationality has given to the social life of the children of this country, I will cite only two examples:

The first: The factor which has enabled this Muslim state to survive, despite its population of only twenty or thirty millions, to maintain its vitality and existence, in the face of all the great powers of Europe is the conviction:

'If I die, I will die a martyr; if I survive, I will survive as a holy warrior of Islam'. This conviction comes from the light of the Qur'an and is enjoyed by the army of this state. Equipped with this conviction, that army has welcomed death with a perfect enthusiasm and terrified Europe for centuries. What else on earth could inculcate such a sublime quality of self-sacrifice in the minds of the soldiers, make them single-minded and pure-hearted? What kind of nationalistic zeal can be substituted for it and cause a soldier to sacrifice his life and all he has for its sake?

The second: Whenever the dragons – the great powers – of

Europe have afflicted this Muslim state with a misfortune, it has deeply affected and shaken the whole Muslim world. And the imperialist powers who governed Muslim lands usually felt, for fear of the Muslim revolts in those lands, compelled to restrain their urge to attack this state. What other force can be pointed to as a substitute for that continual spiritual support (Muslim brotherhood) which it is impossible to regard as trivial? So, those who offer that mighty spiritual support should not be offended by projecting a negative nationalism and patriotism which cause us to be indifferent to other Muslims.

The seventh matter

To those who offer patriotism as an argument for negative nationalism, I would like to say: If you feel a sincere love and affection for this nation, your national and patriotic zeal should be of a kind to embrace the great majority of the people. Otherwise, if it only serves to enhance, briefly, the social life of a small minority who live carelessly of Divine commandments, bringing unpitying disadvantage to the majority, it is neither nationalism nor patriotism – and those who follow this way do not deserve our compassion. Any patriotic zeal coming from negative nationalism may benefit at most two out of eight citizens. While these two may benefit from that kind of patriotic zeal, which, in fact, they do not deserve, the other six are neglected: the old, the ill, the afflicted, the weak, the children, and pious individuals seeking light, consolation and well-being, not in this world, but in the intermediate and other worlds for which they labour, and these individuals need the help of people blessed with public-spiritedness and compassion. What sort of patriotism is it that allows the light of such individuals to be put out, their consolation to be removed? Where is the fellow-feeling for the whole nation? Where is self-sacrifice for the sake of the nation?

It is not permitted, nor is it proper, to despair of God's Mercy. I hope that God Almighty will not ruin, because of some temporary setbacks, the mighty community of the citizens of this country and their magnificent army which He appointed as the bearer of the 'flag' of the Qur'an and employed in its service for a thousand years. He will again enable them to disseminate the light of the Qur'an everywhere, and thereby continue to perform their essential duty.

***

THE THIRD TOPIC

(Note: Like the topics of the *Twenty-sixth Letter*, the subject-matters of this third topic are also not related to one another. Since they were written as answers to the questions of a disciple, any relevance should not be sought between them.)

The first matter

Second: You ask about the number of the worlds which the interpreters mention as eighteen thousand in the interpretation of the phrase, *the Lord of the Worlds* in the *Surah al-Fatiha*, the Opening Chapter of the Qur'an.

Brother, I do not know what they mean by 'eighteen thousand'. What I can say on this question for the time being is as follows:

The expressions of the Wise Qur'an should not be restricted to one meaning only. Rather, each has a universal content addressing each learning level of mankind at all times. So, any interpretation put forward during history points to only one aspect of that universal content. Every interpreter or every gnostic, depending on either his spiritual discovery or intuition, or the evidence he obtains, or his natural disposition, prefers one of those aspects. A group of interpreters have, through their insight or research, judged the number of the worlds to be eighteen thousand. For example, in the Qur'anic expression, *He let forth the two seas that meet together, between them a barrier they do not overpass*[14], which are emphatically repeated by saintly people in their daily recitations, there is an indication to all of the pairs of 'seas' or realms, spiritual or material, figurative or actual, from the realms of Lordship and servanthood to the spheres of necessity and contingency, from this world to the Hereafter, including the visible corporeal world and the World of the Un-

---

14. *al-Rahman*, 55. 19-20.

seen, the Pacific and Atlantic Oceans, the Mediterranean and Red Sea, and the Suez Canal, salt water and sweet water in the seas and under the earth, and the big rivers such as the Euphrates and Tigris carrying sweet water and salty seas to which they flow. All of these, together with many others I do not deem necessary to mention here, are included in the content of the aforementioned Qur'anic expression, whether in the literal or figurative sense.

Likewise, the expression, *Praise be to God, the Lord of the Worlds,* has numerous aspects. Because of this, men of truth and discernment, each depending on his own insight and spiritual discovery, explain it differently.

Such is my understanding of this expression that there are thousands of worlds in the sky; some of the stars, for example, each may be a particular kind of those worlds. Also, on the earth, each species of creatures constitutes a world; and each human being is a little world. The expression of *the Lord of the Worlds* means that every world is directly trained and administered by God's Lordship.

Third: God's Messenger, upon him be peace and blessings, declared:

When God wills a people well, He makes them watchful of their defects.[15]

Also, the Wise Qur'an narrates the Prophet Joseph to have said:

I claim not that my soul is always innocent; surely the soul of man incites to evil.[16]

One who is self-conceited and self-confident is unfortunate, while the one who sees his defects is fortunate. That being so, you are among the fortunate. But it sometimes happens that, though the evil-commanding soul is refined and transformed into 'self-accusing soul' or even 'the soul at rest', it moves its

---

15. al-Ajluni, *Kashf al-Khafa'*, 1.81.
16. *Yusuf*, 12.53.

line of attack to the nerves so that man cannot be free of anger and irritation until his death. There have lived many pure and saintly people who, though their souls were at rest, complained of the temptations of their selfhood and wailed over spiritual ailments, although their hearts were quite illuminated and pure. What they actually complained of is not having an evil-commanding self, but the transferral of those evil commands to the nerves: the spiritual ailments which they bewailed were only imaginary.

I hope, my dear brother, that it is not your evil-commanding self or spiritual diseases which afflict you, but that you are suffering, rather, from nerves, so that you may go on struggling in order to go on making spiritual progress.

The second matter

The detailed answers to the three questions asked by that old prayer leader are found in some treatises of the *Risale-i Nur Collection*. However, I will give here a brief summary of them.

His first question

In his letter to Fakhr al-Din al-Razi, Muhy al-Din ibn al-'Arabi says:

Knowledge of God is different from knowledge of His existence.

What does this mean?

First: The parable designed in the Introduction to the *Twenty-second Word* in order to show the difference between an apparent belief and real belief in the unity of God is enough to understand the meaning of that saying. You can also refer to the First and Second Stations, and Aims of the *Thirty-second Word*.

Second: Since the explanations of the scholars of methodology and theology concerning the principles of the Islamic creed and Existence and Unity of the Necessarily-Existent Being are not sufficient in the view of Muhy al-Din ibn al-'Arabi to establish the essential reality, he wrote that to Fakhr al-Din al-Razi.

Indeed, the knowledge of God acquired through theology is not perfect and thereby does not give satisfaction. If the necessary information is given in the way followed in the Qur'an of Miraculous Exposition, then it will suffice to give both perfect knowledge and complete satisfaction. I hope that each treatise of the *Risale-i Nur Collection* functions as a lamp on the illuminating highway of the Qur'an of Miraculous Exposition.

Also, in the same way that (in the view of Muhy al-Din ibn al-'Arabi) the knowledge of God which Fakhr al-Din al-Razi gained through theology is imperfect, the knowledge gained through the way of Sufism is so too, when compared with the knowledge acquired directly from the Wise Qur'an through direct inheritance to Prophethood. For in the way of Muhy al-Din ibn al-'Arabi, some belonging to his school have gone so far, in order to gain a permanent satisfaction, as to deny the existence of the universe in their assertion that *there is no existent but He.* While some others have, again so as to gain a permanent satisfaction, followed a strange way and completely ignored the creation in their proposition that *there is no witnessed but He.* As for the knowledge acquired from the Wise Qur'an, besides giving a perfect and permanent satisfaction, it neither condemns the universe to non-existence nor ignores it with total indifference. Rather, it elevates the universe from being chaos to the rank of cosmos, and employs it in the name of God Almighty. Thus, each thing becomes a mirror to the knowledge of God, as Sa'di al-Shirazi says:

> In the view of the discerning people, each sheet of the book of the universe opens a window on the knowledge of God Almighty.

In some parts of *The Words*, I have explained the difference between the way, obtained from the Qur'an, and the way of theologists, by means of the following comparison:

There are two ways to supply water for a town: one constructing canals or drainage by digging through hills to carry water from a great distance; the other obtaining water by digging wells everywhere. While the first way is very difficult and laborious, the other is easy for those capable of doing that. It is just as in this comparison that, by interrupting the chain of 'cause and effect' at some point in the past – on the premise that a never-ending chain of 'cause and effect' is inconceivable because it demands at the very beginning a Creator of that chain of causes – theologists go a long distance in order to demonstrate the existence of the Necessarily-Existent Being. But there is an 'inexhaustible source of water' everywhere along the highway of the Qur'an. Each Qur'anic verse can, like the staff of Moses, make 'the water of life' gush out wherever it strikes, and demonstrates the truth, *In each thing there is a sign showing that He is One.*

Besides, belief is acquired not only through learning; it should also be imbibed and appropriated by many other faculties of man. As food is distributed, after digestion in the stomach, among all the members of the body in different ways and doses, so also are the matters of belief, after being received by intellect through learning, assimilated by the spiritual faculties such as the spirit, heart, soul and other innermost senses according to the need and capacity of each. If any of them does not receive its share, belief cannot be perfected. It is this point which Muhy al-Din ibn al-'Arabi brings to the attention of Fakhr al-Din al-Razi.

The third matter

How can we reconcile the Qur'anic expressions, *Surely We have honoured the children of Adam*[17] and *he (man) is very unjust and ignorant?* [18]

Answer

It was explained in the *Eleventh* and *Twenty-third Words* and the

---

17. *al-Isra'*, 17.70.
18. *al-Ahzab*, 33.72.

'Second Fruit' of the 'Fifth Branch' of the *Twenty-fourth Word*. The following is only a brief summary:

God Almighty makes many things from a single substance to cause that substance to serve many purposes, and inscribes on a 'page' the content of a thousand 'books'. Likewise, He has created man, as a single, comprehensive species in place of many; that is, He has willed to make each single man perform the duties and functions that could be done by all the species of the animal kingdom, and therefore He has not put a natural restriction on his feelings and faculties. Although the senses and faculties of all animals have naturally been restricted, every faculty of man functions in an infinite space. Since man is a mirror reflecting the endless manifestations of the Creator's Names, his faculties have been endowed with infinite potentials. For example, if man were to be given the whole world, he would, because of his greed, ask:

'Is there any more?'

Also, because of his selfishness, he would agree to thousands of people's suffering harm for the sake of his interest. And so on. As he makes so much 'progress' in evil conduct as to be a Nimrod or Pharaoh, and becomes a most unjust individual, so also does he realize so great an evolution in good conduct as to attain the rank of the truthful ones or the Prophets.

In addition, man, unlike animals, is ignorant of the necessities of life, and therefore obliged to learn everything. Since he is in need of an unending number of things, any of which he does not know of when he is born, he is most ignorant. Whereas, an animal needs only a few things when it is born, and it acquires their knowledge in a few months or in a few days, or sometimes in a few hours. It is adapted to the conditions of life in so short a time that you would think that it was born after it had been perfected in another world. But man, by contrast, learns how to walk in one or two years and can distinguish between benefit and harm in fifteen years. The verse mentioned above alludes, by mentioning man's ignorance, to this fact.

The fourth matter

You ask about the meaning of, *Refresh your faith with 'there is no deity but God'.*[19] Its meaning has been explained in many sections of *The Words.* One from many aspects of its meaning is this:

Man needs to renew, to refresh, his faith because both he and his personal world are being continually renewed. An individual acquires or is transformed into a different individuality every year or every month, or even every day or every hour. Being subject to the passage of time, he puts on, like a model, the form of individuality every day.

As man himself undergoes such changes and renewals, so too, the transient world he inhabits passes and is replaced by a new one: every day a new world opens its doors to man.

Faith is the light of the life of each and every individuality which a man acquires during his lifetime, and it is also the light of each of the worlds that he inhabits. As for the formula, *There is no deity but God,* it is the key with which to obtain that light.

Also, man is constantly under the influence of his carnal self, his fancies and desires which, together with Satan, resort, enabled by the man's own heedlessness, to many devices to injure his faith and cut off its light through evil doubts and suggestions. Furthermore, since it is contrary to Shari'a (and, according to some leading scholars, indicative of unbelief) to leave go of certain words and actions, it is wise for a believer to refresh his faith again and again, every day, even every hour.

Question

Theologists, in order to prove the Oneness of God, constrain the

---

19. Hakim, *al-Mustadrak,* 4.256; Ibn Hanbal, *Musnad,* 2.359.

universe between a contingency and a beginning: since it is the same for the universe that it is brought into existence or that it is not, its existence is described as not necessary; since it exists and has a beginning, there must be a Necessarily-Existent Being, Absolute and Eternal, Who willed to originate it. Some of the Sufis seek to obtain a perfect satisfaction in the belief of Divine Unity by ignoring the existence of the universe in their assertion, *There is no witnessed but He*. Another school of Sufis accord only a nominal or imaginary existence to the universe and seek perfect satisfaction through their proposition, *There is no existent but He*. By contrast, you assert, differently from those three ways, the existence of a main highway in the Qur'an and show it through the formulas, *There is no worshipped but He*, *There is no one wished for except He*. Could you, then, demonstrate a proof of Divine Unity contained by this highway or a short path leading to it?

Answer

All the *Words* and *Letters* point to that highway, but I will, upon your request, give a brief summary of a mighty, comprehensive proof of it.

Each thing in the universe demonstrates that it is its Creator Who has created all things. Each deed or effect in the world shows that it is its Author Who produces all deeds or effects. Likewise, each act of invention in the universe proves that all acts of invention are inventions belonging to its Inventor. Also, each Name manifesting in the creation points out that all the Names belong to the same Being to Whom it also belongs.

This means that each thing is directly a proof of Divine Unity and also a window opening to the Knowledge of God. Indeed, each deed or effect, especially if it is a living exsistent, is a miniature of the universe, a seed of the creation, and a fruit of the earth. If this is so, then it is necessarily the same Being Who has created both that miniature, that seed or that fruit and the universe itself. For the One Who has created the fruit cannot be other than the One Who has created the tree. That being the case, as each work demonstrates that its Author is the same Being Who produces all the other works, so too, each act shows that its Agent is also the Doer of all the other acts. For we see that each act of creation shows itself to be a tip indicative of the Law of Creativity which is so comprehensive as to encompass all the universe from minute particles to the sun. So, it is the same Being Who is the Agent of both that single act of creation and all the other acts of the same function dependent on that universal Law.

Certainly it must be the same Being Who both revives a single insect after its hibernation and creates all insects and other kinds of animals, and also quickens the earth for spring. Also, whoever whirls particles, also moves the whole creation in a continuous succession and has put in motion the sun together with its planets. For a law is like a string stretching out through the universe, and deeds and effects are arranged along the whole length of it.

So, also does each Name, manifesting in the universe prove, as each work or act does, that all the other Names also belong to its Owner. For the Names manifesting in the universe are, like concentric spheres, one within the other, interrelated and mutually supportive of each other, mutually perfecting and adorning each other's work. For example, when the Name, the All-Life-Giver manifests Itself in giving life to something, the Names, the All-Wise, the All-Munificent, the All-Compassionate and the All-Provider are also manifest at the same instant, respectively, to arrange the body of that living thing with wisdom, to embellish it with munificence, to prepare its needs with compassion, and to provide the sustenance necessary for its maintenance in ways unexpected by itself. That being the case, the One Who owns the Name the All-Life-Giving also owns the Name, the All-Wise, all-encompassing and radiating in the universe, and the Name, the All-Compassionate, one training the whole creation with compassion, and the Name, the All-Provider, nourishing all living creatures generously.

So, each Name, and each act and work is such a proof of Divine Oneness, a seal of Divine Unity that each demonstrates that all of the words – which we call creatures – written on the pages of the universe and the lines of ages, are the inscriptions of the Pen of its Author.

> O God, grant blessings to him who said, 'The best of what I and the preceding Prophets said is, "There is no deity but God" ',[20]and also to his family and Companions, and grant them peace.

The fifth matter

Second: You ask in your letter whether the confirmation that *There is no deity but God,* without the confession, *Muhammad is the Messenger of God,* is enough to prosper in the Hereafter.

This matter requires elaboration. However, I will restrict myself here to the following reflections:

The two propositions of the confession of faith are not separate from each other; they prove each other, and each requires belief in the other. Since Muhammad, upon him be peace and blessings, is the Last Prophet and thereby the heir to all the previous Prophets, certainly he is the one who leads all the ways reaching God. There can be no way of truth and salvation other than his broad highway. Those most prominent in knowledge of God and meticulous research, proclaim, as Sa'di al-Shirazi does,

> Sa'di, it is inconceivable that there might be a way of salvation other than the way of Mustafa,

and they have also declared:

> All the paths are closed except the path of Muhammad.

---

20. I. Malik, *al-Muwatta', Qur'an,* 32.

However, it sometimes happens that some people follow the highway of Muhammad without knowing it to be his way. And sometimes it happens that some people partly follow the way of Muhammad without knowing the Prophet. And then, there may be some people who are content, unconsciously, of the way of Muhammad, in the ecstatic bewilderment of *There is no deity but God*, in a state of absolute seclusion and trance. However, it is most important to distinguish *unacceptance* from *conscious denial*. The unacceptance of the Prophet by these people of ecstasy and seclusion comes not from their denial but their ignorance of him. What they have of knowledge of God consists in the confession, *There is no deity but God*. Such as those may be included in the people of salvation.

If those, on the other hand, who heave heard of the Prophet and been informed of his message, do not confirm him, cannot recognize Almighty God, and their pronouncement of *There is no deity but God* is not sufficient to express belief in Divine Unity, which brings salvation. For this is not excusable unacceptance coming from ignorance; rather it is rejection and denial. Any one who denies the Prophet Muhammad, upon him be peace and blessings, who is the pride of the creation and the honour of mankind on account of his miracles and accomplishments, can by no means receive any light or gain true recognition of God.

The sixth matter

An important question asked by some seekers of truth:

Each of Qur'anic expressions and formulas of praise and glorification of God illumines, in many respects, the spiritual faculties of man, and provides spiritual nourishment. If, however, their meaning is not known, then only the utterance of them does not suffice to give the same enlightenment. Will it then be more beneficial if each people recite them in their own language?

Answer

The Arabic wording (letters) of the Qur'an and the formulas of God's praise and glorification, especially those belonging to the Prophet himself, are like a living skin, not like a solid outer garment. A garment can be changed, but if a skin were to be changed, it would be harm to the body. The wording (letters) of the recitations in prescribed prayers and the call to prayer, functions to the effect of being a title or epithet to their meaning. Neither a title nor an epithet is not changed.

I should tell, by the way, of a point which I have personally experienced concerning the subject:

I used to recite the *surah al-Ikhlas* (the Chapter Sincerity) a thousand times hundred by hundred on the eve of the *'Id* (religious festivals. I noticed that some of my spiritual faculties received their 'nourishment' after a few times and became satisfied. Some of them like the faculty of contemplation took their share after some concentration on the meaning, and also became satiated. After a few recitations, some others like the heart took their share of satisfaction through some understanding of the conceptions giving spiritual pleasure. There remained only the faculties not yet bored of recitation without needing the meaning and even its subtleties any more. Heedlessness did not mar them, though it did mar the faculty of contemplation. The wording and the simple, literal meaning intended by it sufficed them for their enlightenment. Those faculties, which are fed up with further concentration on the meaning, only need remembrance and encouragement, not learning and understanding. So, the Arabic wording, which has the same function for the meaning as the skin has for the body, gives them constant enlightenment especially because it continuously attracts the attention of the person reciting to the fact that what he is reciting is the Word and Speech of God.

This experience of mine shows that it does considerable

harm to attempt to express in another language the truths contained in the *adhan* (the call to prayer), in God's praise and glorifications repeated after the prescribed prayers, and in the Qur'anic chapters like *al-Fatiha* and *al-Ikhlas*. For, once the Divine and Prophetic wording, that inexhaustible source of enlightenment, has gone, the most important of human faculties will no longer receive their share of satisfaction or enlightenment. Moreover, the rewards as many as at least ten per letter will be lost, and, besides, since everyone is not able to find uninterrupted peace during prayer, human wording in translated form may well, in heedlessness, darken the soul.

Imam A'zam Abu Hanifa said: 'The formula of Divine Unity – *There is no deity but God* – is a title or epithet to Divine Unity.' So are the words of God's praise and glorifications, especially those recited in the *adhan* and prescribed prayers are also a title and epithet, which should be taken into consideration with respect to their terminological meaning, not literal, and therefore are not religiously allowed to change. Their clear, pithy sense, which every believer should know, can easily be learned by even the most ordinary individual.

How can it be excusable for those Muslims who, despite spending a lifetime in a Muslim community, fill their minds with useless things, that they should fail to learn the clear, pithy sense of those blessed words that are the key to eternal life? How could they be called true Muslims and considered to be sensible? It is in no way reasonable to shatter the 'case' of those sources of light for the sake of the laziness of such people!..

Also, a believer, no matter which people he belongs to, understands that he is glorifying God when he utters '*Subhan-Allah* (Glory be to God!). Is this not enough for enlightenment? If he considers its meaning in the terms of his own language, a single occasion of study will suffice. However, he repeats it every day as many as a hundred times and, besides the intellect's share of understanding, this blessed phrase is the means, through its wording and brief content, of many lights and effusions of enlightenment.

In short: Nothing can replace or be substituted for, or function as, the blessed Divine wording, which is the 'case' of the religious obligations or fundamentals. Although a translation may seem at first sight to be adequate, it really is not permanently and sublimely, and with the appropriate holiness.

As for the wording which is the 'case' of secondary religious principles, there is no need to change it, for people are instructed in those principles through advice, preaching and other methods of teaching in whatever language they speak.

In conclusion: The Arabic language, which is a grammatically and syntactically strict language, is so comprehensive and the Qur'anic expressions are so miraculous and unique that it is impossible, even inconceivable, to replace them in another language. The existing translations are rather interpretations, rather simple and quite imperfect. How far are such interpretations from the true meaning of a verse which has numerous connotations, resonances, and layers upon layers of meaning!

The seventh matter

(This is a special, important discussion concerning sainthood.)

The *Ahl al-Sunnah wa'l-Jama'ah* (those who follow the way of the Prophet and the Companions), who are the people of true guidance and truth, and constitute the greater portion of the world's Muslims, have preserved and maintained the truths of the Qur'an and faith in strict obedience to the blessed way *(Sunnah* of the Prophet, upon him be peace and blessings. Although the great majority of saints have always emerged among these Muslims, a very few of them have sometimes felt the need to follow a way at odds with some principles of the *Ahl al-Sunnah wa'l-Jama'ah.* Those who look at this second group of saints have, however, differed in their judgement. One group have denied their sainthood on account of their way being opposed to that of the *Ahl al-Sunnah,* and even gone so far as to accuse them of heresy. Another group have blindly followed them and, since they have accepted their sainthood, claimed that the way of the *Ahl al-Sunnah wa'l-Jama'ah* is not the only way true. Thus they have formed a heterodox faction, and have even become people of misguidance, unaware of the fact that not every man of guidance can be a true guide. So, even though their leaders may be excused because they are people of excessive ecstasy, they themselves cannot be excused for their unorthodoxy.

A more reasonable group, however, have neither rejected their sainthood nor accepted their way. They have judged that the untrue utterances of such saints should be taken either like sayings of an ecstatic or as errors resulting from spiritual intoxication.

The first group, particularly such scholars as judge by outward words and acts, have, in order to defend the way of *Ahl al-Sunnah,* unfortunately felt compelled to deny many significant saints and even accuse them of misguidance. The second group, consisting of their followers, have, because of their excessively good opinion of such spiritual masters forsaken the way of truth and become unorthodox, even misguided.

This matter once preoccupied my mind so much that I called God's curse at some significant time upon some of such heterodox saints. However, a powerful spiritual drive repelled my malediction and forced me to renounce it. Later, I came to understand that such saints carry their followers away along their misleading way by the help of a spiritual force, and certain believers do not regard it as too bad to follow a misleading master, because of the attraction of the spiritual force of the master When I felt that truth, I was startled and asked myself: 'Glory be to God! Can sainthood be achieved through ways other than the way of truth? In particular, is it possible for truth-seekers to support a grave trend of misguidance?' Then, on the eve of an 'Id (religious festival), through the blessings of the *Surah al-Ikhlas*, which I recite a thousand times, hundred by hundred, because it is an approved Islamic tradition to do so, the following truth occurred to me as a gift of Divine Mercy:

Some saints, like Jibali Baba, who is narrated to have lived during the reign of Sultan Mehmet the Conqueror, are in a state of spiritual intoxication although they seem to be conscious and reasonable; others are sometimes in a waking state but at other times lose their self-control and go into ecstasy. Some of this latter group cannot distinguish between what they experience during their waking state and in ecstasy. They tend to apply their ecstatic experiences in the waking state and fall into error without knowing that they are doing so. Some of these saints are protected by God against sins and misguidance, but others may be found among the people of deviation, and of heresy.

Since those saints are in a state of spiritual intoxication or ecstasy whether permanently or briefly, they are counted as 'blessed ecstatics', and are therefore not held liable for not carrying out the religious obligations, nor are they held responsible for what they have done. However, although they continue to preserve their ecstatic sainthood, they may support misguidance and unorthodoxy and, by promoting their way, they may, sadly, cause some believers and truth-seekers to adopt their way.

The eighth matter

(The following is to explain a principle regarding visitors, which some friends have reminded me of.)

It should be known that those who want to visit me come either for a worldly purpose – the door to such is closed – or for a matter concerning the next life. Some from this second group regard me as a blessed one of some spiritual rank and when they come, the door is also closed to them. For I neither like my-self nor those who like me. Thanks be to God, He has not caused me to like myself. Those, from that second group, who would like to visit me on account of my being the herald of the Qur'anic truths, will receive a warm welcome. They, however, fall into three groups: friends, brothers and disciples.

In order to be a *friend,* one should earnestly support *The Words* and our service in the way of the Qur'anic lights, and try to benefit from them. He should also oppose, by heart, wrong-doing, misguidance and heresy.

In order to be a *brother,* one should try, truly and seriously, to multiply and promulgate *The Words,* perform the five daily prayers and refrain from the seven major sins.

One should be a *disciple* by sponsoring *The Words* as if they were his own work and dedicate his life to their service and promulgation.

Those three groups are connected to three aspects of my personality. The friend relates himself to me through my personality as a common man. The brother relates to me on account of my being a worshipping servant of God. As for the disciple, he has a connection with me on account of my being a herald of the Wise Qur'an and a religious teacher.

Whether be a friend or a brother or a disciple, one may bene-fit from our meetings in the following three ways:

First: He finds, even if only once, the possibility of learning some of the diamond-like truths of the Qur'an.

Second: He gets some share in my spiritual earnings through worship.

Third: We turn to the Divine Court together with the same feelings and cooperate in the service of the Wise Qur'an to seek help and guidance from God.

I feel the disciple present near me every morning through remembrance of his name or imagination of his person, and he gets some share in my spiritual earnings.

I remember the brother at times either through his name or his person and include him in my prayer and earnings. He is also included in the whole body of the brothers when I mention them in my prayers as 'my brothers and sisters-in-religion', and introduce them into the Divine Mercy. Even if I do not know them each by name or in person, the Divine Mercy certainly knows and sees them.

The friend is also included in my prayer in the whole body of brothers, on condition that he performs the five daily prayers and refrains from the seven major sins.

Those three groups should also include me in their prayer and in their spiritual earnings.

O God, bestow blessings on him who said, 'The believers are like a firm building, one part of which supports the other', and on his family and Companions, and bestow on them peace.

Glory be to You! We have no knowledge save what You have taught us. Surely You are the All-Knowing, the All-Wise.

They say: 'Praise belongs to God, Who guided us unto this; had God not guided us, we had surely never been guided. Indeed, our Lord's Messengers came with the truth.'

O God, O One Who answered the prayer of Noah among his people! O One Who helped Abraham against his enemies! O One Who returned Joseph to Jacob! O One Who relieved Job of his affliction! O One Who answered the call of Zachariah! O One Who accepted the supplication of Jonah, the son of Matta! We entreat you, through the mysteries of those whose prayers were accepted, to protect me, and to protect the publishers and promulgators of these treatises, and their friends, from the evil of devilish persons and jinn; and help us against our enemies; do not leave us to ourselves; remove our griefs and afflictions, and provide remedy for our spiritual ailments! Amen! Amen!

The
Twenty-eighth
Letter

The meaning of dreams
Thanksgiving to God
Explanations on different issues

(This letter consists of six issues.)

THE FIRST ISSUE WHICH IS THE FIRST TREATISE

In the Name of God, the Merciful, the Compassionate
If you know how to interpret dreams...

Second*: You would like me to interpret your dream the meaning of which already became manifest three days after we met three years ago. Concerning that good, promising dream of yours, which has become a thing of the past, is it right, I wonder, for me to say as to follow?

I am neither of the night nor a worshipper of the night;
Rather I am a child of the day and therefore give tidings of the day.

Those fancies that are the traps of saints;
Are the reflections of the moon-faced ones of Divine gardens.

Such being the case, dear brother, and since I am accustomed to

---

* The first part of this Letter is not included in the published text. (Tr.)

discuss with you the truth and since it is not fit for the way of truth-seeking to discuss dreams which usually have to do with human fancies, I will, on this occasion, explain in six points certain truths alluded to in some Qur'anic verses about sleep, which is a 'brother' of death. In the seventh point, I will, however, interpret your dream.

The first point: Like the dream of the Prophet Yusuf (Joseph), which is the kernel of the Qur'anic chapter of Yusuf, several verses (such as, *We have appointed the night for you as a rest.*[1]) show that there are some important hidden truths in sleep and dreams.

The second point: The people of truth do not approve of using the Qur'an as an 'oracle' to consult and of relying on dreams. Since the Qur'an gives to unbelievers severe and frequent blows, it may cause despair when the verses that threaten unbelievers appear before one who opens the Book to receive counsel. Likewise, since dreams are often opposite to the reality, they may also cause despair or demoralization even if they are essentially good and promising. There are many dreams which, though bad and dreadful in appearance, prove to be good and pleasing in actual life. Since not everyone is able to find the true relationship between a dream and its actual meaning, people become uneasy and anxious. It is for this reason that in the beginning I said as the people of truth say and quoted Imam Rabbani: *I am neither of the night nor a worshipper of night.*

The third point: God's Messenger says in an authentic narration that true dreams are one out of the forty-six aspects of Prophethood. [That is, since God's Messenger had true dreams in the initial six months of his twenty-three years' Prophethood, true dreams are some kind of Divine inspirations.] This means that true dreams contain some truths and have some connection with the Prophetic mission. This is, however, a lengthy

---

1, *al-Naba'*, 78.9.

matter, profound and significant and related to Prophethood, so I will cut it short here, leaving its elaboration to some later occasion.

The fourth point: Dreams are of three kinds. Two are included in the category of (in the Qur'anic expression) *jumbled dreams.* Either the imagination gives form to the deviations of a bad temper or the mind remembers an exciting event which happened some time ago, and gives it a new different form, and the dreams a man has in such moods are 'jumbled ones', not deserving of interpretation.

The third kind of dreams are true dreams. When the senses of man connected with the outer, material world stop functioning in sleep, his inner spiritual faculty, innate in him, finds an opening to the World of the Unseen. That faculty has a look at the impending events through that opening and, happening to encounter one of the manifestations of the Guarded Tablet or the examples of the 'letters' of Destiny, sights some real events. However, since man's imaginative faculty gives some form out of its own to what the spiritual faculty has grasped from the record of Destiny, those incidents are reflected upon the tablet of mind in diverse kinds or forms. Because of this, such dreams require interpretation although their meanings are sometimes manifest in the forms they had in the dreams.

As reported in a Prophetic tradition, the meanings of the dreams which God's Messenger had in the initial days of his Prophethood were manifest just as they were, without needing any interpretation.

The fifth point: A true dream is the result of the elaboration of a presentiment. Presentiment is found in everybody to some extent; it is possessed even by animals. I have even discovered that man and animals have, in addition to their inner and outer ones, two other senses that may be called 'motivating and enticing senses or impulses'. Although the people of misguidance and corrupt thinking foolishly call those unperceived senses 'instincts', they should rather be regarded as 'inborn inspiration' through which Divine Destiny directs man and animals. It is through such direction of Destiny that, for example, when its eye is blind, a cat goes and finds the herb with which to heal its eye, and, by rubbing it against that herb, its eye is healed.

Likewise, such flesh-eating birds as vultures, which may be regarded as the sanitary officials of the surface of the earth because of being creationally charged with removing the corpses of wild animals, are informed of the existence of a carcass tens of miles away through that direction of Destiny or the inspiration of presentiment or through Divine orientation and are able to locate that carcass.

It is in the same way that some days-old bee can fly miles away and, without losing its way, return to its hive. It even happens frequently that a man unexpectedly appears before you at the moment you have mentioned him. This is because your spiritual faculty has felt, through presentiment, the coming of that man. Such occurrences are so common and often that it is said in Turkey as a proverb: 'When you mentioned a wolf, get hold of a staff to hit it with.' You are, in fact, unaware of the coming of the man or a wolf, nor could you have been informed of it by reason. Rather, it is because you felt it through presentiment that you mention it unintentionally. This presentiment develops so far in men of piety, especially in saintly people, that it becomes the source of wonders.

Since the common people are also endowed with some kind of sainthood, they grasp in true dreams some things of the future or the Unseen World. Just as sleep is like a rank of sainthood in respect of true dreams, so also it is a time or space of recreation in which magnificent Divine moving pictures are shown.

Now, a man of good conduct thinks of that which is better, and he who thinks of that which is better sights beautiful tablets. By contrast, a man of evil conduct thinks of that which is worse and thereby sights ugly tablets.

Sleep is, again on account of true dreams, also a window opening on the World of the Unseen in the corporeal world. Further, it is a field of release and freedom for mortal man confined in a restricted area, and also a theatre which has a kind of permanence and where time consists in the present only in which past and future are united. In addition, sleep is a period of repose for living beings crushed under the burdens of life. It is because of such aspects of sleep that the Wise Qur'an teaches us the truth of sleep in such verses as, *We have appointed sleep for you as a rest.*

The sixth and most important point: True dreams have long convinced me through direct experience and provided a decisive proof for me that Divine Destiny encompasses everything. Those dreams have, in fact, come to mean for me that what will happen to me tomorrow, down to the most insignificant event or business or conversation, has already been predetermined. I learn of them at night in dreams as if I read them with my eyes. It has happened not once or a hundred times, but perhaps a thousand times, that the people I have seen or the matters I have talked about in dreams, turn out the following day to be true with only a slight interpretation. This means that nothing is accidental or coincidental in the universe, nor it is random; rather, everything down to the most insignificant events, has already been destined and predetermined.

The seventh point: Your beautiful dream is really significant for us and the Qur'an. Time has interpreted it, and continues to do so; it is being manifested in an auspicious way, and if you discern it with some care, you will be able to understand it. However, I will explain a few aspects of it to show its truth. The events which are of the same kind as the reality of your dream demonstrate that truth.

The vast quarter which you saw in your dream is the Muslim world. The mosque at the far end of the quarter is Isparta. The muddy water is today's marsh of dissipation, laziness and religious innovations. That you reached the mosque in security without being dirtied by that water signifies that you obtained the lights of the Qur'an earlier than anybody else and thereby maintained your natural purity. The small congregation in the mosque is the conveyors of the *Words*, such as Haqqi, Hulusi, Sabri, Suleyman, Rusdu, Bekir, Mustafa, Ali, Zuhdu, Lutfi, Husrev and Rafet. The small pulpit in the mosque is a small village like Barla. The loud voice you heard signifies the power and influence of the *Words* and their fast dissemination. The place which was assigned for you in the first row is the seat left vacant for you by 'Abd al-Rahman. The desire of the congregation to transmit the *Words*, like through radio transmitters, to the whole world will, by God's will, come true in the future. Even if the members of that community are like seeds for the time being, they will, by God's help, grow into a tall, elaborate tree in the future. The boy with a turban is someone expected to be included among the disciples and disseminators to serve the Qur'an on the same level as Hulusi, or even ahead of him. I guess he will appear among certain ones I know but I cannot say certainly who he is. That boy will appear with the power of sainthood. You may interpret the other aspects of the dream on my behalf.

Since it is both approved and pleasant to converse with friends like you, I have dwelt on this matter a bit longer; perhaps I have wasted my speech. But since I began with the intention of pointing out a kind of interpretation of the Qur'anic verses related to sleep, I hope God will forgive me that waste of speech, or He will not regard it as a waste of speech.

THE SECOND ISSUE WHICH IS THE SECOND TREATISE

(This treatise has been written to remove the doubts as to the authenticity of the *hadith* which says that *the Prophet Moses slapped the Archangel Azrail, the angel of death, on the eye.*[2])

I was shown in a reliable book a *hadith* at the end of which there is the sign to represent the agreement of the two masters of Tradition, Bukhari and Muslim, on the authenticity of a tradition, and was asked whether it was an authentic tradition.

I gave the following answer:

We should rely upon the judgement of the person who inserted, in a reliable book such as this, that sign to show the agreement of the two masters on the authenticity of a tradition. So, that *hadith* is an authentic one. However, like some Qur'anic verses, some Prophetic traditions are also allegorical and have many levels of meaning, which can be perceived only by the elite among (distinguished) scholars. That tradition may, in respect to its literal meaning, be among those allegorical ones.

Later, I heard that a discussion had been held in Egridir about this tradition. Such discussions are harmful, especially at this time. If I had been informed of the discussion before, I would not have restricted myself to the answer above, rather I would have answered as follows:

First: Such discussions may be permissible on condition that they are carried on between qualified persons for the purpose of finding out the truth, and without causing any misconception. A discussion may be for the sake of truth if the disagreeing parties can admit the truth even if it is reached by their opponents. If that happens, the party in the wrong has learned what he was ignorant of or corrected his mistake. If he is right, then he has not learned anything new; rather, he may be boastful of himself.

2. Bukhari, *Anbiya'*, 31; Muslim, *Fada'il*, 157.

Second: If a discussion is about the *hadith*, the parties should know the degrees of traditions and implicit revelation and the categories of the Prophetic sayings. It is not permissible to discuss about the difficulties of *hadith* in the presence of common people, to defend, like an advocate, his own opinion in a way to display his virtues and to try to find evidence in his favour in preference for his egoism over the truth. Anyway, once that matter was made a subject of public discussion, and since that discussion is most likely to have left some ill-effect upon the minds of people so as to lead them to deny many authentic traditions which they cannot understand because of the allegorical traditions unununderstandable to them, or since the acceptance by ordinary people of such allegorical traditions in their literal meaning may cause the people of misguidance to reject them as 'superstitions', it is certainly necessary to explain the truth so as to remove the doubts about such traditions. This truth should be expounded in any case whether the tradition concerned is an authentic one or not.

Although it has already been elaborated in some other treatises such as the Third and Fourth Branches of the *Twenty-fourth Word* and the Introduction to the *Nineteenth Letter* concerning the categories of revelation, I will, nevertheless, discuss it here briefly, as follows:

Angels are not, like human beings, restricted to single forms; when an angel takes on form, it may represent the whole of its kind. The Archangel Azrail is the angel of death, and it is therefore a matter of debate among scholars whether the soul of every being is taken by Azrail himself or whether there are other angels subordinate to Azrail in the taking of souls. There are three opinions on this question. In mentioning these opinions, I shall try to explain also the meaning of the *hadith* which says, *The Prophet Moses, upon him be peace, slapped Azrail on the eye.*

First opinion: The Archangel Azrail, upon him be peace, takes the soul of every body. Since he was created from light, he can be present and take on form in numberless places at the same time and his engagement in a particular task does not prevent him from carrying out many other tasks at the same moment. The different forms of a being created from light possess the properties of that being and are therefore identical with the essence of that being. As the reflections of the sun in mirrors display the heat and light of the sun, so the ideal forms of spirit beings, like angels, in various mirrors of the World of Ideas are identical with their essences and possess their properties. Nevertheless, they take on forms according to the reflecting capacity of 'mirrors'. The Archangel Gabriel, for example, was present in thousands of other different places in different forms at the same time as he was prostrating before God's Greatest Throne of Honour with his magnificent wings stretching from east to west, and again at the same time as he was seen among the Companions of the Prophet, upon him be peace and blessings, in the form of Dihya, one of the Companions. He takes a different form according to the reflecting quality of the place and can be present in thousands of places at the same moment.

Thus, according to this opinion, it is neither inconceivable nor unreasonable for the Prophet Moses, who was quick-tempered and one of the five greatest Prophets, to have slapped on the eye a particular, human form of the Angel of Death when he appeared before him to take his soul.

Second opinion: The Archangels like Gabriel, Michael and Azrail, upon them be peace, each has subordinates of his kind resembling him, and supervised by him. Those subordinates differ according to the species of creatures. For example, the subordinate angel who takes the souls of the righteous is different from the one who is charged with taking the souls of the wicked.[3] The verses, *By those who pluck out violently; by those who*

---

3. When the angel of death who is in charge of taking the souls of saintly people came to a great saint renowned among us with the title of 'Sayda', he was witnessed by those beside his death bed to pray aloud: 'Let an angel from the group in charge

draw out gently,[4] indicate that the angels who take the souls are of different kinds. Thus, according to this opinion, it is quite reasonable that the Prophet Moses, upon him be peace, slapped, on account of his natural sharp-temper and might, and inborn courage and his being beloved by God Almighty, not the Archangel Azrail himself, but the ideal, energetic envelope of a subordinate of Azrail, upon him be peace.[5]

Third opinion: As explained in the Fourth Fundamental of the *Twenty-ninth Word* and indicated by some Prophetic traditions, there are some angels with forty thousand heads, each with forty thousand tongues – also with eighty thousand eyes – and forty thousand praises sung by each of the forty thousand tongues.

Thus, since some angels have been deputed to supervise the species of creatures in the visible, corporeal world, representing their praises and glorifications in the World of Spirits, they should be as described by the tradition mentioned above. For example, the earth is a creature and glorifies God. There are not forty thousand, but hundreds of thousands of species on the earth, each corresponding to a head in the Prophetic description. Each species have, in correspondence to tongues, hundreds of thousands of individual members. That being so, the angel that has been deputed to supervise the earth should have hundreds of thousands of heads, each with hundreds of thousands of tongues. So, according to this opinion, the Archangel Azrail, upon him be peace, has a face turned, and an eye directed, towards each individual member of the human species. In which case, the Prophet Moses, upon him be peace, slapped not – God forbid – the person of Azrail in his essential nature to re-

of taking the souls of the students of religious sciences take my soul because I like those students very much'.

4. *al-Na'zi'at,* 79.1-2.

5. A very brave man from our province is narrated to have seen the angel of death while in the throes of death, and said to him: 'You have siezed me in bed!' That man mounted his horse, took his sword in his hand and challenged the angel. He died on the horse in a brave manner.

ject and humiliate him, but only one eye of him that willed to put on end to his (Moses') mission because he desired to continue his duty of Messengership.

God knows the truth. No one, except God, knows the Unseen. Say: 'Knowledge is with God only'.

It is He Who has sent down upon you the Book, wherein are clear verses; they are the Mother of the Book, and others allegorical. Those with a swerving in their hearts pursue the allegorical, seeking dissension, and seeking its (distorted) interpretations. Yet no one knows its (true) interpretation except God. And those firmly grounded in knowledge say, 'We believe in it; it is all from our Lord'; yet none heeds, but men possessed of minds.

***

THE THIRD ISSUE WHICH IS THE THIRD TREATISE

(This is a private answer to a question asked by all my brothers, explicitly by the majority of them and tacitly by the rest.)

Question

You say to your visitors: 'Do not expect any miraculous help or spiritual support from me, and do not regard me as someone blessed. I do not have any spiritual rank. Like a private delivering the commandments issuing from the office of a marshal, I am communicating the commandments issuing from the office of a spiritual marshal, or like a penniless person advertising the jewellery of a very rich jeweller, I am advertising the jewellery of the sacred Qur'an.' You say so, but as our minds require knowledge, so our hearts and souls need enlightenment and spiritual satisfaction. We visit you in the hope that you can meet our needs. We need, rather than a religious scholar, a man of sainthood and perfections, one who will satisfy our spiritual needs. If you are not the man we are in quest of, then is our visiting you in vain?

Answer

Heed the following five points and then judge whether your visit is in vain or beneficial:

The first point: If an ordinary servant or a poor private of a king were to deliver to generals and commanders the royal gifts of the king or hand over to them their medals of honour in the name of the king himself, would it be a haughty foolishness that those generals and commanders should object, saying, 'Why shall we lower ourselves to receive those gifts and medals from the hands of an ordinary private'? Equally, if that private did not stand up, on other occasions, before those commanders in respect for them, it would be sheer stupidity on his part. Further, if one of those generals were to show so much kindness as to pay a visit of thanks to the poor barracks of that private, the king would certainly send a table from the royal kitchen to the respected visitor of his faithful servant so that the latter would not be embarrassed at having nothing except some dry bread to offer to his visitor.

In the same way, a faithful servant of the Wise Qur'an, however ordinary he is, communicates the commandments of the Qur'an to men of even the highest virtue without hesitation, in the name of the Qur'an, and offers the invaluable jewellery of the Qur'an to men of spiritual wealth, not in a lowly manner but with pride and with indifference to their ranks. However great the addressees or 'customers' are, they have no right to put on an air of superiority over that servant while he is doing his job. Equally, that servant cannot boast of himself because of their application to him, in transgression of the bounds of modesty and forgetting his place. If some aspirants to the sacred treasury of the Qur'an regard that poor servant as a man of sainthood, it certainly befits, and is a characteristic of, the compassion of the Qur'an that, in order not to leave its servant in embarrassment, it will give from the Divine treasury enlightenment to their hearts and satisfaction to their souls, without the knowledge and contribution of the servant.

The second point: Imam Rabbani Ahmed Faruqi, the greatest of those coming after the first thousandth year of *Hijra* to revive Islam, says: ' I would prefer to grasp a single matter of faith and make it known in plain terms, than attain thousands of spiritual pleasures and ecstasies, and work miracles.' The final station in all kinds of spiritual journeying is full perception of the truths of faith. If this is the judgement of a hero of spiritual quest, then the *Words* (which spring from a reading of the Qur'an) to explain the truths of faith in a most clear and convincing way can provide what is expected from sainthood.

The third point: Thirty years ago, I suffered fearful blows to my mind, and pondered the reality that death must one day come. Having found myself in a 'swamp', I sought help, looked for a way out and searched for a guide. I saw that there are various ways, and, hesitating over which one to follow, consulted the book *Futuh al- Ghayb* ('Discovering the Unseen'), by Ghaws Azam Shaykh 'Abd al-Qadir al-Jilani. This sentence appeared before me: *You are in the Dar al-Hikma (House of Wisdom); seek a (spiritual) doctor who will heal your heart.*

Curiously enough, I was indeed a member in the House of Wisdom. I was regarded as a 'doctor', as a spiritual guide, and expected to heal the spiritual diseases of Muslims; whereas, it was I who was spiritually ill more than others, and I had to treat myself as a patient ahead of others.

Following the advice of the Shaykh, I requested him to treat me, and began to read the book. However, the book seemed too strict and wounded my pride severely. It functioned as a major operation on my carnal self. I could not bear to read it to the end and put it back in the book-case half-way. After some while, the pains of operation were replaced by the pleasures of being healed. I read the book of that first teacher of mine to the end and derived great benefit from it. I also paid heed to his daily glorifications and supplications and received much enlightenment and spiritual satisfaction.

After that, I saw the book of *Maktubat* (The Letters) by Imam Rabbani, and consulted it with a pure intention. Curiously enough, there were two letters in it addressed to Mirza Badi' al-Zaman. 'Glory be to God', I said; as the name of my father was Mirza, and Badi' al-Zaman was one of my titles at that time, I concluded that both of those letters also addressed me.

Since that person, whom the Imam addressed, was, as it seemed, in the same state as I was, I found a cure in those letters written to him. As in those two letters, the Imam insistently ad-

176

vises also in many other letters of his, 'Unite the directions towards which you turn', that is, 'take only one master or one way to follow to truth'. However, this most important advice of his was not in accordance with my disposition and temper. I was not able, for some time, to make up my mind about which one to follow above others. Since each way has some attractions of its own, it was difficult for me to prefer one to follow. While I was in bewilderment, it occurred to me through God's Compassion that the head of all these ways, the source of all these channels, the 'sun' around which all these 'planets' turn, is the Wise Qur'an, and all the directions can be unified into it. The Qur'an is the greatest of guides and the most sacred of masters. I took hold of it firmly, but however imperfect and inadequate is my capacity to absorb the bounteous gift, the 'water of life', overflowing from that true guide, I hope I will be able to offer, by its guidance and enlightenment, that gift, that water of life, to men of purity and some spiritual state according to the receptivity of each. The *Words* and lights emanating from the Qur'an do not only consist in some scientific matters addressing minds but also in the matters of belief addressing hearts and souls, and involving spiritual states. They also provide knowledge of God at the highest degree.

The fourth point: Those of the greatest sainthood among the Companions, and the two generations following them, successively absorbed from the Qur'an the share for each of their faculties, and the Qur'an became a true and sufficient source of guidance for them. This shows that the Wise Qur'an expresses the truths at all times and radiates effusive light enough for those qualified to attain the greatest sainthood. Those who adhere sincerely to the outward practice of religion can penetrate to the truth of it in two ways:

One: by entering the 'intermediate world' of spiritual orders and rising through the higher ranks until the truth is reached;

Two: through Divine grace without entering the 'intermediate world' of spiritual orders. This is a most direct and exalted way peculiar, especially, to the Companions and those succeeding them. If this is so, then the lights radiating from the Qur'anic truths and the *Words* making them known can be said to have, and actually do have, enough in them to enable the talented to penetrate the truth in the way followed by the Companions and the succeeding generations.

The fifth point: I will point out through five examples that the *Words* also perform the duty of guidance as they teach the truths.

The first example: I have had the conviction through thousands of experiences that the *Words* and the 'lights' emanating from the Qur'an, besides nourishing my mind, inspire faith in my heart and give the pleasure of belief to my soul. What is more, as a disciple of a spiritual guide working wonders seeks help from his guide for his needs, so I frequently witness that my urgent needs are met through the miracle-working of the Wise Qur'an in an unexpected way. To cite two insignificant examples out of many:

One: I am a poor man living economically, to the extent that three loaves of bread and two pounds of rice sufficed me during the previous Ramadan. I spent the three months of last summer in the mountain of Barla, where I managed, although I sometimes had visitors, with two pounds of butter and some bread. Once I had a blessed guest, named Suleyman. He desired to accompany me to the top of the mountain on a Friday night. We sat at the top and I told him to make some tea. While he was busy with tea, I sat under a wild poplar tree looking down into a deep valley, and began to think sadly: We have only one piece of stale, old bread which will suffice us only tonight; how can we manage for the remaining two days and how shall I explain the situation to that pure-hearted man! Just at this juncture, I happened to look up at the tree. Lo, a large loaf of bread was looking down at us from the tree! I told Suleyman! 'Good tidings for us! God Almighty has sent us our food!' We took the bread, which had not been touched by birds or wild animals. No one had climbed there for the last twenty or thirty days. That bread sufficed us for two days, and just at the end of those two days Mustakim Suleyman, for four years my faithful companion, turned up unexpectedly with some bread.

Two: This is an insignificant but highly interesting incident which took place recently.

I had told a man something which might give him some suspicion about a matter. I also wished at the same time I had a book of mine which I had sent to Nis. I was sitting after the morning prayer when – Lo! that man entered with something in his hand. 'What is that?' I asked. He said: 'Someone from Nis gave me this book at your door'. 'Glory be to God!' I said, and thought: It cannot be coincidence that the man I desired to see has turned up with the book I wished to have. It is certainly through the help of the Wise Qur'an that that man has come with that book. Praise be to God! The One Who is aware of a hidden, most insignificant desire of my heart has pity on me and protects me. So, I take no account of the help which might come from worldly people.

The second example: My nephew 'Abd al-Rahman, whom God took into His Mercy, had an excessively high opinion of me, although he left me eight years ago to be engaged in worldly affairs. He expected me to give him, for his spiritual needs, extraordinary help beyond my capacity. However, the Wise Qur'an went to his aid. It caused the *Tenth Word,* which is about the Resurrection, to reach his hand three months before his death. That *Word* purified him of all his spiritual dirt, doubts and heedlessness, and, in addition, he displayed three wonders in his last letter as if he had attained the rank of sainthood.

The third example: I had a brother-in-religion from Burdur, named Hasan Effendi. He was a man of God. Because of his extremely good opinion of me, he used to expect me to give him spiritual help as extraordinary as a great saint can give. One day, I happened to give the *Thirty-second Word* to someone from a village in Burdur to read and, recalling Hasan Effendi, said to him: 'If you go to Burdur, give this to Hassan Effendi to study for five or six days.'

That man went directly to Hasan Effendi and gave the treatise to him. Hasan Effendi gave himself over to reading it with the excitement and eagerness of a thirsty man who has seen a spring of sweet water. He found so much pleasure and enlightenment in that treatise that, in particular, the section about love of God in its Third Station became a cure for his ailments. It was not forty days after he had read that treatise that he went to the mosque and, although he did not have any obvious illness, died there after the prayer (May God's mercy be upon him).

The fourth example: Hulusi Bey, as he himself admitted, has found much more enlightenment and radiance, and spiritual pleasure in the *Words,* which explain the mysteries of the Qur'an, than the Nakshbandi way, one of the most influential and widespread among the spiritual ways.

The fifth example: My brother 'Abd al-Majid suffered greatly from the death of my nephew 'Abd al-Rahman (may God's mercy be upon him) and from other grievous circumstances. Although he expected from me extraordinary spiritual help beyond capacity, I had no contact with him. One day I sent him, with no particular purpose, a few significant treatises from the *Words.* After reading them carefully, he wrote to me: 'Praise be to God that I have been relieved of my troubles. I was about to go crazy! Each of the treatises has become a guide for me. Although I parted with a guide, I have found several guides all at the same time and been relieved.' I found out that 'Abd al-Majid was really improved and attained a better state.

There are, besides those five, other examples which show that, when taken directly from the Wise Qur'an in case of need, the knowledge related to belief and spiritual remedies is enough for those needy of them if they apply themselves sincerely.

It therefore makes no difference who is the herald who announces them or who is the 'druggist' who offers them, whether ordinary or distinguished, rich or poor, or a man of some spiritual rank or someone of common people.

There is, indeed, no need, where there is the light of the sun, to seek illumination with the light of candles. If I show you the sun, then it is meaningless to ask me for the light of a candle, particularly when I do not possess it. You should, rather, come to my help through praying for me and with your spiritual power. I think I have a right to seek help from you. And you should be content with the enlightenment and spiritual satisfaction you get from the *Treatises of Light*.

Glory be to You, We have no knowledge save what You have taught us. Surely You are the All-Knowing, the All-Wise.

O God, bestow blessings upon our master Muhammad in a way that gains Your approval and gives him his due, and upon his family and Companions, and also bestow upon them peace.

***

THE FOURTH ISSUE WHICH IS THE FOURTH TREATISE

In His Name
There is nothing that does not glorify Him with praise.

(This is an answer to a question asked by some brothers of mine concerning a small incident of a warning nature.)

Question

We have heard that, on Friday night, they (the local police force) invaded your privacy in your mosque because someone visited you. Why did they do so? Why do they continually molest you?

Answer

I will explain in four points and, as I am forced to, in the language of Old Said, hoping that my brothers will take warning from it, and that you will have the answer to your question.

The first point: That incident was a violation done by hypocrites following a Satanic instigation on behalf of heretics. It was done in order to give us trouble, to dishearten the congregation, as well as to prevent me from having guests. Curiously enough, on the Thursday before that night, I went out, by way of recreation, for a walk and, on the way back, a long, black snake, looking as if it were two snakes joined together, came up from my left and crawled between me and my companion.

– Did you see it? I asked him.

– See what? he asked.

– That horrible snake.

– No, he said, I didn't see it.

– Glory be to God, I responded, and went on: How could it be that you did not see that long snake crawling by between us?

I did not give it much thought at the time. But later it occurred to me that that event was a warning for me. It was of the same kind as the snakes that I see in dreams at nights. That is, whenever an official comes to me with an evil intention, I see him in a dream in the form of a snake. Once I told the governor of the district: 'When you come with an evil intention, I see you in the form of a snake, so be careful!' I had frequently seen his predecessor in the same form. So, that snake I saw clearly was a warning that they would not restrict their mischief to intention only, but they would make an assault on us.

However insignificant they try to make it seem, that attack was a violation – both of the sanctity of the mosque and of the prayer, and of my natural right to meet people and have guests. Instigated by an unscrupulous teacher, that official gave the gendarmes the order to apprehend my visitors while we were reciting the glorification of God after the night prayer. He intended to arouse my anger and provoke me to return that unlawful, hostile action by sending the gendarmes back in indignation. That unfortunate official did not, however, know that Said carries in his tongue 'a diamond sword', manufactured by the Qur'an. Therefore he would not defend himself with 'a broken piece of wood'*. The gendarmes were sensible; they knew that no government in the world troubles people while in prayer in the mosque. They waited until the end of the recitation of the glorification. Angered by the delay of the gendarmes, the official sent the field watchman.

I give thanks to God that He does not oblige me to struggle with such snake-like people. So, this is my advice to you, my brothers:

Do not struggle with them unless you are definitely compelled to. Do not lower yourselves to speak to them, in compliance with the rule that the best response to a stupid individual is to hold one's tongue. Nevertheless, be prudent also: for, just

---

* i.e. in the wrong way, using the wrong means – anger and hostility. (Tr.)

as displaying helplessness before a wild animal encourages it to attack you, so also does weakness prompt beastly persons to assault those who exhibit weakness before them in the form of flattery. That being so, our friends should always be on the alert so that the supporters of heresy cannot exploit their possible indifference or heedlessness.

The second point: As declared in the verse, *Do not incline to those who do wrong, lest the Fire touch you,*[6] God severely threatens not only those who bend themselves to or support wrongdoing, but also those who show the least inclination to it. For, as approval of unbelief if also unbelief, so approval of wrongdoing is itself wrongdoing.

A man of perfection interpreted one of many aspects of that verse as in the following couplet:

The helper of wrongdoers in the world is from among the people of meanness;

Only a dog takes pleasure in serving an unjust hunter.

Both the one who informed against the blessed guest while he was in prayer on a blessed night as though he were committing some crime, and the one who arranged the assault, definitely deserve to be the referents of that couplet.

The third point: You ask: 'You rely on the help of the Qur'an to reform and guide to the truth even the most stubborn of heretics through the enlightenment of the Qur'an's Wisdom, and we see that you actually do succeed in that. That being so, why do you not invite those aggressive people and guide them'?

Answer: It is one of the basic principles of the canon law of Islam that the one who wilfully condones the harm done to him does not deserve compassion.

---

6. *Hud,* 11.113.

I claim, relying on the strength of the Wise Qur'an, that I can silence, if I cannot convince, the most stubborn heretic in a few hours unless he is one of the meanest kind and one who takes pleasure, as a snake does, in spitting poison (that is, giving people harm). However, it is disrespect to the truth itself to tell it to those snake-like, unscrupulous, unjust people of so mean a disposition, who wilfully display such hypocrisy as to sell their religion deliberately for worldly gain, who exchange diamond-like truths for the befouled pieces of old glass, namely, material profit in this world. Or, it is like adorning the necks of cattle with necklaces of pearls. For, such people as those have heard the truths from the *Risale-i Nur* many times, but they try intentionally to refute them in favour of heresy. They take pleasure, like snakes, from spitting poison.

The fourth point: Their treatment of me for seven years is completely arbitrary and unlawful. The exiled, even the imprisoned, in some circumstances, are allowed, by law, to meet their relatives, and are not banned from social intercourse. Besides, there is absolute freedom of prayer and worship in every other country, except the Communist ones. The others who were, like me, sent to exile lived in cities together with their relatives or loved ones, and they were banned from neither social intercourse nor from communication nor travel. But none of these rights have so far been allowed to me. What is more, they have attacked my house and interfered with my prayer. Although it is a prophetic tradition, according to the Shafi'i school, to repeat the declaration of God's Unity after every prescribed prayer, they have tried to prevent me from doing this. Further, they have not permitted my fellow-citizens to meet with me even in the mosque. An illiterate man, called Shabab, who emigrated to Burdur, once came here with his mother-in-law for a change of air and visited me in the mosque on account of being my fellow-citizen. He was taken out to the presence of the official by three armed gendarmes. In order to veil that unlawful act of his, the official, on releasing him, said: 'Excuse me, I was just doing my job!'

Considering overall what they have done to me, such as the incident on Friday night, it will be readily understood how altogether arbitrary and unlawful their treatment of me is. They let snake-like people assault me, but I do not lower myself to struggle with them. I refer them to the All-Mighty to ward off their evil.

Those who provoked the incident which led to my exile are now in their homes, and the powerful chieftains are at the head of their clans; all have been allowed to return home. Although I have nothing to do with their world, they made an exception of me and of two others. However, I have recently heard that one of those two has been appointed *Mufti* [7] to a town and is free to travel everywhere except his home town, and he is permitted to go to Ankara. The other is living in Istanbul among his fellow-citizens, free to meet anybody as he wishes. Further, those two are not, like me, without relatives or support; they are, by God's grace, very influential and have many supporters. In contrast to those two, I have been forced to live in a village, surrounded by some of the most uncaring people. During those six years, they have not allowed me, except on two occasions, to go to any neighbouring villages, even for recreation; in addition, they have been crushing me under increasing despotism. But a government should have the same laws and not discriminate between people or places of residence. That being so, their treatment of me is wholly unlawful and arbitrary. The officials of this district use the power of the government to satisfy their own grudges.

However they treat me, I give thanks to the Most Compassionate of the Compassionate hundreds of thousands of times, and proclaim, in order to declare His blessings on me, that their

---

7. *Mufti*: The religious officer who, when asked, explains to people the decree of Islam on a legal or religious matter. (Tr.)

despotic and increasingly aggressive treatment of me serves us, the students of the *Risale-i Nur*, as pieces of wood to make flare up ever more brightly the fire of our zeal and our efforts to disseminate the lights of the Qur'an. Those lights, brightening more and more through increasing pressure each passing day and through the 'wind' of incessant efforts, have made not only this district of Barla, but also this province and even most of this country, a school where the Qur'an is studied with the help of the *Risale-i Nur*. They think that I am a prisoner in a village but, contrary to the will of those heretics, Barla has become a chair of the Qur'anic lessons, and many provinces, like Isparta, have each become a school.

All praise be to God that this is from my Lord's bounty.

***

THE FIFTH ISSUE WHICH IS THE FIFTH TREATISE

The treatise of thanksgiving

In the Name of God, the Merciful, the Compassionate
There is nothing that does not glorify Him with praise.

The Qur'an of Miraculous Expression urges in reiterated phrases like,

Will they not be thankful? We will reward the thankful. If you are thankful, I will give you more. Nay, but God do you serve, so be among the thankful.

that what the All-Merciful Creator asks most importantly of His servants is thanksgiving. In the Wise Criterion – the Qur'an – He insistently calls them to thanksgiving and, proclaiming that unthankfulness means the denial of bounties, reproaches them severely, in *Surah al-Rahman,* no less than thirty-one times, asking, *Then, which of your Lord's bounties do you deny?*

Like the Wise Qur'an, this universe, of which the Qur'an is a microcosm, also demonstrates that the most important result of creation is thanksgiving. For we can discern with a little attention that the universe has been arranged in a way to arouse thanksgiving. Everything in the universe calls for thanksgiving. It seems that the most important fruit of this 'tree' of creation is thanksgiving, and it is also thanksgiving which is the best 'product' of this factory of the universe. This is so, because the universe has been created in the form of a circle, the centre of which is life. The design of the whole creation is directed towards life; everything in it serves life and works for the provision of its necessities. This means that the Creator of the universe drew up life from the universe.

Then, we also see that God has created the worlds of living beings again in circular forms and put man in the centre. The purposes for the creation of living beings are concentrated toward him; the other beings have all been subjected to man's service. This means that the Majestic Creator has chosen man out of living beings and made him rule over them.

Again we witness that the human kingdom, as well as the world of animals, has also been designed in a circular form, in the centre of which there is providence. The Creator has inculcated in mankind and animals love for providence and urges them to work for it. He has made providence a treasury so vast and rich that it encompasses infinite kinds of bounties. In order that mankind and animals sould recognize the taste of only one of those kinds, He has equipped the tongue with the power of distinguishing as many tastes as there are edibles and drinks. That being so, providence is the most manifest, most comprehensive, most curious and most pleasing reality in the universe.

Then, as everything has been concentrated around providence and directed towards it, providence itself comes through thanksgiving, subsists on it and points to it. For the need and desire for providence are a natural kind of thanksgiving, and the pleasure and satisfaction coming from providence are an unconscious thanksgiving, both common to all animate beings. However, man changes the nature of those kinds of thanksgiving through misguidance and unbelief and drifts from thanksgiving to associating partners with God.

The beautiful forms of bounties, and the tastes and smells they have, are invitations to thanksgiving and, by arousing desire in living beings and directing them through desire to appreciation of, and respect for, providence, these forms, tastes and smells urge living beings to thanksgiving, animals through disposition, and human beings with the tongue and actions. And they make living beings experience the greatest pleasure and satisfaction through thanksgiving itself.

That is, by showing the most pleasurable and permanent grace and favour of the All-Merciful, All-Generous Owner of the treasuries of Compassion behind the temporary enjoyment of bounties, they make man experience a permanent pleasure of Paradise while here in the world. Nevertheless, while being, through thanksgiving, an invaluable and rich treasury, providence is reduced to almost nothing through unthankfulness.

As explained in the *Sixth Word*, if the sense of taste possessed by the tongue is used for the sake of God, that is, if used to distinguish the kinds of providence with the intention of performing the duty of thanksgiving, it becomes a thankful examiner and a highly esteemed supervisor of the numberless treasures of the infinite Mercy of God. If, by contrast, it is used for the carnal self without considering the thanks due to the Provider, then the sense of taste is reduced to being a watchman of the factory of the abdomen or the doorman of the workshop of the stomach. As that servant of providence is reduced, because of unthankfulness, to that rank, so too, the nature of providence itself, together with its other servants, like air, light and water, is likewise reduced to the lowest rank, and assumes a quality contrary and opposed to the Wisdom of the Creator of the universe.

Thanksgiving is recognized by contentment, thrift, consent and gratitude, while unthankfulness by greed, waste, ingratitude and consuming without distinguishing between the lawful and unlawful.

Indeed, greed, besides being unthankfulness, is both a cause of depravity and a means of humiliation. It might even be said that the ant, that blessed animal having a social life, is trodden under foot because of greed. For it tries to collect thousands of grains without contentment when a few might suffice it. The bee, on the other hand, flies over heads due to – so to speak – its contentment, and offers, by God's command, its honey to human beings.

The Divine Name, the All-Merciful, which is the greatest Name of the Sacred Divine Essence coming after God – His proper Name and the greatest of the Greatest Names – relates to providence. The first and most manifest meaning of the All-Merciful is the All-Provider. It is through thanksgiving that one can secure a connection with that Name.

There are many kinds of thanksgiving, the most comprehensive of which is the daily prescribed prayers.

Thanksgiving contains a sincere belief and a genuine declaration of God's Unity. For the one who has eaten an apple and then uttered, *All praise and thanks be to God*, proclaims through that thanksgiving that that apple is a direct souvenir of the hand of Power and a gift from the treasury of His Mercy, and thereby ascribes everything, whether particular of universal, to God's Hand of Power and sees in everything the manifestation of His Mercy. Thus, he declares, through thanksgiving, a true belief and a sincere acceptance of God's Unity.

I will point out only one aspect of the loss which a heedless man is certain to suffer because of unthankfulness.

When a man thanks God for something delicious he has eaten, that thing will produce, through thanksgiving, a light and become a fruit of Paradise. It gives, besides its material pleasure, a spiritual enjoyment still greater and permanent because it causes man to reflect on it as a favour of Divine Mercy.

Thus, any food given by God as a bounty, sends to the higher, incorporeal worlds its spiritual outcome from thankfulness, and itself is digested to nourish the body and then excreted to be re-transformed into elements in the soil. Without thanksgiving, the material pleasure given by that food ultimately results in grief because of its consequential disappearance, and the food itself becomes waste matter. Consumable bounties produce permanent pleasures and yield permanent fruits through thanksgiving, but without thanksgiving, they become the lowest form of the worst nature because, in the view of a heedless, unthankful man, they are no more than things to be eaten and then excreted.

Providence is something deserving love. While this love is

elevated, through thanksgiving, to the rank of a sublime, permanent love, love of God, the love of heedless and misguided people for providence is of animal kind and nature. Consider, then, how great a loss the people of misguidance and heedlessness are in!

Among the species of living creatures, man needs providence more than the others. God Almighty has created man as a mirror reflecting all of His Names, as a miracle of Power having the faculties with which to weigh and recognize the contents of the treasuries of His Mercy, and as a vicegerent on the earth endowed with the faculties to measure even the subtlest manifestations of all of His Names. For this reason, He has made him needy of all kinds of material and spiritual providence. Only through thanksgiving can man, a being of such comprehensive nature, attain the rank of being the 'best pattern' of creation, which is the highest of the ranks. Without thanksgiving, he commits a most dire crime and falls to the lowest of the low.

In short: There are four pillars of the way of being a worshipping and (thereby) beloved servant of God, as stated in the following:

In the way depending on awareness of one's impotence before God, four things are essential;

They are, O beloved one, acknowledgement of one's absolute impotence and poverty, and absolute thanksgiving and absolute zeal.

Thus, the most essential of these pillars is thanksgiving.

O God, make us, through Your Mercy, among those who are thankful, O the Most Compassionate of the Compassionate!

Glory be to You! We have no knowledge save what You have taught us. Surely You are the All-Knowing, the All-Wise.

O God, bestow blessings and peace on our master Muhammad, the lord of the thankful and the praising, and on all of his family and his Companions! Amen!

The last of their call is saying, All praise be to God.

THE SIXTH ISSUE WHICH IS THE SIXTH TREATISE

(This treatise consists of points in the form of answers to some questions.)

The first point

You ask in your first question containing five or six points:

How will the Place of Mustering be built, and how will people be gathered together there? Will they be naked? How will we be able to meet friends there and find God's noble Messenger to request his intercession? How will God's Messenger meet countless people personally? How will the people of Paradise and Hell be clothed? Who will show us the way?

Answer

The answers to those questions are found very clearly in the books of *Hadith*. So, I will only mention a few points relevant to our way:

First: It has already been explained in the *Tenth Letter* that the earth draws a huge circle through its annual movement and empties every year into the tablets of that circle the immaterial outcome of its yearly life – the immaterial consequences of what has happened on it throughout the year. On the Day of Judgement, the total outcome of the earth's whole life will take on the form peculiar to the Hereafter. As the earth will submit, on the Last Day, the minor hell in its centre, it will also empty its contents into the Place of Mustering, which will be built on the annual orbit of the earth.

Second: In *The Words,* including primarily the *Tenth and Twenty-ninth,* it has been decisively proved that the dead will be resurrected on the Day of Judgement and assembled in the Place of Mustering.

Third: How a single person – God's Messenger – will meet everyone has been proved in the *Sixteenth, Thirty-first and Thirty-second Words.* Just as a single sun can be present, by virtue of being a luminary, at the same moment in countless different places, so too, God's Messenger can, through the luminosity of his spirit, be present at the same time in thousands of different places and meet millions of people.

Fourth: God Almighty supplies in this life a natural covering for His living creatures except man. So, as a requirement of His being All-Wise, He will provide a natural covering in the Place of Mustering for people who will be naked of artificial clothes. Man wears artificial clothes in this world not only to shelter from cold and heat or to cover his private parts but also as a sign of his commanding position over other species of creation and disposal of them. If this was not so, he would be clothed quite simply. Without this wisdom, requiring man to be clothed somewhat elaborately, a man dressed in rags would be ridiculed among other conscious beings. However, since this wisdom will not be sought in the Place of Mustering, there will be no need for man to be dressed in artificial clothes.

Fifth: The guide for those who, like you, sheltered in the world under the light of the Qur'an, will be the Qur'an itself. Look at the opening verses of the Qur'an beginning with *Alif-Lam-Mim, Alif-Lam-Ra* and *Ha-Mim*, and see what an acceptable intercessor, what a true guide and what a sacred light, the Qur'an is.

Sixth: Concerning the clothes of the people of Paradise and Hell, what was told about the seventy-times-pleated garment of the *houris* in the *Twenty-eighth Word,* is also true for the people of Paradise and Hell.

A man of Paradise desires to get, at the same time, uninterrupted pleasure from every section of Paradise. Paradise has innumerable kinds of beauties with which he has continual intercourse. So, he clothes himself and the *houris* belonging to him in specimens of those beauties, thus each becoming a miniature paradise. In the same way as a man grows in his own garden a sample of each kind of flower in his country, or a shopkeeper lists the examples of the items in his shop, or a man makes a piece of furniture out of the specimens of the creatures with which he has a relation, a man of Paradise and his *houris* will be dressed by God's Mercy in a special garment showing the beauties of Paradise in a way to please each sense and feeling, and satisfy each faculty, of theirs, especially one who has been able to worship God in the world with all his senses and faculties and therefore deserves all the pleasures of Paradise. The *hadith, Houris wear seventy celestial garments one over the other but the marrow in their legs is still perceptible,*[8] shows that the garments to be worn by the people of Paradise will not be of the same kind; every one of them, from the most outer to the most inner, is of a different level to please senses and feelings in a different way with its different particular beauties. It is likewise in accordance with wisdom and justice that, since the people of Hell committed in the world sins with their eyes, ears, hearts, hands, intellects and so on, they will be dressed in garments of different kinds which will each cause them to suffer a special torment and be like a miniature hell for them.

The second point

You ask whether the ancestors of God's Messenger, upon him be peace and blessings, were devoted to a certain religion during the interregnum – the period when no Prophet came.

Answer

There are traditions that they acted according to what survived of the religion of the Prophet Abraham, upon him be peace, which continued in some particular persons under the veils of heedlessness and spiritual darkness. It is certain that the mem-

8. Bukhari, *Bad'u'l-Khalq*, 8; Tirmidhi, *Qiyama*, 60.

bers of an illustrious lineage beginning with the Prophet Abraham and resulting in God's Messenger, upon him be peace and blessings, cannot have been indifferent to the light of the true religion, or been overcome by the darkness of unbelief. Besides, those who lived in the interregnum will not be called to account for their faults in the secondary commandments of religion and, as stated in the verse, *We do not torment unless We send a Messenger*[9], be exempt from Hellfire. Further, according to Imam Shafi'i and Imam Ash'ari, they will be saved from the torment of Hell even if they were in unbelief, unaware of the pillars of faith, since God holds His servants responsible for His Commandments only after He has sent a Messenger and, what is more, responsibility is established after people become aware of belief and Divine Commandments. So, because the passage of time had covered the religions of the preceding Prophets, the people of the interregnum can not be held to account for not following those religions. However, those who carried out some commandments of those religions consciously or unconsciously will be rewarded, while the others who did not will not be tormented.

The third point

Did a Prophet appear among the ancestors of God's Messenger, upon him be peace and blessings?

Answer

It is not traditionally certain whether there appeared one after the Prophet Ishmael, upon him be peace. There were however, two Prophets named Khalid ibn Sinan and Hanzala, but not from the lineage of God's Messenger. Nevertheless, the couplet of Qa'b ibn Luayy, who was from that lineage,

> *The Prophet Muhammad will appear in the time of heedlessness,*
> *He will give tidings, in all of which he is truthful.*

---

9. al-İsra', 17.15.

seems to be miraculous and therefore belonging to a Prophet. Imam Rabbani, based on both evidence and spiritual discovery, said: 'Many Prophets appeared in India, but, since no one or only a few followed most of them, they either did not become famous or were not recognized as Prophets.'

Thus, from the viewpoint of that illustrious Imam, some Prophets resembling those of India, might have appeared among the lineage of God's Messenger, upon him be peace and blessings.

The fourth point

You ask: 'What is the most true and acceptable opinion concerning the belief of the parents of God's Messenger and of his grandfather, 'Abd al-Muttalib?'

Answer

I have had no books, except the Qur'an, with me for ten years, and I do not have enough spare time to make a thorough search in the books of *Hadith* to find the most acceptable opinion on matters like this one, relating to the details of the religion. What I can here say on this point is that the parents of God's Messenger, upon him be peace and blessings, are among the people of belief and Paradise. God Almighty will certainly not hurt the feelings of His most noble beloved of filial affection towards his parents.

If you ask why they were not allowed to live long enough to witness the Prophethood of God's Messenger to be able to believe in him, I will give this answer:

In order to please the filial feelings of His most noble beloved, God Almighty may have willed not to make his parents indebted to him. Since His Compassion required, in order to please both His noble beloved and his parents, that the parents of God's Messenger should not be reduced from parental rank to the position of being his children-in-religion, and that they should only be indebted to His Lordship, not to any created being, God Almighty did not make the grandfather and parents of God's Messenger among his community, but He granted to them the virtues, merits and happiness shared by the community. If, for example, a noble marshal's father, who has the rank of a captain, enters the presence of his son, that son will be under the influence of paradoxical feelings. So, the monarch does not include his father in the company of the marshal, who is his honourable aide-de-camp, because of his compassion for him.

The fifth point

You ask about the most accurate opinion about the belief of Abu Talib, the uncle of God's Messenger.

Answer

The Shi'ites are of the opinion that he believed, while the majority of the *Ahl al-Sunnah* hold the opposite. It occurs to me, however, that Abu Talib sincerely loved God's Messenger for his person, not on account of his Messengership. That sincere and solemn love and affection will certainly not go to nothing. Even if Abu Talib would go to Hell because he did not actually believe for such feelings as shame and tribal zeal, not for wilful denial and sheer obstinacy, God Almighty could create a particular paradise in Hell for him in reward for his good deeds, as he loved God's noble Messenger and protected and supported him. As He sometimes makes people live in mid-winter a weather of spring or even creates spring in some places, or He changes a dungeon into a palace for some by means of sleep, He may change a particular abode in Hell into a particular paradise.

Knowledge is with God. No one but God knows the Unseen.

Glory be to You! We have no knowledge save what You have taught us. Surely, You are the All-Knowing, the All-Wise.

The
Twenty-ninth
Letter

Some points to note concerning the Qur'an
The holy month of Ramadan
God is the Light of the heavens and the earth
The intrigues of human and Satanic devils
Six questions about the freedom of worship
The symbols of Islam cannot be changed
Nine clarifications about *tariqa*

(The *Twenty-ninth Letter* consists of six sections. This first section comprises nine points.)

> *In the name of God, the Merciful, the Compassionate*
> *There is nothing that does not glorify Him with praise.*

My dear, truthful brother and earnest friend in the service of the Qur'an,

In that last letter of yours, you request a response to an important matter, concerning which neither my time nor the conditions I am in, permit me to write.

Dear brother, praise God that the number of those copying out the *Treatises* has increased this year. I am editing them for a second time. I am engaged in the task from morning to evening. Although this causes me to delay many other important tasks of mine, I regard that duty as more important. However, since the heart is, rather than the intellect, apt in Shaban and Ramadan to receive Divine effulgence and the soul is active, I will try to write to you whenever something occurs to me from God's Mercy. For the time being, I will make some explanations about three points.[1]

The first point

There are two aspects of the claim that the mysteries of the Wise Qur'an are not known, and the interpreters have not perceived the truths of the Qur'an, and those who make this claim are two groups:

The first group comprises the people of truth and investigation. They say that the Qur'an is a boundless treasury and therefore people of each century, after acknowledging its principles and unchangeable commandments, receive their share from its complementary, implicit truths without interfering with the share of others.

It is true that the truths of the Wise Qur'an are being understood better with the passage of time and in more detail, and the dimensions of its meaning are being clarified. However, this does not mean at all throwing doubt on the literal, explicit truths of the Qur'an expounded by the righteous predecessors. To believe in them is obligatory. They are certain and incontrovertible, and the fundamentals of the Qur'an and Islam.

The Qur'an explicitly states by declaring its being in *clear Arabic* that its meaning is manifest. The Divine address concentrates on those manifest meanings, reinforcing them and elaborating them. Their rejection means – God forbid! – the contradiction of God Almighty and the understanding of the holy

---

1. Later enlarged to Nine Points.

Messenger. The explicit meanings which form the fundaments of the Qur'anic truths were derived from the source of Messengership, and they were transmitted to following centuries through established reliable channels. This is so undeniably established a fact that Ibn Jarir al-Tabari related the meaning of each verse of the Qur'an to the source of Messengership through reliable chains of transmission, and wrote, in this connection, a most comprehensive interpretation of the Qur'an.

The second group comprises either single-minded friends who make matters worse with the intention of doing something good, or devilish enemies who desire to oppose the commandments of Islam and the truths of belief. They want to make way through the fortified *surahs* of the Wise Qur'an, which are, in your words, each like a steel citadel around the Qur'anic truths. In order to throw – God forbid – doubt upon the truths of belief and the Qur'an, those people spread such false claims.

The second point

God Almighty swears by many things in the Qur'an. There are many mysteries, many subtle points in these oaths.

For example, the oath in By *the sun and his morning brightness,*[2] points to the truth expressed in the magnificent comparison in the *Eleventh Word,* and presents the universe as a palace or a city. We are reminded in the oath, Ya Sin. By *the Wise Qur'an,*[3] that the Qur'an has a miraculousness so sacred that it is worth swearing by.

The oaths, in By *the Star when it sets off downward ,*[4] and No! I *swear by the locations and fallings of the stars and that is indeed a mighty oath, if you but knew!*[5], point out that the fallings of the stars are a sign for the banning of the *jinn* and devils from hear-

---

2. *al-Shams,* 91.1.

3. *Ya Sin,* 36.1-2.

4. *al-Nacm,* 53.1.

5. *al-Wa'qi'a,* 56.75-76.

ing the tidings of the Unseen so that there should be no doubt about the authenticity of Revelation. These oaths are also to remind us of the greatness of the power and perfection of the wisdom in establishing the stars – such mighty heavenly objects – in their places in perfect order, and in turning the planets with an amazing speed.

In the oaths by the angels responsible for winds in the verses, *By the scattering and winnowing,*[6] and *By the emissaries sent,*[7] the attention is drawn to the significant instances of wisdom in the whirling winds and in air waves, and we are reminded that the elements thought to move randomly are, in fact, employed for important services and subtle purposes.

In short, there are numerous subtleties in the Qur'anic oaths. However, since I have no time to explain them one by one, I will only point out one of the fine points in the oath, *By the fig and the olive.*[8]

By reminding man of the greatness of His Power, the perfection of His Mercy and His important bounties, through swearing by the fig and the olive, God Almighty points out that the man who is heading toward the *lowest of the low* can realize, through thanksgiving, contemplation, faith and good deeds, spiritual evolution as high as to reach the *highest of the high.*

The reason for the particularization of the fig and the olive among bounties is that, besides being very useful, those two blessed fruits have in their creation many subtleties worthy of note. As everybody knows, the olive has a particular, important place in social and commercial life, as well as being rich in sustenance. As for the fig, besides demonstrating a wonderful miracle of Divine Power in that God encapsulates the members of a huge fig tree in its seeds which are as tiny as particles of sand, it displays many aspects of Divine Providence in its being food

6. *al-Dhariyat,* 51.1.
7. *al-Mursalat,* 77.1.
8. *al-Tin,* 95.1.

and useful for man, and more enduring than most of other kinds of fruits, and also in its other properties that should be studied by food engineering.

The third point

Al-huruf al-muqatta'at, the abbreviated letters at the beginning of several Qur'anic *surahs*, are a Divine cipher, through which God gives His particular servant some signs of the Unseen. The key to that cipher is in the hand of that particular servant and his heirs.

Since the wise Qur'an addresses every level of understanding in every age, it must have numerous aspects and folds of meaning comprehensive of the share of each level and age. The righteous predecessors have the primary share, which they disclosed. The people of sainthood and truth-seeking have found in those letters many indications to the treatment of the Unseen in the spiritual journey. I have explained those letters from the viewpoint of their miraculousness of eloquence at the beginning of *Surah al-Baqara* in *Isharat al-I'jaz (The Signs of Miraculousness)*, to which you may refer.

The fourth point

It was proved in the *Twenty-fifth Word* that a true and exact translation of the Qur'an is impossible. Its sublimity of style, which is an element in its miraculousness of meaning, cannot be imitated at all in translations. Far from imitating it, even explaining and making understood the truth and pleasure derived from that sublimity of style is impossibly difficult. However, I will cite a few points in order to show the way to its understanding:

In verses such as,

And of His signs is the creation of the heavens and earth and the variety of your tongues and colours. And the heavens shall be rolled up in His Right Hand. He creates you in your mothers' wombs creation after creation in threefold shadows. He created the heavens and the earth in six days. God comes in between the man and his own heart. Not an atom's weight or less than that or greater, escapes from Him in the heavens or in the earth. He makes the night to pass into the day, and makes the day to pass into the night, and He is the knower of all that is in the breasts.[9]

the Qur'an of Miraculous Exposition portrays the truth of God's creativity sublimely and with a miraculous conciseness. It shows that the Builder of that universe establishes the particles in their places – in the pupils of the eyes, for instance – with the same instrument and simultaneously as He fixes the sun and the moon in their locations. He makes and places exactly the eyes and removes their veils according to the same measure, and using the same immaterial instrument with which He arranges and unfolds the heavens. The Majestic Maker establishes the distinguishing marks of a man's face and his outer and inner senses in their places with the same immaterial hammer with which He fixes the stars in the sky. As is understood from the verses quoted, that Majestic Maker, in order to have the eyes see and the ears hear His acts while He is at work, strikes, through the verses of the Qur'an, a hammer on a particle, and then strikes it at the same time, through another word of the same verse, on the sun, and thus shows, with a sublime style, Oneness in Unity, the Infinite Majesty within the Infinite Grace, the boundless Might in utter secrecy, the limitless extent in complete subtlety, the infinite Grandeur within the infinite Compassion, and endless distance in exact nearness. He demonstrates the ultimate unity of the opposites to the farthest extent, which is, although regarded as impossible, absolutely necessary for the existence and life of the universe. It is before this

9. *al-Rum*, 30.22; *al-Zumar*, 39.67; *al-Zumar*, 39.6; *al-A'raf*, 7.54; *al-Saba'*, 34.3; *al-Anfal*, 8.24; *al-Hadid*, 57.6, respectively.

sublimity of the Qur'anic style that the greatest of literary men could not help but prostrate themselves in admiration.

Also, through the verse,

And of His signs is that the heaven and the earth stand firm by His Command; then, when He calls you once and suddenly, out of the earth, lo you shall come forth.[10]

the Qur'an demonstrates, again in sublime style, the majesty and grandeur of the Sovereignty of God's Lordship, as follows:

The heavens and the earth are like the barracks or training grounds of magnificent armies. The creatures, who lie behind the veils of non-existence and mortality, appear in the Place of Mustering with a perfect speed and in perfect obedience to a trumpet blown or the command of *Rise up for the Last Judgement!*

The verse quoted refers to the final destruction of the universe, together with the Resurrection, in a miraculously exalted style and points to a convicing proof, as in the following:

The seeds covered and having rotted away in the bosom of the earth, and the drops of water having evaporated and concealed in the atmosphere, re-appear every spring in the place of testing and trial with perfect order and speed, and show an example of the Resurrection. It is in just the same way that the dead will be resurrected following the final destruction of the universe.

You can compare the degree of eloquence in the other verses of the Qur'an to those quoted above and answer the question whether a true translation of the Qur'an is possible. What can be done as a first step is only to make either a brief or relatively long verse-by-verse interpretation.

The fifth point

For example: *al-hamdu li-llah* (All the praise be to God) is a

10. *al-Rum*, 30.25.

Qur'anic sentence, the most brief meaning of which, according to the rules of the sciences of syntax and semantics, is:

Every praise and thanks communicated by everyone to everyone from past eternity to future eternity is, in reality, for, and deserved by, the Necessarily-Existent Being, God.

The meaning 'every' derives from the *al* (the), and 'by everyone' from 'praise' itself, for the Arabic original of praise is *hamd*, which is in the infinitive form. When the subject is omitted before an infinitive, it expresses a general meaning. Again, since the omission of the object in a sentence spoken to the addressee, in his presence or absence, is also for generalization, the meaning 'to everyone' is derived from this short sentence. 'From past eternity to future eternity' comes from the rule that the transition from a verb clause to a noun clause is indicative of persistence and duration. 'For' and 'deserved by' are expressed in the preposition *li* – 'to' or 'for' God – which is used for particularization and to express deserving. And, since the Name *Allah* (God) is the Greatest Name of the Divine Being, including all the other Divine Names and Attributes, and since existence is essential and indispensable to the Divine Being, and a tableau to help in reflecting on the Majestic Being, *Allah* necessarily connotes the Necessarily-Existent Being.

If the explicit, briefest meaning of so short a sentence as *al-hamdu li-llah*, which is agreed upon by linguists of Arabic, is as explained above, how can it be translated into another language with the same strength and miraculousness?

Further, there is, other than Arabic, one language in the world syntactic like Arabic, but it cannot compete with Arabic in comprehensiveness. How can it then be possible that the sacred words of the Qur'an which appeared miraculously through Arabic, a syntactic and comprehensive language, in an All-Encompassing Knowledge penetrating everything at the same time, are substituted by the words chosen by those with partial and confused minds and adulterated souls in other languages, synthetic and inflectional? I can even claim and prove that each letter of the Qur'an is a treasure of truths, so rich that its explanation may cover at least a page.

The sixth point

In order to express this meaning better, I will describe what once occurred to me to enlighten me.

Once, I pondered over 'we' in *You alone do we worship and You alone do we ask for help*,[11] and tried to find out why 'we' was preferred instead of 'I'. The merits of congregational prayer suddenly dawned upon me through that 'we', and I noticed that every member of the congregation in which we prayed in the mosque was a kind of intercessor for me and a witness and supporter of the causes and truths that I openly declared in my recitation. I felt encouraged to offer my faulty prayer to the Divine Court in the company of the comprehensive prayer of the congregation.

This was followed by the removal of another veil, and I imagined all the mosques of Istanbul as one mosque, with the people praying in them becoming a huge, single congregation. I felt I was included in their supplications and confirmation.

Afterwards, I imagined myself to be in the circular lines of worshippers around the Ka'ba, and I said, *al-hamdü li-llahi Rabbi'l-alemin* (All praise be to God, the Lord of the Worlds), seeing that I had so many intercessors repeating and confirming every word I recited during the prayer. This thought led me to seeing the Ka'ba as the niche *(mihrab)* and, entrusting to the blessed Black Stone the words of the confession of faith, *I bear witness that there is no deity but God, and I bear witness that Muhammad is God's Messenger*, which I uttered together with the whole congregation, I noticed that the congregation I was in comprised three circles:

---

11. *al-Fatiha*, 1.5.

The first circle was the mightiest congregation formed by all the believers and monotheists on the earth.

The second circle was composed of all the creatures in a most comprehensive prayer and glorification of God, each species being engaged in supplications and litanies of praise particular to themselves. The services they render, called the functions or duties of things, are the form of their worship. Aware of this fact, I uttered, *Allahu akbar* (God is the greatest), and bowed my head in wonder.

The third circle of congregation was my body – a world amazing and seemingly slight and insignificant, but in reality, on account of the task it performs, very great and significant – each part of which, from the cells to the outer senses, is busy with the duty of worship and thanksgiving. In this circle, I felt the spiritual faculty in my heart reciting on behalf of that congregation, *You alone do we worship,* and *You alone do we ask for help,* as my tongue did on behalf of the two other congregations.

In sum: 'We' in *You alone do we worship* refers to those three congregations. Still in this state, I imagined that the spiritual personality of God's Messenger, the conveyor and transmitter of the Wise Qur'an, took on a form in all its grandeur in Madina al-Munawwara, which could be regarded as his pulpit in the world, and was reciting, *O mankind! Worship your Lord!* I imagined everyone, including myself, in those congregations responding to his command and reciting, *You alone do we worship!* Then, according to the rule, *When something is established, it is established with all that is needed for it to be established,* the following truth came to my mind:

Since the Lord of the Worlds addresses mankind and, through them, speaks to all creatures, and God's Messenger, upon him be peace and blessings, communicates that speech of honour to mankind, even to all beings having spirit and consciousness, all time, including the past and future, can be regarded as the present time, and therefore, the whole of mankind, in the form of a congregation composed of various lines, are listening to this address.

This truth, however imaginal it be, showed me each verse of the Qur'an having a radiance of miraculousness in its subtlety of style, eloquence and fluency coming both from the Eternal Speaker of Infinite Grandeur and Majesty through the illustrious transmitter who has the greatest rank of being beloved by God, and from the variety and multitude of its listeners. This made, not only the Qur'an itself in its entirety, or a chapter, or a verse, but every word of it, miraculous. I uttered, 'All praise be to God for the light of faith and the Qur'an', and, emerging from the imaginal world I had entered through the letter *nûn* (-n-) (prefixed to a verb in the present tense to mean 'we' as in *na'budu*, 'we worship'), understood that not only the verses and words of the Qur'an, but also some of its letters, like the *-n-* of *na'budu* are radiant keys to significant truths.

It was when the heart and imagination came out of the - *n* - of *na'budu* that the reason came across them, saying: 'I want my share. I have no wings with which to fly like you. I walk on the feet of evidence and argument. You should clearly show me the way to the Creator, the Worshipped One, Whose help is asked for, through *We worship* and *We ask for help*, so that I can accompany you.' In response, I told the heart to say to the bewildered reason:

Look at all of the creatures in the universe, whether animate or inanimate, how, by doing their duties in perfect order and obedience, they worship God! Some of them, despite being unconscious or dumb, unfeeling, perform duties in perfect order as if they were conscious and worshipping God. This means that there is One, Truly Worshipped and Absolutely Commanding, Who employs them in worship of Him.

Look again, and see that all the creatures, including especial-

ly the animate ones, have numerous, diverse needs and demands necessary for their existence and sustenance, even the
most insignificant of which they are unable to meet by themselves. Whereas, we witness that those many needs of theirs are
regularly met for them at just the proper time from an unexpected place.

Thus, that infinite poverty and neediness of creatures, and
the extraordinary help of the Unseen and the aid of Mercy
reaching them to satisfy their needs, all shows self-evidently
that they have a Protector and Provider, absolutely Rich, Generous and Powerful, to Whom all things, especially all living beings, turn for help. That is, through the language of asking for
help, they say: *You alone do we ask for help.*

The reason responded, saying: 'I have also believed and af-
firmed.'

The seventh point

Then I said, *Guide us to the Straight Path, the path of those whom
You have blessed,* and I saw that among the caravans of people
who have passed away into the past, the illustrious caravan of
the Prophets, the truthful ones, the martyrs, and the saints and
the pious ones are going to eternity along a straight highway,
removing the darkness from the future. This supplication
guides me to join that caravan. I suddenly uttered: *Glory be to
God!* One with slight consciousness should know what a great
loss and perdition it is not to join that illustrious caravan pro-
gressing in utmost security to illuminate the future. I wonder
where those who have turned away from that caravan by intro-
ducing pernicious innovations to the religion of Islam can find
light and what it is that they can follow to salvation.

God's Messenger, who is our guide, declared: *Every innovation is a deviation, and every deviation leads to Fire.*[12] Again, I wonder what kind of benefit those unfortunate ones, deserving the

---

12. Muslim, *Jum'a*, 43; Abu Dawud, *Sunnah*, 5.

title of evil scholars, hope to find in innovations in the face of that decisive declaration, and on what principle they base their pernicious opposition to the self-evident marks or symbols of Islam regarding them as changeable. They must be deluded by a transient, illusory light caused by an aspect of meaning. For comparison: if a fruit is peeled, it may show more clearly its delicacy, but all too briefly – before long it gets bruised and rots. It is in the same way that the Prophetic and Divine expressions and concepts in the symbols of Islam are like a living and protecting skin. When this skin is taken off, that is, when, for example, the original phrases of the *adhan* are recited in another language, the meaning may first seem brighter or more understandable. But, like a fruit peeled, the blessed meaning soon loses its freshness and spirit, leaving its 'carcass' in dark minds and souls; its light is extinguished, with its smoke left.

The eighth point

I should explain an important principle in this point, which is as follows.

As there are two spheres of law, normally the law of individual rights and the public law, which deals with the public rights, regarded, in one respect, as the rights of God, so too, some matters in the Islamic law – the Shari'a – are related to personal rights and duties, while some others to the public. The latter are called, in the language of the Shari'a, the public symbols or banners of Islam. Since the whole body of world Muslims is concerned with these symbols, any interference in them without the consent of all Muslims is a transgression of their rights. Even the minor ones of these symbols, like the commended duties, are of as great importance as a most major matter of Islam. Therefore, those who try to change or abolish these symbols, and those who assist them in this ominous undertaking, should reflect that these matters are the concern of the whole Muslim world, they are the radiant links which, from the Time of Happiness, have joined the Muslims to Islam and to each other; they should reflect that what they are undertaking is a most dreadful crime. If they have a bit of consciousness, they should tremble at the dire consequences to which they must eventually succumb!

The ninth point

Some matters of the Shari'a are related to worship, so that, being independent of human reasoning, they are performed because God has commanded them. The cause for their performance is that they are God's commands.

Other matters of the Shari'a are those whose meanings are comprehensible. That is, they are of the kind that some purpose or comprehensible benefit has been preferred in their legislation. Nevertheless, the real cause for their legislation is, again, the Divine ordinance.

The public symbols of Islam related to worship cannot be made dependent on any imagined or fancied benefits, however numerous such benefits may be supposed to be. It is not right or permissible to interfere in them. In addition, the wisdom in or Divine purposes for the legislation of the symbols, or the uses they bring are not restricted to their known benefits. For example, no one should claim that the purpose of the *adhan* is to call Muslims to prayer – firing a gun would suffice for that purpose. Rather, it should be known that calling Muslims to prayer is only one of the numerous benefits of the *adhan*. Firing a gun might suffice for calling to prayer, but how could it substitute for the *adhan*, which is also a means, on behalf of the people of the town or district where it is recited, of declaring God's Unity, which is the greatest purpose and result of the creation of mankind and the universe, and a means of also expressing servitude and worship for Divine Lordship?

In short: Hell is not for nothing; many things are being done about which one feels compelled to shout, 'Long live Hell!'. And Paradise does not come cheap; it requires the payment of a very high price.

Not equal are the inhabitants of the Fire and the inhabitants of Paradise. The inhabitants of Paradise – they are the triumphant.[13]

***

---

13. *al-Hashr*, 59.20.

THE SECOND SECTION
COMPRISING THE SECOND TREATISE

The holy month of Ramadan

(Having said something about the public symbols of Islam at the end of the first section, I will mention in this section some Divine purposes for ordering the fasting during Ramadan, which is the brightest and most splendid of those symbols.

This second section consists of nine points to explain nine of those purposes.)

In the Name of God, the Merciful, the Compassionate

The month of Ramadan in which the Qur'an was revealed, a guidance for mankind, clear signs of guidance and the criterion.[14]

The first point

Fasting in the holy month of Ramadan is one of the foremost of the five pillars of Islam, as well as being among the greatest of the symbols of Islam. That fasting has many purposes relating both to the Lordship of God and thanksgiving for His bounties, and to man's individual and collective life, as well as to his self-training and self-discipline.

One of the multiple purposes of fasting connected with the Lordship of God is that God manifests the Perfection of His Lordship and His being the All-Merciful and All-Compassionate upon the surface of the earth which He has designed as a table upon which He has laid out all the varieties of His bounties in a way beyond the imagination of the inhabitants of the earth. Nevertheless, people cannot perfectly discern the reality of this situation because of heedlessness and the blinding veil of causality. But in the holy month of Ramadan, the believers, like an army waiting for the order 'March!', display a manner of wor-

---

14. *al-Baqara*, 2.185.

shipping in expectation of the command of 'Help yourself!' towards the end of the day, and they thus respond to that magnificent and universal Mercy with a comprehensive and harmonious act of collective worship. I wonder whether those who do not participate in this sublime act of worship and share in the honour of being so favoured deserve to be called human.

The second point

One of the numerous purposes of fasting in the holy month of Ramadan concerning thanksgiving for the bounties of God Almighty is that, as stated in the *First Word*, there is a price for the food brought from the kitchen of a king by the servant carrying the trays of food. Obviously, it would be folly of an infinite degree to tip the servant but not to recognize the king who sent the food – an act which would mean disrespect for that gift of precious food. In the same way, God Almighty has spread for mankind His countless bounties of infinite variety on the face of the earth. These bounties require the payment of a price, which is thanksgiving. The apparent causes of those bounties, or those who bring them to us are like the food-carrying servant in the example above. We pay the servants, feel indebted to them, and sometimes thank them and thereby show them a degree of respect they have not merited. The true Giver of Bounties is infinitely more deserving of thanks for those bounties received than the causes or the means by which they come to us. One thanks Him by acknowledging one's need for the bounties, and being fully appreciative of them and ascribing them directly to Him.

Fasting during the holy month of Ramadan is the key to a true, sincere, comprehensive and universal thanksgiving. Many people are unable to appreciate most of the bounties they enjoy since they suffer no hunger. A piece of dry bread, for example, means nothing as Divine bounty for those who are full, especially if they are rich, although it is, as even testified by his sense of taste, a very valuable bounty of God in the sight of a believer at the time of breaking his fast. Everyone, whether a king or the poorest of people, are favoured, in the holy Ramadan, with a heart-felt thanksgiving by understanding the value of Divine bounties. Also, because of being forbidden to eat during daytime, a believer thinks: those bounties do not originally belong to me, and I am not free to regard them as mere food or drink. One Other owns them, and He grants them to me. So, I should wait for His permission to eat them. By thus acknowledging whatever he eats and drinks to be a gift of God, the believer thanks God tacitly. On account of this, fasting becomes a key to thanksgiving, which is a real human duty in many respects.

The third point

Fasting has many purposes in connection with man's collective life, one of which is this:

God has created human beings differently in respect of their livelihood. Because of this, He calls the rich to the help of the poor. However, only through the hunger of fasting can the rich feel the hunger and tragic situation of the poor. Without fasting, many rich and self-indulgent people cannot perceive how painful hunger and poverty are, and to what extent the poor need care. Whereas, care for one's fellow-beings is a foundation of true thanksgiving. There is certainly one poorer than each individual, so everyone is obliged to show care for the one poorer than him. Unless, therefore, one is obliged to suffer hunger, it is nearly impossible for him to do good or give help to his fellow-beings as required by that duty of care. Even if he does, he cannot do it as perfectly as he should, since he does not feel the condition of the hungry to the same extent.

The fourth point

There are many Divine purposes for the obligation of fasting during Ramadan related to self-training and self-discipline. One of those purposes is as follows:

The carnal self desires to be free and unrestricted and regards itself to be so. It even wishes, by its very nature, for an imagined lordship and free, arbitrary action. Disinclined to thinking that it is being trained and tested through the countless bounties of God, it swallows up, like an animal, those bounties in the manner of a thief or robber, especially if it has a degree of wealth and power accompanied by heedlessness.

It is in holy Ramadan that the selfhood of everyone, whether the richest or the poorest, understands that, rather than owning itself, it is owned by One Other, and rather then being free, it is a servant. Unless it is ordered, or permitted, it is unable to do even the most common thing like eating and drinking, and thereby its illusory lordship is shattered, it can admit to servanthood and performs its real duty, which is thanksgiving.

The fifth point

Fasting during Ramadan also prevents the carnal self from rebellious acts and adorns it with good morals.

Man's carnal self forgets itself through heedlessness. It does not see, nor does it want to see, the infinite impotence and poverty and the defects of the utmost degree in its very nature. It does not reflect how it is exposed to misfortunes and subject to decay, that it consists of flesh and bones tending to rapid disintegration and decomposition. It rushes upon the world with a violent greed and attachment as if it had a steel body and would live forever. It clings to everything profitable and pleasurable. In this state, it forgets its Creator, Who trains it with a perfect care. Being immersed in the swamp of bad morals, it thinks about neither the consequences of its life in this world nor about its afterlife.

Fasting during holy Ramadan, however, causes even the

most heedless and stubborn to feel their weakness and innate poverty. Hunger becomes an important consideration for them and reminds them how fragile their bodies are. They come to perceive to what extent they need compassion and care and, giving up haughtiness, feel a desire to take refuge in the Divine Court in perfect helplessness and destitute, and rise to knock at the door of Mercy with the hand of tacit thanksgiving, provided, of course, that heedlessness has not yet corrupted the individual completely.

The sixth point

Fasting during Ramadan has a connection also with the revelation of the holy Qur'an. As is generally known, the Qur'an began to be revealed in Ramadan. This connection has many implications. One of these is that – just as if the Qur'an were to be revealed in every Ramadan, a believer should seek to be like the angels and abandon eating and drinking, and divest himself of the vain preoccupations and gross needs of his carnal self. During Ramadan, he should recite or listen to the Qur'an as if it were being revealed for the first time or, if he is able, listen to the Qur'an as if he were hearing it recited by the Prophet Muhammad, upon him be peace and blessings, or by the Archangel Gabriel to Muhammad, or revealed by God Himself to Muhammad through Gabriel. Also, he should respect the Qur'an in the actions of his daily life and, by conveying its message to the others, demonstrate the Divine purpose for revealing the Qur'an.

The Muslim world becomes in Ramadan like a huge mosque where millions of reciters recite the Qur'an, that heavenly address, to the inhabitants of the earth. Demonstrating the reality of the verse, *The month of Ramadan, in which the Qur'an was revealed*, Ramadan proves itself to be the month of the Qur'an: while some members of the vast congregation in that great mosque of the Muslim world listen to its recitation with solemn reverence, others recite it themselves. As it is most disagreeable to forsake that heavenly spiritual state by giving in to the prompting of the carnal self to eat and drink in the sacred 'mosque', an action that is bound to provoke the dislike of the whole congregation – it is also most disagreeable and must, plainly, provoke the dislike and contempt of the whole Muslim world to oppose the Muslims who fast during the holy month of Ramadan.

The seventh point

Fasting during Ramadan has also many purposes related to the spiritual rewards of man, who has been sent to the world to sow it with the seeds of the next life. The following paragraphs explain one of those purposes.

The rewards for the good deeds done in Ramadan are multiplied by a thousand. According to one *hadith*, ten rewards are given for each letter of the Wise Qur'an. The recitation of a single letter means ten good deeds, and brings forth ten fruits of Paradise. However, in the whole month of Ramadan, the reward for each letter of the Qur'an is multiplied not by ten, but by a thousand, even by thousands for some particular verses like the 'Verse of the Throne'. The reward is still greater on the Friday nights of holy Ramadan. Furthermore, the reward for each letter of the holy Qur'an recited in the Night of Power is multiplied by thirty thousand. Thus, the Qur'an, each of whose letters yields thirty thousand permanent fruits of Paradise, becomes in Ramadan like a huge blessed tree which produces for believers millions of permanent fruits of Paradise. Consider, then, how holy and profitable a trade this is, and know in how great a loss those are who do not appreciate the letters of the Qur'an!

So, the holy month of Ramadan is the most proper time for

carrying on that most profitable 'trade' in the name of the after-life. It is like a most fertile field to cultivate for the harvest of the afterlife. For the multiplication of the reward for good deeds, it is like April in spring. It is also a sacred, illustrious festival for the 'parade' of those who worship the Sovereignty of God's Lordship. Because of this, fasting is made obligatory for believers in Ramadan so that they should not gratify the animal appetites of the carnal self and indulge in its useless fancies. Since they become like angels while fasting or engaged in a trade for the next life, each acts as a mirror reflecting the Self-Sufficiency of God by moving in the direction of becoming a pure spirit manifested in corporeal dress through the abandonment of the world for a fixed period. In fact, the holy Ramadan contains, and causes a believer to gain, through fasting, a permanent life in a short period in this world.

One Ramadan may enable a believer to gain as much reward as could be earned in a life of eighty years. This can be decisively proved by the fact that the Night of Power is, as declared by the Qur'an, more profitable than eighty years in which there is not a Night of Power. A worldly king may announce a few days' festival in the year to mark some special occasions like his accession to the throne, and he honours his faithful subjects on those days with special favours. Likewise, the Eternal, Majestic King of the eighteen thousand worlds sent down in holy Ramadan the Wise Qur'an, which is His exalted decree to all of those eighteen thousand worlds. For this reason, wisdom requires that Ramadan should be a special Divine festival in which the bounties of God's Lordship will be poured out and the spirit beings will come together. Since, then, Ramadan is a Divinely ordained festival, it is proper that fasting in it would be commanded so that people should withdraw to some extent from their bodily preoccupations. Excellence in fasting, aside from its preventing the satisfaction of the stomach, is possible through refraining from sins committed by the senses or members of the body, such as the eyes, ears, heart, mind, and imaginative and contemplative faculties, and using them, instead, in the acts of worship particular to each. For example, the one who fasts, should prevent his tongue from lying, backbiting, bad language and indecent talk, and make it busy with the recitation of the Qur'an, glorification of God, seeking His forgiveness, and calling His blessing upon the Prophet Muhammad, upon him be peace and blessings. In the same way, he should prevent his eyes from looking at, and his ears from listening to, the forbidden things. He should, instead, use his eyes to see such things as those which, for example, will give a spiritual lesson or moral warning; and use his ears to listen to the Qur'an and truths. When the stomach, which is like a big factory in the body, is stopped from working, the other members, which may be likened to very small workshops in comparison with the stomach, can, in fact, easily be made to follow it.

The eighth point

One of the purposes of fasting related to man's individual life is as follows:

Fasting is a diet from the viewpoint of both the physical and spiritual health of man. If the carnal self acts in eating and drinking in whatever way it wishes, this is harmful to man's physical health, as well as being a poison for his spiritual life because of the absence of discrimination between what is lawful and unlawful. It becomes very difficult for such a carnal self to obey the heart and spirit. Without recognizing any principles, it takes the reins of man and drives him in whatever direction it desires. But, in Ramadan it gets accustomed to dieting through the fast and, in self-discipline, it is trained to learn to obey orders. Further, it does not cause the poor stomach to suffer illness because of over-eating without enough time allowed for proper digestion. In addition, since it has learned to forsake eating even what is lawful, it gains the ability to follow the decree of reason and religion to refrain from the unlawful. Thus, the carnal self tries not to corrupt the spiritual life of its owner.

Also, the great majority of mankind frequently become subject to hunger. In order to endure a long-lasting hunger with patience, people should train themselves in self-discipline and an austere lifestyle. Fasting during Ramadan provides just such a training based on patience with hunger of fifteen hours, or even twenty-four hours if the meal before dawn is missed. This means that fasting is a cure for the impatience and want of endurance, which double the misfortune of mankind.

Many members of the human body are either in direct or in indirect service of the factory of the stomach. If that factory is not made to stop working in daytime during a certain month of the year, it keeps those members busy with itself, forgetful of the kinds of worship and sublime duties peculiar to each. It is for this reason that, since the oldest times, saints have usually preferred to get themselves used to an austere lifestyle for the sake of spiritual and human perfection. Fasting in Ramadan reminds us that the members of the body have not been created only for the service of the stomach. In Ramadan, many of those members take pleasure in the angelic and spiritual pleasures, instead of the material ones. This is the reason why in Ramadan, believers receive, according to the extent of their spiritual perfection, different degrees of spiritual pleasures and enlightenment. The heart, the spirit, the reason and innermost senses of man are refined through fasting in Ramadan. Even if the stomach wails during fasting, these senses rejoice greatly.

The ninth point

Fasting during Ramadan breaks the illusory lordship of the carnal self and, reminding it of its innate helplessness, convinces it that it is a servant.

The carnal self does not like to recognize its Lord, and claims lordship in great obstinacy. However much it is made to suffer, it preserves that temperament. It is only hunger which can alter that temperament. Fasting during Ramadan breaks the obstinacy of the carnal self and, by showing to it its intrinsic helplessness and poverty, reminds it that it is only a servant.

It is related from God's Messenger that God Almighty asked the carnal self: 'Who am I and who are you?' The carnal self replied: 'You are Yourself, and I am myself.' However much God tormented it and asked the same question, He received the same answer: 'You are Yourself, and I am myself.' At last, God subjected it to hunger, and when asking the same question, the reply came: 'You are my All-Compassionate Lord; I am Your helpless servant'.

O God, grant peace and blessings to our master Muhammad in a way to please You and to give him his due, to the number of the rewards for reciting the letters of the Qur'an in the month of Ramadan, and to his family and Companions.

Glorified be your Lord, the Lord of Honour and Power; exalted above what they falsely ascribe to Him! And peace be upon the Messengers! And all praise be to God, the Lord of the Worlds. Amen!

***

THE THIRD SECTION COMPRISES THE THIRD TREATISE

In the name of God, the Merciful, the Compassionate
God is the Light of the heavens and the earth.[15]

In the holy month of Ramadan, I experienced, in a different mood, one of the numerous radiances of mystery of the light-diffusing verse, *God is the Light of the heavens and the earth*. It is as follows:

I felt in my heart a convincing vision that all living creatures make the same supplication to God, of the kind made by Uways al-Qarani, like

O God, You are my Lord, and I am Your servant;
You are the Creator, and I am the one created;
You are the All-Provider, and I am the one provided...

and I felt that each of the eighteen thousand worlds receives its light from one of the Divine Names.

The world may be likened to a multi-petalled rose-bud, made up of many kinds of worlds one wrapped within the other. Behind or under the veil of each world, I saw a new one. Each world manifested itself to me in darkness and frightening gloom, as depicted by the verse, *Or like the veils of darkness in a vast deep ocean, overwhelmed by a great wave topped by a great wave, topped by dark clouds, one darkness over another, such that if a man stretches out his hand he can hardly see it. For whomsoever God has not appointed light, for him there is no light.*[16]

In my vision, a Divine Name was suddenly manifested and enlightened whichever world appeared to me in darkness because of heedlessness. This journey of the heart or the imagination lasted for a long time. What follows is a summary:

15. al-Nur, 24.35.
16. al-Nur, 24.40.

The world of animals appeared to me very gloomy because of their impotence and weakness along with innumerable needs and severe hunger. But the Divine Name of *al-Rahman* (the All-Merciful) suddenly appeared like a shining sun above the tower of the All-Provider, that is, with the function of all-inclusive provision, and illuminated that world thoroughly with the light of Mercy.

After that, I saw within that world another one in a pitiful condition, where the young desperately struggle in impotent neediness. All of a sudden, the Name, the All-Compassionate rose above the tower of the All-Caring, that is, with the function of all-comprehensive caring, and illuminated that world so beautifully that it changed the tears of pitiful wailing and sorrow to tears of joy, happiness and the pleasure of thanksgiving.

Then, like a film screen, a new screen appeared to me, where the human world manifested itself. That world was so dark and gloomy, and so terrifying that I was filled with panic and exclaimed, 'How pitiful it is!' For I saw that human beings have infinite desires and ambitions, universal ideas and imaginations, and very grand inclinations and dispositions to eternity and eternal happiness in Paradise. Nevertheless, in addition to their infinite weakness and impotence and the multiplicity of their needs, they are exposed to innumerable misfortunes and the attacks of many enemies, and are flowing, one by one or in groups, through a short, tumultuous life, a miserable livelihood, and under the tragic blows of continual decay and separation, to the grave, which (to the people of heedlessness) appears as a gate opening on to eternal darkness whence they are hurled into a dark pit. I was on the point of collapsing in tears, with all my human senses including the intellect, heart and soul, even every particle of my body, at the sight of that world in such pitiful darkness and gloom, when the Divine Name, the All-Just, was suddenly manifested in the meaning of the All-Wise, and the

Name, the All-Merciful in the meaning of the All-Generous, the Name, the All-Compassionate in the meaning of the All-Forgiver, the Name, the Raiser of the Dead in the meaning of the Heir-to-All, the Name, the Reviver in the meaning of the All-Beneficent, and the Name, the Lord in the meaning of the Master. Those Names illuminated many spheres within that human world and, opening windows on them out of the luminous World of the Hereafter, diffused light upon that human world of darkness.

Afterwards, another huge screen brought into view the earth and everything on it. The obscure laws of science and the principles of corrupt philosophy showed the earth as terrifying and gloomy. The condition of miserable humanity, floating in infinite space on the old earth in a state of continuous volcanic eruption inside and apt to disintegration, moving at such great speed as to revolve around the sun in a year, seemed to me frighteningly gloomy. I was dazed and felt dizzy. But all at once, the Names of the Creator of the universe and the earth, the All-Powerful, the All-Knowing, the Lord, God, and the Lord of the Heavens and the Earth and the Subduer of the Sun and the Moon appeared in the manifestation of Mercy, Grandeur and Lordship. They illumined that world in such a way that I saw the earth as a safe, perfect and beautiful ship of voyage, one subjected to humankind to travel in for pleasure or business.

In sum: I saw that each of one thousand and one Divine Names is like a sun illuminating one of those worlds, containing many spheres within it, and that all the other Names manifest themselves on account of God's Oneness, in some degree of ordered relation to the full manifestation of that Name. Having discerned a different light behind each veil of darkness, I felt the desire to make a spiritual journey upwards, to the eternal world of the heavens. I saw that those radiant planets which appear to be smiling to us are bigger than the earth, revolving in space faster than it. If a single one of them were to confuse its way, it would collide with another and cause the destruction of the universe. So, I saw the heavens as a dark, boundless and frightening space, with the stars moving or fixed, radiating fire and light. I felt much regret at having come up here, when the Divine Beautiful Names, the Lord of the Heavens and the Earth and the Lord of the Angels and the Spirit, manifested themselves in a way to disclose the meaning of, *And indeed We have adorned the nearest heaven with lamps*,[17] and *He has subdued the sun and the moon*[18]. Each of the stars, which were located in darkness, received a gleam from the mighty light of those Names, and the heavens were illuminated as if as many lamps as the stars had been lighted. That space, which had been imagined to be dark and empty of any beings, were thronged and cheered by the angels and spirit beings, and the suns and stars, which, serving as one of the numerous hosts of the King of Eternity, seemed to me to demonstrate, as if performing an exalted manoeuvre, the magnificence of the Majestic King and the splendour of His Lordship. With all my strength and, if it had been possible, together with all the particles in my body and, if they could have obeyed me, in the languages of all creatures, I would have recited:

> *God is the light of the heavens and the earth. The parable of His Light is as if there were a niche and within it a lamp, the lamp enclosed in glass, the glass as it were a brilliant star, lit from a blessed tree, an olive, neither of the east nor of the west, whose oil would almost glow forth of itself though no fire touched it. Light upon light! God guides to His Light whom He wills.*

However, I recited that verse on behalf of all creatures and, awakening from that state, I came back down to earth, uttering: *All praise be to God for the light of faith and the Qur'an.*

***

17. *al-Mulk*, 67.5.
18. *al-Ra'd*, 13.2.

THE FOURTH SECTION
COMPRISING THE FOURTH TREATISE

The intrigues of human and Satanic devils

(This part has been written in order to warn the pupils and servants of the Wise Qur'an against delusions.)

In the name of God, the Merciful, the Compassionate

Do not incline toward those who do wrong lest Fire should touch you.[19]

This fourth section brings to nought the six intrigues of human and Satanic devils and blocks up six of their routes of assaults.

The first intrigue

Human devils desire, based on the lesson they learn from Satan, to delude the self-sacrificing servants of the Qur'an through the love of post and positions and thereby to cause them to give up that exalted service and spiritual holy struggle.

Every worldly individual suffers some degree of ambition for fame, some love of position and, through that fame and show, the desire to acquire a status in the eyes of people. He is so fond of fame that he may even sacrifice his life for its sake. However, this desire, perilous for the people of the afterlife, is also destructive for the worldly-minded; it is the origin of many bad morals, and the weakest point in human character. By exciting this desire for public recognition, by working on this weak point in human character, the human devils can subdue a man and make him attached to themselves. What I fear most for my brothers is that the heretics are most likely to make use of that weak spot in them. It troubles me greatly. They have deceived a number of my poor friends and put them in danger.[20]

---

19. *Hud*, 11.113.

20. Those poor people, misled into the assertion that they are with their teacher by

O my brothers and companions in the service of the Qur'an, say to the intriguing agents of the worldly people, and the heralds of misguidance and the disciples of Satan:

'God's approval, the compliments of the All-Merciful, the acceptance of the Lord is so great a station or position that, when compared with it, the favour and commendation of people mean almost nothing. If God likes and approves us, then the approval or commendation of people may be accepted provided it is a reflection of God's approval. Otherwise, it should not be desired, for it is of no use at the gate of the grave.'

If, despite this, you are not able to overcome the love of position and the desire for status in the eyes of people, you can channel it into another direction, as will be explained below:

Such desire may be permissible if directed to gain a spiritual reward or founded on the intention of earning the prayers of people and of securing the influence of the service on others. The following comparison will clarify the point:

Let us suppose that the mosque of Aya Sofia is full of pious worshippers, and there are some idle boys and vagabonds at the gate or the antechamber and foreign lookers-on, fond of amusement, at the windows. If a man entered the mosque and recited beautifully a page of the Qur'an, the hundreds of the pious, truth-loving worshippers in the mosque would welcome, approve and commend him, and, by calling God's blessing on him, cause him to gain spiritual rewards. Only those urchins, and sinful vagabonds, and the few foreigners would disapprove of him. If, by contrast, that man were, instead of reciting the Qur'an, to chant obscenities and dance violently in the mosque, he would amuse the idle boys, delight the sinful tramps by inciting them to more indecencies, and attract the ironical ap-

___

heart, think they are not at risk. However, such an assertion of a man carried along with the propaganda of heretics and open to being used as a spy unconsciously, and who supports them even, is like the response of one who, when reminded that he has lost his ritual purity because of the escape of wind in prayer, says: 'Why, how could I lose my state of purity? My soul is purified!'

proval of foreigners, who take pleasure in witnessing the misery of Islam and Muslims. However, he would be disliked and condemned by every member of the huge blessed congregation, and seem to them among the lowest of the low.

The mosque in the comparison corresponds to the Muslim world in general, or Asia in particular. The believers and people of truth are the congregation. The idle boys represent foolish people, and the immoral vagabonds stand for the irreligious and heretical imitators of the West. As for the foreign lookers-on, they are the journalists who spread the foreign ideas. Every Muslim, especially the one of piety and perfection, has, according to his degree of practising his religion, a place in the mosque and a position in the eyes of Muslims. If he does deeds and acts in compliance with the sacred truths and commandments of the Qur'an, with sincerity and for the good pleasure of God, which is the basis of Islamic life, and the meaning of the Qur'anic verses is demonstrated through his conduct, he is included in the supplication, *O God, forgive all the believers, male and female,* always said by all the world Muslims, and establishes a brotherly relation with all of them. He is only disapproved by some people of misguidance far below the rank of humanity, or by the single-minded who may be regarded as 'bearded children', that is, adults in appearance but children in mind and character.

If, on the other hand, that man breaks away from all his ancestors, whom he recognizes as the means of honour and pride, and breaks from the illustrious way of the righteous precedents, which he takes as a spiritual source of support, to become, instead, engaged in whims and fancies, and occupied with irreligious novelties for show and fame, he will be degraded to the lowest of the low in the eyes of the people of faith and truth. However ignorant and ordinary a believer may be, nevertheless, according to the Prophetic judgement, *Fear the insight of the believer, for he looks with the light of God,*[21] he unconsciously turns

---

21. Tirmidhi, *Tafsir Sura 15.6.*

away in disgust from such vainglorious people.

Thus, the one who acts to please and indulge the worldly and the heretics for the sake of fame or to gain a position in their eyes, falls to the lowest of the low in the eyes of a huge congregation, the great majority of the Muslim community. He achieves only a transient and inauspicious position in the eyes of a small minority of people suffering delirium and derision – according to the Qur'anic verse, *Friends on that day will be foes one to another except those who fear God and avoid evil*,[22] he finds only some false friends, harmful in this world, a means of torment in the Intermediate World of the grave, and foes in the Hereafter.

If a man, influenced by a desire for public recognition, acts like the one in the comparison above who prefers to recite the Qur'an in the mosque, he achieves a kind of spiritual position, both considerable and harmfree, to gratify that desire for fame and position – provided that he acts in sincerity and for God's good pleasure, and does not see the fame and position as his main aim. In comparison with what he gains, what he loses is quite insignificant. He may lose a few snake-like people, but will find so many blessed friends that he receives, through their supplications, numerous Divine blessings like the water of life flowing to his soul from all over the Muslim world, and those blessings are added to the record of his deeds.

When a public figure once took a very important worldly post and became a laughing-stock in the eyes of the Muslims of the world because of the grave errors he indulged in to obtain fame, I preached this lesson to him most forcefully. It shook him, but since I was unable to rid myself of the love of position, my warning did not suffice to rouse him from it.

The second intrigue

Fear is one of the most basic human emotions. The intriguing wrongdoers, the agents of the worldly, and the heralds of mis-

---

22. *al-Zuhruf*, 43.67.

guidance, make much use of this weak spot of ordinary people and particularly of religious scholars, inculcating in them fear and anxiety. Suppose an anxious, fearful man is on the roof, but then an intriguer goads him by increasing his groundless suspicions and anxieties till, finally, he falls head first and breaks his neck. Similarly, the worldly people cause Muslims to sacrifice many important things by arousing in them groundless fear and anxieties.

There was a significant man – may God's mercy be upon him – who was afraid of travelling by boat. One evening, we came down to the bridge together to go to Ayub by boat. He did not want to get on the boat.

– I fear I will drown, he said.

– How many boats are there in this Golden Horn? I asked him.

– As many as one thousand, he answered.

Our conversation continued as follows:

– Roughly, how many boats sink in a year?

– One or two. There are years when no boats drown.

– How many days are there in a year?

– 365 days.

– Then, the chance of drowning is one out of 365 thousand. What on earth should a man fear from so unlikely chance? Besides, how many years more do you expect to live?

– I am an old man. I may live at most ten more years.

– The appointed hour of death is unknown to us. That is, you may die at any time; death may come to you on any of three thousand, six hundred and fifty days. Therefore, the chance of your death is not one out of 365 thousand, which is (perhaps) the risk of this boat sinking; rather you may die today at a chance of one out of 3650. That being so, repent of your sins and weep, and write your last will and testament!

He came to his senses and got on the boat, though trembling. On the boat, I said to him:

'God Almighty has placed the sense of fear in man's nature so that he might preserve his life, not ruin it. He has not given us fear so that man should make his life an unbearable burden and a pain, full of torment for himself. If there is a risk of one chance out of two or three or four, or at most, five or six, then it may be religiously permissible to fear and to avoid the risk. But, to fear a chance of one out of twenty, thirty or forty is a groundless suspicion, a sort of paranoia, which changes life into a torment.'

Therefore, dear brothers! If the sycophants and the heretics, seeking to prevent you from your holy spiritual struggle in the way of God, attack you through fear, say to them:

'We are the people of the Qur'an, and, according to God's declaration, *No doubt We have sent down the Qur'an and surely We will guard it,*[23] we are within the stronghold of the Qur'an. Our firm conviction is that *for us God is sufficient, and how good a Being He is to trust in and rely on,* and our trust is a strong citadel around us. So, by urging us to fear of a danger, the chance of which affecting us in this our short, transient life is one in a thousand, you cannot direct us willingly to a way a hundred per cent harmful to our eternal life, hereafter.

You should also say to them:

'Which among the people of truth who are, like us, friends to Said Nursi in the way of truth, has so far suffered harm on account of him? He is our companion in the service of the Qur'an and our teacher in the administration of this sacred service. Who among his sincere disciples has so far suffered a misfortune such that we should be anxious lest something undesirable happens to us? This brother of ours has thousands of brothers and friends in religion. Even when, in the past, he was heavily en-

---

20. *al-Hijr*, 15.9.

gaged in public life over almost twenty years, we never heard of anyone among his friends having suffered harm. They claimed his participation in the revolt of March 31, and crushed some of his friends. But it was soon clarified that he had nothing to do with that revolt and the harm coming to his friends was not on his account, but on their own account. Indeed, he saved many of his friends from some misfortunes. Besides, he held at that time the 'mace' of politics in his hand. It is now a long time since he threw away that 'mace'; now he holds the light of the truth. For all these reasons, human devils, like you, should never think that they can deprive us of an eternal 'treasury' for fear of a danger the chances of which befalling us are one in a thousand.

You should speak to those who fawn on the people of misguidance in that manner and repel them. And say to them also:

Let alone for fear of a misfortune which is almost impossible to befall us, even if there were a certain danger promised to us in this way, we would still never desert him while we preserve a bit of sense. For, as has been witnessed many times, a misfortune happens first to those who betray their master in the event of a danger. Such are pitilessly punished and condemned as base people; some of them have suffered a material as well as a spiritual death. Those who punish them feel no compassion for them. For they think:

'Since these men have betrayed their faithful and affectionate master, they must be of the basest character and therefore deserve condemnation, not compassion.'

When a cruel, unjust man throws someone to the ground meaning to trample him to death, if that trampled man kisses the other's foot, he will first die spiritually, and in addition to losing honour and dignity, will not be able to save himself from a degrading death. By displaying helplessness before that cruel man, he encourages him to crush him to death. If, by contrast, that wronged man spits in the face of the cruel man, he will die as a martyr and remain spiritually alive in honour and dignity.

When foreign forces invaded Istanbul and destroyed the cannon at the Bosphorous, a religious representative of them asked six questions of the office of the Shaikh al-Islam, then the highest religious office in Turkey. I was at that time a member of the House of Islamic Wisdom *(Dar al-Hikma al-Islamiyya)*. They requested me to answer those questions. The representative of the foreign clergy wanted the questions to be answered in six hundred words. I replied:

'Not with six hundred words, nor with six words, nor with one word even, I will answer them with a ... . For you see how, when a nation's government puts its foot on our neck, its religious officer gets up to ask us some questions in a boastful way. Therefore, his due is a single ... !'

Now I say:

'Dear brothers! Even though it was a hundred per cent dangerous to give response in that way publicly in the press following the invasion of Istanbul by tyrannical powers, the Qur'an sufficed for my protection. It will also suffice for your protection to a hundred-fold degree against any danger of which there is but a slight chance at the hands of those insignificant people of wrongdoing.

Also, dear brothers! Most of you have completed your military service. Those who have not yet joined the army must have heard – if they have not, let them hear it from me – that those who flee the battlefront receive many more wounds than those who persevere at the front. The verse, Verily, *the death from which you flee will surely meet you,*[24] hints that those who flee are actually hastening to meet death.

The third intrigue

They deceive many because of greed. Based on decisive proofs I

---

24. *al-Jumu'a*, 62.8.

have obtained from the verses and clear explanations of the Wise Qur'an, I have written in several treatises that the lawful provision comes in accordance, not with the extent of capacity and will-power, but with the degree of poverty and impotence. Out of countless signs and evidences concerning this truth, the following are only a few:

Trees are a kind of living creatures in need of provision. They stand still in their places and the provision they need reaches them. Animals, by contrast, are not provided with food as perfectly as trees because they seek their food impatiently.

The fish are fed perfectly and usually become fleshy though they are the least intelligent of animal species, whereas the animals more clever and powerful, like apes and foxes, are mostly weak because of insufficient nutrition. This also shows that the means of provision is need or destitution, not power or ability.

Also, the infants of both animals and human beings are fed very well and extraordinarily, especially with milk, the best food and the sweetest gift of the treasury of Mercy bestowed on them in an unexpected way out of care for their weakness and incapability. Wild beasts, by contrast, have usually to be content with the scarce food they obtain through tiring effort. This again illustrates how the means of lawful provision is impotence and poverty, not intelligence and capability.

Again, there are no people in the world in as passionate pursuit of worldly provision as the Jews, who are famous for the force of their greed. But no people in world history have suffered privation and shortage of livelihood as much as the Jews, and lived in humiliation. Even the wealthy among them live in misery and under stress. However, the wealth they obtain through unlawful means like usury is not religiously sanctioned so that it does not refute the general argument.

Further, the poverty of most of the literary men and scholars as against the richness of many ignorant people also shows that what attracts provision is not intelligence and ability, but it is weakness and need, and submission to God in reliance on Him, and petitioning Him by tongue, disposition and lawful effort.

The verse, *Verily, God is the All-Provider, the Owner of the Strength, the Steadfast*[25] which proclaims this truth, is so strong and firm a proof for my argument that all the vegetation, animals and babies announce it. Every living family in need of provision recites this verse through the tongue of their disposition.

Since provision has been pre-determined and is supplied by God Almighty, who is the All-Compassionate and the All-Generous, it is extreme folly to humble oneself in a way to deride God's Mercy and belittle His Generosity, to offer one's conscience and sacred things as a bribe in return for some wealth, albeit not forbidden by religion.

The worldly people, especially the misguided, do not pay out money except for a high return. In exchange for some wealth which might contribute to a year's livelihood, they may cause one to lose his eternal life of the Hereafter. Unfortunately, there are always some who attract the Divine wrath because of that disgusting greed and by trying to please the misguided.

Dear brothers! If those who fawn on worldly people and hypocrites among the misguided are to capture you by greed – another weak spot of mankind – ponder over the truth I have explained above and follow the example of this poor brother of yours! I assure you with all my strength that it is thrift and contentment, rather than wages or salaries, with which you can preserve your life. Moreover, in return for the money given to you unlawfully, they will demand from you a high repayment. Your involvement in their world may also hinder your service of the Qur'an, each hour of which can open for you the gates of an eternal treasury-house. Being deterred from this service is so great a loss that no salaries or wages, however high, can compensate for it.

25. *al-Dhariyat*, 51.58.

Note: Unable to resist by ideas and argument or defend themselves against the truths of the Qur'an and their dissemination, the people of misguidance, being also hypocrites, use the trap of cheating and deception. They try to deceive my friends through the love of position, greed and fear, and resort to false imputations to present me as someone unreliable. We always act in our service in a positive way. However, in order to remove the obstacles put before our good activities, unfortunately we have to sometimes act in a negative way.

It is for this reason that I warn my brothers against those three intrigues of the people of hypocrisy mentioned above, and try to repel the attacks made on them.

More than my brothers, they are attacking my person, and say:

'Said is a Kurd; so, why do you hold him in such high esteem and follow him so warmly?'

In order to silence them, I feel compelled to write a fourth Satanic intrigue in the language of Old Said:

The fourth intrigue

Instigated by Satan and inspired by the people of misguidance, some heretics who occupy certain high positions attack me with false accusations and, in order to deceive my brothers and stir up their national zeal, say to them:

'You are Turkish. There are among Turks – God bless them – scholars in every field and men of perfection; this Said is Kurdish. How do you reconcile co-operation with a non-Turk with your national zeal?'

Answer: O unfortunate heretics! I am – praise be to God – a Muslim. My holy nation – it is the Muslim nation – has long had hundreds of millions of members. I take refuge in God a hundred thousand times from sacrificing for the sake of racism and negative nationalism those hundreds of millions of brothers between whom and me there is eternal brotherhood and who help me through their prayers, among whom are the great majority of the Kurdish people. I also take refuge in God from securing, instead of those countless blessed Muslim brothers, the support of a few atheists or heretics considered as belonging to the Kurdish race. O unfortunate heretics! According to your corrupt logic, the eternal brotherhood of a huge, illustrious community composed of hundreds of millions of true brothers should be sacrificed for the sake of the temporary, useless friendship of few westernized and apostatized Turks or Hungarian or Bulgarian unbelievers who are considered as belonging to the Turkish race.

Referring the reader to the 'Third Matter' of the *Twenty- sixth Letter* to see the nature and injuries of negative nationalism, I would like to elaborate here a truth briefly discussed at the end of the Third Matter.

I say to those heretics who, although being in reality enemies of the Turks, conceal themselves behind the veil of Turkish nationalism.

I have a deep and true connection with the believing people of this country through a genuine brotherhood and belonging to the same Muslim nation. I support and love, and take pride in, in the name of Islam, the children of this country, who carried the flag of the Qur'an victoriously throughout the old world for nearly a thousand years. As for you, O hypocrites, who falsely claim Turkish nationalism! With ulterior motives you make show of feeling a short-lived brotherhood with the Turkish people in order to make them forget their true national honours! I ask you whether the Turkish nation is made up of only fanciful and heedless young men between twenty and forty years of age? Does your nationalism require that they should adopt for their national interests a West-imposed kind of education which increases their heedlessness, habituates them to immorality and encourages them to commit religiously forbidden things? Does your service of them mean amusing them in a way that will make them, in old age, wail and repent over their sins of youth? If your nationalism requires, and progress and happiness consist of, all these, and if you are Turkish nationalists of this sort, then I am infinitely far from this kind of nationalism, and you may keep yourself away from me. If you have some trace of conscience left and true national zeal, and if you are at least a little fair-minded, consider the following discussion and then answer me:

The children of this country – the Turkish nation – comprise six groups of people. The first group are the people of piety and righteousness. The second group are the afflicted and the ill. The old form the third group, and children the fourth. The fifth group consists of the poor and weak. The sixth and last group is the youth. Are the first five groups not Turks to be offered your kind of national zeal? Is it true nationalism to wound their feelings and deprive them of their means of consolation in order to amuse the sixth group? According to the principle, *The majority is considered in giving the judgement,* something harmful to the majority comes from enmity – not friendship – so your nationalism is enmity for the nation.

I ask you: Does the interest of the people of piety and righteousness lie in blindly imitating Western civilization in its corrupt aspects? Or does it lie in finding true consolation in following the way of the truth to which they are passionately attached because of their belief in eternal happiness? The way of those misguided people who, like you, falsely claim national zeal, would extinguish the light of pious believers, deprive them of their means of consolation and present death as absolute annihilation and the grave as a gate to infinite separation.

Does the interest of the second group comprising the afflicted and the ill and those hopeless of their life lie in imitating Western civilization in its irreligious and immoral aspects? Rather, those wretched people hope for consolation and desire some return for their suffering. They seek vengeance upon those who have wronged them and wish to enter the grave happily. Nevertheless, through your false nationalism, you wound the feelings of those afflicted ones in dire need of care, hope and consolation, you keep them under restraint, and drive them without pity to absolute despair. Is this what national zeal really requires?

The old, who comprise the third group, are one third of the total population. Every day, they are more and more far away from this world and approaching death. In preparation for emigrating to the other world, they are gradually breaking with this life. Does their interest or consolation lie in listening to the dreadful adventures of certain tyrants, supposedly belonging to the Turkish race, and in the present direction of your movement which you claim as progress but is, in reality, neglect of the Hereafter, and attachment to this world, and therefore spiritual decay? Can a man find in a cinema the light with which to illuminate his other world, or find true consolation in the theatre? If to deceive those poor old people (who expect due respect from national zeal), into believing that death is absolute annihilation and the grave, which they believe to be a gate to mercy, is like the mouth of a dragon into which they are going to be thrown, is national zeal, I seek refuge in God a hundred thousand times from such kind of national zeal.

The fourth group of people consists of young children. They expect mercy and care from national zeal. Since they are feeble and impotent, it is only through recognizing an All-Merciful and Powerful Creator that they can be spirited and develop their potential. They can look at life lovingly and hopefully only by being inspired with belief in, and reliance on, God, and Islamic submission to Him. That will enable them also to resist the awful circumstances and calamities of their future in this world. That being so, does their interest and happiness lie in attaching themselves to the material progress they are only lightly interested in, and to the principles of materialistic philosophy which will demoralize and dispirit them? If man were no more than a biological entity, like the animals, one devoid of intellect, that West-imposed education, which you call a national education for civilization, might provide certain of their worldly interests and temporarily amuse them as a new toy amuses a child. But, since those innocent infants are human, and since they will find themselves in the tumults of life, they will certainly cherish long-term desires in their hearts and have great objectives in their minds. That being so, in order to compensate for their weakness and impotence, we should establish in their souls, as a requirement of our care of them, belief in God and the Hereafter as a strong point of support and an inexhaustible source of help. This is what mercy and care for them really demands. Otherwise, like an insane mother slaughtering her child with a knife, we will kill them spiritually, intoxicated with national zeal. Or we will commit a great, pitiless crime like taking out their brains and hearts and offering these to them as food in order to fatten their bodies.

The fifth group consists of the poor and weak. Surely national zeal should not ignore the poor, who are crushed, because of their poverty, under the heavy burdens of life, and the weak, who are very much affected by the terrible convulsions of life. Does your national zeal require that you should move, under the name of nationalism, to a shameless and tyrannical kind of civilization which must increase the grim hopelessness of their situation, which serves as a game to satisfy the fancies of certain, dissolute wealthy people, and as a means for some tyrannical, powerful individuals to gain notoriety and commit crimes? The remedy for the poverty of the poor does not lie in the notion of racism; rather, it is to be found in the sacred 'medicine store' of Islam. The source of the resistance and strength to endure of the weak lies in Islamic zeal and sacred Islamic nationalism, not in a materialistic philosophy which attributes everything to blind coincidences and chance accidents.

The sixth group is the young. Were youth permanent, the 'wine' you offer them through negative nationalism might be of temporary use for them. But when they recover in old age from the drunkenness of youth, when they awake in the morning of old age to the pains and realities of life, the troubles that drunkenness has caused will make them weep bitterly, and the pain coming from the end of that sweet dream will drive them to regret, saying:

'Alas! Youth has gone, life almost ended, and I am approaching the grave bankrupt of good deeds. I wish I had collected myself earlier!'

That being so, does national zeal require that this group should lament in regret for a long time in exchange for a transient merriment? Or is it that the happiness, even the pleasure, of their lives lies rather in spending their youth, not in dissipation, but on the Straight Path so as to thank God for the blessing of youth, to be enabled to use their transient youth to gain permanence through worship, to secure an eternal youth in the World of Happiness by spending youth in faith and good deeds?

In short: If the Turkish nation were composed of only the young, if youth were permanent, and were it not for another world, your imitation of the dissipated life-style of certain portion of the West, behind the veil of Turkish nationalism, might be considered as true national zeal. You might have a right to say of me – a man who gives little importance to worldly life, considers the idea of racism as a disease like syphilis, and tries to prevent the young from indulging in religiously forbidden pleasures, and who was born in another province – 'He is Kurdish, so do not follow him!'

However, since the people of this country, called the Turkish nation, consist of six groups, it is not friendship, but sheer enmity, for this nation, to harm and trouble five out of the six groups in exchange for amusing the sixth for a limited period, for intoxicating them in a way that must drive them to regret and despair in old age.

They do not consider me as belonging to the Turkish race. However, I have been striving with all my strength and perfect zeal, and with deep affection and brotherly feelings, for the good of the righteous among the Turkish people, as well as for the old and the afflicted, for the poor and weak, and for the children. I have also been trying to prevent the youth from religiously forbidden acts which poison their worldly life and will cause the ruin of their next life, and which cause one to weep for a whole year in exchange for an hour's pleasure. The works I have had published in the Turkish language, not over the last six or seven years, but over the last twenty years or so, are all in the open. All praise be to God that, through those works which I have derived from the source of the Qur'anic lights, the old are offered the light of which they are in such dire need. The most useful remedy for the afflicted and the ill is shown to be found in the sacred 'medicine store' of the Qur'an. The grave is demonstrated as a gate opening to infinite mercy, not to eternal annihilation. The children are offered, from the treasure of the Qur'an, a very strong point of support against countless misfortunes of life, and a source of help to satisfy their innumerable desires and ambitions. And the weak and the poor are relieved, through the Qur'anic truths of belief, of the heavy burdens of life under which they are crushed.

As for the youth, I feel a heart-felt brotherhood with the good among them. Nevertheless, I do not recognize as Turks those who have fallen into heresy and want to break with the Muslim nationality, which is the real source of all the national pride of Turkish people; I regard them as some hostile foreigners disguised as Turks. They cannot deceive the people of truth even if they claim a hundred thousand times that they are Turks and Turkish nationalists. For their acts and attitudes contradict their claim.

Now, O you who try to make my true brothers chilly in their relations with me! What use do you have for this nation? You extinguish the light of the people of piety and righteousness. You deepen the injuries of the second group, the ill and afflicted, who deserve compassion and attention. You deprive the third group, the old, of their means of consolation and drive them to despair. You completely demoralize the fourth group, the children, who are in such need of care, and extinguish their humanity. By bringing to nought the hopes of the fifth group – the poor and weak – who are in such need of help and consolation, and by drying up their source of help, you change life in their eyes into something more dreadful than death. Lastly, you intoxicate the sixth group, who should be warned and awakened to collect themselves, from the sleep of youth, with such a 'wine' that the resulting drunkenness is extremely painful and dreadful. Thus is your national zeal of a sort that you would sacrifice for its sake many sacred things of this nation! Does your Turkish nationalism benefit the Turks in the ways mentioned? I seek refuge in God a hundred thousand times from your Turkism or Turkish nationalism!

Gentlemen! I know very well that you resort to force when you are defeated on a point of truth. According to the principle, *right is might*, not *might is right*, this head of mine, ready to be sacrificed for the truths of the Qur'an, will never be bowed before you. Also, I inform you that even if, not only those few persons, like you, who are disliked by the people, but also thousands of others of the same sort were to antagonize me, I will not care for them at all nor attach them any more importance than to certain harmful creatures. What can you do to me? You can either put an end to my life or impede my service. I have no relations in the world with anything else other than these two things: my life and my service of the faith and the Qur'an. I am unshakeably convinced that the appointed hour of death never changes. So, if I die at your hands as a martyr, this is what I

have been expecting eagerly. In addition, I am old, not antici-
pating that I will live longer than one more year. It is the most
exalted objective and aim of those like me to exchange one year
of life for eternal life through martyrdom. As for my service, all
praise be to God Almighty, He has made such people friends or
brothers to me in this service of the faith and the Qur'an that
this service, which is done in one centre only, will be done after
my death in many other centres. If I am silenced through death, '
many others more will speak, and much more loudly, on my
behalf, and continue this service. I can even argue that in the
way a seed rotted away under the soil grows into an elaborate
tree, yielding thousands of seeds in exchange for one, it is my
hope that my death will be, much more than my life, the means
for this service.

The fifth intrigue

Supporters of the misguided desire, by making use of human
egotism, to separate my brothers from me. Indeed, the most
dangerous temperament common to all, which is also the weakest spot, of a man, is egotism. By exciting this sentiment, they
urge men to do very bad things. Dear brothers, take care that
they do not captivate you through egotism. Know that the people of misguidance, carried by their ego, wander in the alley-
ways of deviation. Therefore, the people of truth have no way
other than to forsake 'ego' in order to serve the truth – even if
they are sometimes right to make use of 'ego', since this will
make the people of truth resemble the others, making them
seem as egotists like the others. For the service of the Qur'an,
around which we come together, does not accept 'egotism'; rather it demands co-operation in sincere brotherhood. You must
have been convinced that this poor brother of yours did not
come forward to satisfy his ego or to invite you to serve it; rather, he showed himself to you as a servant of the Qur'an with no
feelings of egotism. He has chosen self-denial and altruism as

the way to follow. He has also proved to you that the works put forward for the benefit of people were derived from the Qur'an and belong to everyone. No one can claim ownership of them, attributing them to himself. If we were to suppose the inconceivable that they belong to me, then – as a brother of mine said – once this gate of the Qur'anic service has been opened, the people of perfection and knowledge should not hesitate to follow these works, giving no consideration at all to my defects and shortcomings. However great a treasury useful for everyone and a cure for every intellectual or spiritual disease the works of the righteous precedents and scholars of truth are, it sometimes happens that a key can open several treasure-houses. I think that those who have a forceful ego based on knowledge have also understood that *The Words* are each a key to the truths of the Qur'an and a 'diamond sword' with which to strike those who try to deny these truths. Those people of knowledge and perfection boastful of their knowledge should know that, by following my works, they will become the disciples of the Wise Qur'an, not of me, and that I am their fellow-student. Supposing the impossible that I claim mastership, since the *Risale-i Nur* removes the doubts of the believers – from the most elect to the commonest – concerning the truths of belief, those scholars should either find a better way of removing those doubts or instruct people in the truths expounded by the *Risale-i Nur*. The scholars who use knowledge, or conceal the truths they know, for worldly interests, are severely warned in sound traditions, so let the knowledgeable people take care.

Supposing I were doing this service, as claimed by our enemies, to satisfy my egotism, even then does this brother of yours have the right to request you to forsake egotism and form a strong unity around the truths of the Qur'an, seeing that numerous people forsake their egotism to come together for worldly aims around a Pharaoh-like man with utmost loyalty and work in a strong solidarity? Are even the greatest of your scholars not wrong not to accede to this request?

Dear brothers, the most harmful aspect of egotism is envy. If one's service is not purely for God's sake, envy intervenes and adulterates his service. In the way the hands of a man are not envious of each other, and his eyes feels no envy of his ears and his heart does not compete with his intellect, so every one of you is like a member or a sense of our collective body. So, it is a duty of conscientiousness to take pride, and take spiritual pleasure, in each other's merits, not to enter into rivalry with each other.

There is left something else, as yet unmentioned, which is most harmful to our service. Some of you or your friends may cherish envy against this poor brother of yours. There are significant scholars among you. Some scholars are boastful of their knowledge. Even if they are humble in character, they cannot easily get rid of the kind of egotism caused by being knowledgeable. However devout and faithful they are in heart and intellect, their carnal selves desire the distinction of being known to be knowledgeable, to have their merits displayed. It may even be that they desire to compete with the *Risale* (Treatises), that is, though they consciously like and approve the *Risale*, the wish of their carnal selves is to see the *Risale* devalued because of the envy coming from being boastful of their knowledge, so that the products of their intelligence may find as a wide circle of readership as the *Risale* does.

I feel, at this point, compelled to inform you that, as it has become clear through numerous signs and indications, the *Risale-i Nur* have been derived directly from the Qur'an, and this poor brother of yours has been charged with finding out and pronouncing the final truth in the matters of belief. For this reason, we should assume, according to the principle of division of labour, each a different duty and offer those 'drops of the water of life' to those in need, and what falls concerning the sciences of faith to those taking part in these Qur'anic lessons, however great scholars or jurists of the highest level they are, is to explain and expound the *Words*, and to design and arrange them.

The sixth intrigue

This concerns making use of laziness, the fondness for comfort and ease, which is to be found in a man, or giving new duties to those who are really dutiful. Indeed, devils of humankind and *jinn* attack from every direction, and when they see those among our friends who are steadfast, faithful, sincere and zealous and persevering in service, they adapt their strategy. In order to interrupt our service and abate the zeal of our brothers, they choose to exploit laziness, the desire to live an easy life, which is naturally to be found in every person. They resort to such tricks in their efforts to prevent our service that they find such jobs for some of our brothers as leave them no spare time to assign to the service because of overwork, or they give them extra work. They show some brothers of ours the attractions of the world to stir up their worldly desires and aspirations so that they feel indolence in the service.

It will take a long time to note all their methods of attack. Cutting the matter short here, I refer the rest to your insight and understanding.

Dear brothers! Be alert! Your duty is sacred, and the service is exalted. Each of your hours spent in the service is as valuable as to gain for you the reward of a whole day's worship. Be aware of this so that you do not let the opportunity slip.

> *O you who believe! Be patient, and vie you in patience; be steadfast, and fear God; haply so you will prosper.*[26]
>
> *Do not sell My revelations for a trifling price.*[27]
>
> *Glorified be Your Lord, the Lord of Glory, above that they describe!*

---

26. *A. Imran*, 3.200.
27. *al-Baqara*, 2.41.

And peace be upon the Envoys; and all the praise be to God, the Lord of the Worlds!

Glory be to You; we have no knowledge save what You have taught us. Surely, You are the All-Knowing, the all-Wise.

O God, bestow blessings and peace upon our master Muhammad, the unlettered Prophet, Your beloved, most esteemed and noble, and of the highest rank; and on his family and Companions. Amen!

***

ADDENDUM TO
THE FOURTH SECTION COMPRISING THE FOURTH TREATISE

The six questions

(In order to prevent the hostility and insult that may be aimed at us in the future, I have written this addendum. That is, I have written it so that future generations should not reproach us with 'Shame on the lazy fellows of that age!', and so that we may be able to justify ourselves against this or a similar reproach.

Let it go to the ears of certain pitiless leaders of Europe disguised under the mask of humanism – let it be thrust under the blind eyes of the tyrants who have pestered us with those cruel, unjust men! What follows was written to disclose but one of the many troubles they give me to please those leaders of that 'civilization of barbarity' which gives one a hundred thousand reasons to shout, 'Long live Hell!')

In the Name of God, the Merciful, the Compassionate

Why should we not put our trust in God, seeing that He has guided us in our ways? We will surely endure patiently, however you hurt us; and in God let all put their trust who put their trust.[28]

In parallel with the increase and diversification of the attacks of heretics in recent times, such as the cruel assaults they make on the poor people of belief, they raided the little mosque which I have repaired in person to perform my own prayers in, and interfered in the *adhan* and *iqama* – the formal words recited to call Muslims to prayer and to announce the beginning of prayer respectively – while I was praying together with a few brothers. They questioned why we were reciting the *adhan* secretly in its Arabic original and saying the *iqama* in Arabic.

The patience I had to maintain silence has now been exhausted. So I am now addressing, not those unfair, unscrupulous, vile

---

28. *Ibrahim*, 14.12.

fellows from whom understanding is impossible, but the heads of that tyrannical committee which continue their arbitrary and despotic rule of this nation. O people of heresy and irreligious innovations! I demand answers to the following six questions of mine:

The first question

Every people, even cannibals and gangsters, have a certain style and constitution of government. According to what law do you make such assaults? If you have one, show it! Or, do you accept as a law the arbitrary acts of some officers? For no statutes, no laws have been legislated in regard to prayers.

The second question

On what power do you base such acts of yours as breaking and disregarding the principle of religious freedom and freedom of thought, which have been adopted by almost all nations of the world in this century of freedoms, and thereby despising mankind and their general consensus? What power do you have that, though you have adopted secularism which is supposed not to interfere with either religion or atheism, you dare to make such assaults on religion and on religious people in a way that indicates that you have adopted a fanatical irreligiousness as a religion for yourselves? Such attacks of yours will not remain secret. What kind of answer will you give when you are questioned about them? How do you venture to violate religious freedom with force in a manner that disregards the united objection of twenty states (the Western powers) while you have not the courage to resist a single objection of the least of these states on any other matter?

The third question

On the basis of what principle do you try, following the wrong judgements of some evil scholars who have sold themselves for worldly gain incompatibly with the purity and sublimity of the

Hanafi School, to impose your unlawful decisions on people, like myself, of the Shafi'i School? If you compel me to obey your decisions only after you formally outlaw the Shafi'i School and force them to become followers of the Hanafi School, then your action might be viewed having some sense, albeit the sense of the irreligious people that you are. If not, what are you doing is vile and despicable and we will never give in to it.

The fourth question

Again, according to what principle do you compel those, like myself, of a different nationality, to say in Turkish the formal words announcing the beginning of prayer, following a false judgement opposed, in essence, to religion, and in the name of your sort of Turkish nationalism which is absolutely contrary to the essential nature of the Turkish peoples who are sincerely devoted to, and deeply integrated with, Islam? Indeed, I have very friendly and brotherly relations with true Turks, but I have nothing to do with the Turkism of those who, like you, blindly imitate Western style of life. Only if you force your decisions on us after abolishing the other nationalities who have the same citizenship as Turks in this country, and who number millions of members and who have not forgotten for centuries their language and original nationality, who have fought for Islam side by side with Turks, then this could be counted as acting according to a certain style of government, albeit a style of great barbarity.

The fifth question

A government applies its laws to its subjects or the people it accepts as its subjects, but it cannot apply its laws to those to whom it refuses the right to be its subjects, who therefore oppose its laws, saying:

'Since we are not your subjects, then you are not our government.'

Also, a government does not execute two sentences of punishment concurrently. It punishes a murderer either by hanging or imprisonment, not both. These two kinds of punishment are not combined in the law of any country.

Thus, although I have done no harm to this country and nation, you have been keeping me for eight years under so strict a surveillance as would not be justifiable against the wildest criminal from the wildest of foreign peoples. You have pardoned proven criminals, but you have deprived me of every sort of freedom and denied me all my civil rights. Seeing that you do not accept me as a member of this nation, according to what law or principle do you subject me – a man foreign to you in every respect – to such despotic treatment as you deem proper for your helpless people against their consent?

You regard as a crime the personal sacrifices I made, or the self-sacrificing fighting I fought for the sake of the country, as witnessed by the army commanders in the First World War; and you consider as a treason doing one's best to preserve the good morals of this poor nation and to secure their happiness in both worlds; you have sentenced a man who does not accept the Western-style of life and dress, because it is harmful, indulgent and dangerous as it leads to unbelief, sometimes to surveillance and sometimes to imprisonment for twenty-eight years; you have forced me to serve these sentences each time in spite of my objections. Now, according to what law or principle do you double this (unjust) punishment by interfering in my prayer?

The sixth question

Since there is an over-all opposition between us concerning the difference of creed (as is implicit and explicit in your treatment of me), and since you sacrifice your religion and afterlife for the sake of your world, know that we are ready, in opposition to you, to sacrifice our world for the sake of our religion and afterlife. That will be, for us, like drinking of the water of *Kawthar* – the fountain in Paradise – to sacrifice a few years' life of subjection under your unjust and barbarous rule to attain a sacred martyrdom. However, in order to make you tremble with fear, let me say to you forcefully and depending on the enlightenment of the Wise Qur'an:

If you kill me, you will not be able to outlive me by long; rather, taken by an overwhelming hand out of the world, which for you is your beloved and paradise, you will be thrown into eternal abode of darkness. Following my martyrdom, your Nimrod-like chiefs will soon be killed and sent near me. Should they not consider that we will settle the matter in the Presence of God, and they will be cast, by Divine Justice, into the lowest pit of Hell?

O unfortunate ones, who exchange the afterlife for this world! If you would like to live, do not pester me! If you do pester me, be certain, and tremble with fear, that I will be avenged on you in a much more dreadful way, as I hope, through Divine Mercy, in that my death will serve the religion better than my life does, in that my martyrdom will explode like a bomb and eradicate you. If you have the courage for it, you can molest me! Do your worst, then see what I will do! In the face of all your threats, I recite the following verse:

Those to whom the people said: 'The people have come together against you, so fear them!'. This made them firmer in faith, and they said: 'For us God is sufficient. How good He is as the Protector and Helper!'[29]

***

---

29. *A. Imran*, 3.173.

THE FIFTH SECTION

The seven signs

In the Name of God, the Merciful, the Compassionate

Believe in God and His Messenger, the unlettered Prophet who believes in God and His Words, and follow him so that you may be guided.[30]

They will to extinguish the Light of God with their mouths, but God wills to perfect His Light even if the unbelievers be averse.[31]

(This part consists of seven signs as answers to three questions. The first question contains four signs.)

The first sign

Those who seek to change the public symbols of Islam base their attempt, as every evil action of theirs is based, on a blind imitation of the West. This is their argument:

'Those who convert to Islam in London or in the other parts of Europe, recite the *adhan* and *iqama* in their own languages, and the Muslim world does not object to them doing so. Does not this silence of the Muslim world imply a tacit approval, which must be based on an Islamic law?'

Answer

This is a most misleading analogy; indeed it is inconceivable that any intelligent person would seek to imitate Westerners on this point. For the lands where unbelievers (who are at war with Muslims) live dominantly are called the 'domain of war', and there are many things religiously permissible in the 'domain of war' which are impermissible in the Muslim world.

---

30. *al-'Araf*, 7.158.
31. *al-Tawba*, 9.32.

Second, Christianity is dominant in the West. Since the West is not an environment which normally inspires and inculcates the meaning of the Islamic terms and the content of the sacred words or phrases, the Western Muslim may feel compelled to sacrifice the original wording for the sacred meanings. But the whole environment in the Muslim world teaches the Muslim people the brief meaning of those sacred words and phrases. All the discourses about the Islamic traditions, the whole history of Islam and, above all, the symbols or signs and pillars of Islam, always and continually import the brief meaning of those sacred phrases to the people of belief. Besides the mosques and institutions of religious learning, even the gravestones and the epitaphs on them in this country remind, like a teacher, the believers of the sacred meaning of the Islamic symbols. That being so, I wonder whether anyone who calls himself a Muslim and is capable of learning fifty words of a foreign language in a single day, really deserves the name of Muslim if he fails to learn in fifty years such sacred phrases as *Subhana-llah* (Glory be to God), *al-hamdu li-llah* (All praise be to God), *la ilaha illa-llah* (there is no deity but God), and *Allahu akbar* (God is the greatest) – phrases which he repeats each day at least fifty times. For such heedless and indifferent persons, these sacred phrases are not distorted by translation and stripped off their original sacred wording. To change and distort them would mean erasing the epitaphs cut on tombstones, and invite the curse of the dead who tremble with indignation in the face of such an insult.

Evil scholars, influenced by heretics, argue in order to deceive the people: Imam A'zam Abu Hanifa is, in opposition to other Imams, of the opinion that in case of necessity, those who live at great distances from the centres of Islam are permitted to recite in prayer, in accordance with the degree of necessity, the translation of the *Fatiha* – the opening *surah* of the Qur'an – instead of its original. Therefore, we can recite its Turkish translation because we need to.

Answer

The greatest Imams of the Hanafi School and twelve other Imams who had the authority to deduce verdicts on legal matters from the Qur'an and the *Sunnah* are of the opposite opinion in this matter. The highway followed by the Muslim world for centuries is founded on the precedents of those Imams. The mighty congregation of the Muslim *Ummah* can follow only this broad highway; those who try to direct them into other strange byways seek to urge their misguidance. The great Imam, Abu Hanifa, is alone in this opinion of his; moreover his opinion is particularized in the following five points:

One: It relates to those living at great distances from the centres of Islam.

Two: It is valid only in case of absolute necessity.

Three: It relates only to the Persian language, which is, according to a Prophetic tradition, considered as one of the languages of the people of Paradise.

Four: It relates only to the *surah al-Fatiha,* and is intended for those who do not know it by heart so that they do not omit to perform the prescribed prayers.

Five: The great Imam gave this opinion because of his Islamic idealism and commitment, from his strength of faith, so that ordinary people could understand the sacred meaning of *al-Fatiha*.

By contrast, those who would like to substitute in prayer a (Turkish) translation of *al-Fatiha* for its original are acting with motives of destroying the religion of Islam, from weakness of belief, negative nationalism and hatred of the language of Arabic – in sum, their efforts aim to lead people to defect from their religious tradition.

The second sign

The heretics, who have altered the symbols of Islam, first demanded a *fatwa* – a conclusive legal verdict – from evil scholars, and then published the *fatwa*, the oddness of which we have demonstrated above. Second, they borrowed this ominous argument from Western 'revolutionaries':

'The philosophers and revolutionary intellectuals of Europe rejected Catholicism and adopted Protestantism, which could be likened to some sects of religious innovation in Islam, including chiefly the Mu'tazili School. Since Christianity was thus reformed to give birth to Protestantism, and the reformers, though branded as apostates at first, were later accepted as Christians, so too, Islam may be reformed in the same way.'

Answer

This analogy is much more misleading than the one in the First Sign. For only the doctrinal pillars of Christianity were established by Jesus through Revelation, while most of the other principles, legal, social, economic and political, were either laid down by his followers and other spiritual leaders or borrowed from the earlier Divine Books. Since Jesus, peace be upon him, was not a worldly ruler and did not therefore legislate any social laws, the legal system of Christianity is like a borrowed garment fitted on the body of its religious fundamentals. Then, if this garment is altered or changed for a newer or different one, the religion of Jesus remains, without any hint of denying the Prophethood of Jesus, upon him be peace. By contrast, since the Prophet Muhammad, the pride of the world, upon him be peace and blessings, was, besides his religious leadership, also a ruler, the king of both worlds, whose dominion extends from Spain to Philippines, he received, as well as its pillars, all the principal commandments and social, economic and political principles of the religion directly from God through Revelation. This means that the secondary principles of Islam are not like a garment alterable or changeable in a way that, when they are changed for different ones, the essence of the religion can continue to exist. Those principles are rather like the body or at least the skin of the essentials of Islam, organically moulded to each other in a way impossible to separate. Their changing, therefore, amounts to denial of the Prophet of Islam.

As for the differences between various schools or sects of Islam, these originated in the understanding of some theoretical principles laid down by the Prophet, upon him be peace and blessings. The fundamentals of the religion and its incontrovertible principles are never subject to dispute or alteration. Whoever attempts to dispute or alter them becomes an apostate and is included in the meaning of the Prophetic tradition, *They break with the religion in the same way as an arrow leaves the bow*[32].

Trying to find a pretext for their heresy, the heretics argue:

'In the great French Revolution, which caused successive convulsions in the world, priests, spiritual leaders and Catholicism were attacked, and these attacks were later approved. This is one of the factors in the progress of the West.'

Answer

This analogy too, is quite misleading, like the previous ones. For in the West in general, and in France in particular, Christianity, particularly Catholicism, had been, for centuries, in the hands of the elite and ruling classes, a means of oppression and despotism. Through it, the elite and ruling classes had sustained their dominion over the common people. Since Catholicism had also served as a means, in the hands of those classes, to crush the nationalists appearing among the common people, as well as the thinkers among the lovers of freedom who were opposed to their despotic rule, and also since it had been regarded as the cause of revolts which destroyed social life and internal peace for four centuries in the West, it was made the target of attacks not in the name of heresy and atheism, but in the name of Christianity itself. The common people and philosophers had been indignant with and resented the Catholic Church, and

---

32. Bukhari, *Anbiya'*,6; Muslim, *Zakat*, 142-144; Tirmidhi, *Fitan*, 24.

therefore the French Revolution went the way it did. By contrast, neither the common people nor thinkers have any right to complain about Islam. For Islam, far from annoying them, protects them. Its long history is an undeniable proof of this fact. Contrary to Catholicism which provoked internal conflicts and wars for long centuries, there have been no internal wars of religion in Islam except for a very few.

Further, Islam has been a shelter, a stronghold, for the common people rather than for the elite. Through the obligation of alms-giving (*zakat*) and the prohibition of interest-involving transactions, it puts the elite not over the common people, but in their service. Islam also established the principles that *the master of a people is one who serves them,*[33] and *the best of people is one who benefits them.*[34]

Also, through its many appeals in the language of the Qur'an – such as *Will you not use your reason? Will they not ponder? Will they not reflect?* – Islam calls reason to bear witness to its being true, and refers people to reason and investigation. It assigns a high position and attaches importance to the people of reasoning and knowledge. Unlike Catholicism, Islam does not reject reasoning nor seeks to silence the people of reflection; nor does it demand blind imitation.

Since there is, with respect to an important point, an essential difference between Islam and Christianity in its present form – not the original religion of Jesus – they differ from each other in many other respects also. That important point is this:

Islam, being a religion of pure monotheism, refuses means and intermediaries, and, breaking egotism, establishes sincere worship. It denounces and rejects every kind of false lordship, from that of the human carnal self to that of nature. It is for this reason that a pious man from the elite has to give up egotism. Without abandoning egotism and self-conceit, a Muslim cannot

33. al-Ajluni, *Kashf al-Khafa'*, 2.463.
34. al-Munawi, *Fayd al-Qadir*, 3.481.

prevent himself from losing the strength of his religious devotion, even from breaking with religion itself to some degree.

As for the present Christianity, since it accepts the creed of Divine sonship and begetting, it inevitably ascribes creative power to causes and means. Rather than breaking egotism in the name of religion, it sacralizes the egotism of intermediaries by regarding them as the holy representatives of Jesus, upon him be peace. For this reason, the Christian elite who occupy high worldly positions could be perfectly pious. For example, the former president of the USA, Wilson, and again the former prime minister of England, Lloyd George, were as bigoted as any priest. But the Muslim elite who attain such high worldly positions must break their egotism in order to be God-fearing pious Muslims, unlike their Christian counterparts whose piety is not in contradiction with their egotism. This is why Islam has, contrary to Christianity, not been in the hands of the elite a means for oppressing and despising the common people. Rather, in Islam, the standard of belonging to the elite or the common people is knowledge, God-fearing and piety.

Like the difference of piety between the Muslim and Christian elite, while the philosophers appearing in Christendom have, as a second difference, usually been indifferent or even hostile to Christianity, the majority of Muslim philosophers or theosophists have based their thinking on the essentials of Islam.

Also, the common people of Christianity who are afflicted or oppressed do not seek help from religion. Indeed, these used to be mostly irreligious in the past. The famous revolutionaries who brought about the French Revolution and were described as 'irreligious tramps' belonged to the disaffected middle classes. But the case is the reverse in the Muslim world. Those who are afflicted and oppressed usually apply to religion for help and consolation, and become religious. This is also another significant difference between the two religions.

The third sign

The heretics also argue: Religious fanaticism has caused our regressiveness and backwardness. A progressive life in this century is only possible through giving up fanaticism. It is after giving up religious fanaticism that Europe has developed and progressed.

Answer

You are mistaken and deceived, or misleading on purpose. For, first of all, fanaticism, being a violent and unreasoning devotion, is incompatible with Islam. However deep it is, a Muslim's devotion depends on knowledge and reasoning. Even if it is not, it cannot be described as fanaticism. For the deeper and firmer a Muslim's belief in, and devotion to, Islam, whether based on knowledge or reasoning, the further from fanaticism a Muslim is by virtue of Islam being the 'middle way' based on peace, balance, justice and moderation.

Second, fanaticism is peculiar to European Christianity, which has been fed for centuries with hatred and enmity for Islam; so much is this that if you were to tell an ordinary Bulgar or an English private or a French tramp, 'Wear a turban or else you will be thrown into jail', his fanaticism would cause him to respond, 'Even if you kill me, I will not despise my religion and nation by doing so.'

Third, as witnessed by history, whenever the Muslim people have taken firm hold of their religion, they have made considerable progress, and whenever they have shown negligence in their devotion, they have declined. The case is, however, the reverse with Christianity. This also comes from a significant, essential difference between the two religions.

Fourth, Islam cannot be compared with other religions. If a Muslim gives up his religion, he can no longer believe in any of the other Prophets. He can neither admit God's Existence and recognize anything sacred. Since he does not find any point in his soul to be a means for human perfection, he is corrupted or goes bad like butter, and becomes an anarchist. It is for this reason that in Islam a non-Muslim enemy has the right to live: if he is from a foreign country in peace with the Muslim country or if he lives in the Muslim country and pays his tax of protection, his life is under the guarantee of the Muslim government. Whereas Islam refuses an apostate the right to live. For he is inwardly corrupt and like a poison for the Islamic collective life. But a Christian who gives up his religion can remain to be a beneficial element for Christian collective life. He may still recognize some sacred things, have belief in some of the Prophets and confirm, in some respect, the Existence of God.

Now, I wonder what kind of use those people of heresy find in the denial of religion. If they consider government and public security, the administration of ten irreligious tramps is much more difficult than that of a thousand religious men. If they are anxious for progress, irreligious people of such kind are, in addition to being harmful to the government, also obstacles to progress: they destroy public order and security which is indispensable to trade and progress. They follow, in fact, a socially destructive way. So, it is the greatest stupidity to expect from such irreligious vagabonds progress and happiness in life. One of those occupying a high position has unfortunately displayed so much stupidity as to say: 'Our belief in, and reliance on, God has caused us to decline; Europe has developed by means of technology and weaponry.'

According to the principle, *The best answer to give to an idiot question is keeping silent,* I should keep silent in the face of such absurdities, but since there are some reasonable people who should be warned against such absurdities, let me say:

O poor fellows! This world is a guest-house. Hundreds of thousands of those dying every day confirm and testify that *death is a reality.* Can you destroy death and contradict those testimonies? Since you cannot do it, then death calls you to believe in and rely on God. In place of God, what technology or weaponry can illuminate the eternal darkness before him who is in the throes of death, and change his despair into hope? Since death is inevitable and the grave is awaiting us, and this transient life is giving way to the permanent life, then we should mention God a thousand times where we mention technology and weaponry once. Besides, when used in the way of God, both technology and weaponry lead to God; they operate and cease in the name of God.

The fourth sign

The destructive heretics are of two groups. The first group pretend to be on the side of religion and faithful to Islam, and on the pretext of reinforcing the religion with nationalism, they say: 'We want to implant in the soil of nationalism the illustrious tree of religion, which has been weakened, and thereby strengthen it.'

The second group introduce, in order to promote racism in the name of nationalism, innovations into the religion on the pretext of 'grafting nationalism into Islam.'

I would like to say to the first group:

'The illustrious tree of Islam, which is deeply established in the truth of the creation and has sent out roots through the truths of the universe, is not to be implanted in the dark, barren, arid, unstable, and easily scattered, dust-like soil of racism. It is heretical, destructive and unreasonable to try to implant that tree in that soil.'

I say to the second group:

'O insensible ones pretending to nationalism! The previous century was perhaps the century of nationalism. But in this century, nations and countries are coming together to form strong blocks, and feel the need to form unions. Bolshevism and socialism invalidate the idea of racial separatism. Besides, such trends as nationalism or racism and the like are temporary; like a strong wind, they came, sweep over the earth and pass away. Therefore, the Islamic nationality, which is enduring and eternal, cannot be grafted on racism. If you attempt to graft them onto each other, it will only bring about the corruption of Islam and the destruction of racism. Although it may at first gives a temporary pleasure, it will endure too briefly and end in a catastrophe.

Separatist movements may lead in this country to internal conflicts almost impossible to heal. Since, in this case, the sides will break each other's power, the overall strength of the nation will be utterly exhausted. And this will cause this nation to be easily manipulated by any foreign power – just a small stone of force can manipulate two mountains of the same weight if they are put on the scales of a balance.

The fifth sign

This is a very brief answer to an important question.

Question

There are various authentic traditions that a man called the Mahdi will come towards the end of time and reform the world after its corruption. However, this is the time of communities, not individuals. However able and intelligent, having the capacity of a hundred geniuses, an individual may be, without the support or representation of the collective body of a community, he is liable to be defeated by the collective body of the opposing community. So, how can a single man, however strong his sainthood is, reform the world corrupted to such extent by the whole of mankind? If every act of his were to be miraculous, then this is contrary to the Divine Wisdom and laws operating in the world. So, what is the truth of this matter of the Mahdi?

Answer

Each time the Muslim community has drifted into corruption,

God Almighty has sent, out of His perfect Compassion and as a sign of His protection of the Islamic Shari'a until eternity, a reformer or a reviver, a noble caliph or a great saint called *qutb* (pole) or a perfect spiritual guide, and removed the corruption, and preserved the religion of Islam. Since this is the way God acts in this respect, He is certainly able to reform the world in the time of the greatest corruption by means of an illustrious person who will combine in his personality the functions of a greatest jurist, a greatest reviver, a greatest ruler and a greatest spiritual and intellectual guide, and this person will be among the descendants of the Prophet's family, upon him be peace and blessings. As God Almighty fills in a minute the space between the heaven and the earth with clouds and then clears it of them, or calms down a raging sea in a moment, or as He shows in spring an hour of summer weather, and causes an hour of winter-storm to blow in summer, so He can remove through the Mahdi, the darkness over the Muslim world. This is very easy from the viewpoint of the Divine Power. When considered from the viewpoint of causality and Divine Wisdom, it is so inevitable that had it not been related from the Truthful Reporter, upon him be peace and blessings, it must happen as he said it would, and certainly it will happen. This is what the people of reflection are certain to judge because the supplication made by the whole Muslim community five times a day in the prescribed prayers,

> *O God, bestow blessing on our master Muhammad and on the family of our master Muhammad as you bestowed it on Abraham and on the family of Abraham among the whole creation! Surely, You are Most Praiseworthy, Most Glorious.*

has, praise be to God, evidently been accepted. The family of Muhammad, upon him be peace and blessings, have become like the family of Abraham, upon him be peace, and lead all the blessed chains of saints and preside over all the assemblies of spiritual commanders and guides in every part of the world in every century.[35] They are so numerous that those guides and commanders in total make up a mighty army. If they form a certain division through solidarity and make the religion of Islam, in the form of a sacred nationality, a means of awakening and a bond of unity, the army of no nation can resist them. That mighty and irresistible army is the descendants of the Prophet's family and is the core of the army of the Mahdi.

In world history, there is no other lineage, except that of the descendants of the Prophet's family, continuously linked to each other through uninterrupted descent, and distinguished with personal merits and ancestral nobility, or stronger or more important than them. They have included, since the beginning, all the groups of the people of truth and perfection. At present, with millions of members, they are a blessed people, awake and aware, whose hearts are full of belief and love for the Prophet, and elevated and ennobled by priceless honour of attachment to him. Events are taking place in the world to excite and stir up the sacred force in this mighty community. Certainly, this force will burst with a sublime zeal and the Mahdi will direct them to the way of truth. This is our expectation from Divine Laws and Mercy, just as we expect the coming of spring after winter, and we are right in this expectation.

The sixth sign

The illustrious community of the Mahdi will reform the destructive and heretical regime of the committee of the Sufyan – the Anti-Christ to appear in the Muslim world – and revive the Prophetic way of belief, life and government. That is, the committee of the Sufyan, who appear in the Muslim world to destroy the Islamic way of life in denial of the Messengership and

---

28. Among them, Sayyid Ahmad Sunusi commands millions of disciples. Sayyid Idrıs and Sayyid Yahya each has hundreds of thousands of followers. There are many such heroes among the descendants of the Prophet's family, and still greater ones, among them, like Sayyid 'Abd al-Qadir al-Jilani, Sayyid Abu'l-Hasan al-Shazali and Sayyid Ahmad al-Badawi.

leadership of the Prophet Muhammad, upon him be peace and blessings, will be defeated and eradicated by the miraculous, spiritual sword of the community of the Mahdi.

Also, another devoted, self-sacrificing Muslim community which may be called the Muslim followers of Jesus, trying to unite the original religion of the Prophet Jesus with the truth of Islam, will defeat and eradicate the committee of the Anti-Christ *(Dajjal)* who have, in denial of God, corrupted human civilization and violated all the sacred things of mankind, and deliver mankind from atheism.

The seventh sign

They ask me: 'Your defence of Islam, or your struggle for its sake, did not use to be in the way it is now. In addition, you do not follow the way of those thinkers defending Islam against Europe. Why did you change the way of Old Said, and why do you not follow the way of other defenders of Islam?'

Answer

Thinkers accept, as Old Said did, to some degree, the principles of human philosophy and the Western way of thinking, and depend on them in their struggle against Europe. Since they admit some of those principles beforehand, as if they were the established principles of science, they do not succeed in demonstrating the true value of Islam. By grafting the shoots of philosophy, which they suppose deep-rooted, on the trunk of Islam, they imagine that they strengthen Islam. I gave up this way since it is very difficult and an improbable way to overcome the anti-Islamic trends, and since it means degrading Islam to some extent. I have actually demonstrated that the essentials of Islam are too deep for the principles of philosophy to reach. This truth has been decisively proved in the *Thirtieth Word*, *Twenty-fourth Letter* and the *Twenty-ninth Word*. By contrast, those thinkers following the same way as that of Old Said, imagining human philosophy to be deep and the pillars of Islam to be shallow, think that they can preserve those pillars by making them firm through the principles of philosophy. But those principles can by no means reach the level of either the fundamental or even the secondary principles of Islam.

Glory be to You, we have no knowledge save what You have taught us. Surely You are the All-Knowing, the All-Wise.

All praise be to God, Who guided us to this; if God had not guided us, we had surely never been guided. Indeed, our Lord's Messengers came with the truth.

O God, bestow blessings upon our master Muhammad and upon the family of our master Muhammad, as You bestowed blessings upon our master Abraham and upon the family of Abraham among the creation. You are Most Praise-worthy, most Glorious.

***

THE SIXTH SECTION

The nine clarifications

In the name of God, the Merciful, the Compassionate

*Surely God's friends – no fear shall be on them, neither shall they grieve.*36

(This section comprises nine clarifications about the ways of attaining to the rank of being God's friend or sainthood.)

The first clarification

There is a lovely, light-giving and spiritual truth variously called Sufism, *tariqa* (spiritual order or way), sainthood or being God's friend, initiation, following a spiritual order or way. The truth-seeking scholars among the people of spiritual pleasure and discovery have so far written thousands of volumes to describe and explain this sacred truth and taught it to the Muslim community. May God reward them with much good! All that I will attempt to do here, therefore, is to show, in accordance with the present context, a few drops out of that ocean of information.

Question

What is *tariqa?*

Answer

Tariqa is the name of the spiritual way by which a man initiated into it seeks to acquire knowledge of God and attain full perception of the truths of belief, and by which he is elevated, at the end of his spiritual journeying, under the auspices of the Prophet's Ascension, to the rank of the perfect man.

---

36. *Yunus*, 10.62.

Since man is an all-comprehensive index of the whole universe, his heart is like an immaterial map of thousands of worlds. As the mind of man is, as shown by sciences, like a centre of telecommunications, a sort of immaterial centre of the universe, so his heart is, as explained in many enlightening books written by countless men of sainthood, the receiver of innumerable universal truths, as well as being their source or seed.

Since, then, the mind and heart of man are of such a nature – a seed in which are encapsulated the members of a huge tree and the wheels and other parts of an eternal and splendid machine – the Creator of this heart, Who made it so, willed that it should operate and flourish by putting its potentials into practice. Since He willed it to be so, the heart will, like the intellect, work, and the most practical and important means to make it work is repeating different Names of God in the gradations toward sainthood and seeking to attain the truths of belief alongwith the spiritual journeying.

The second clarification

The two keys to, or means of, this spiritual journeying or movement, are repeating God's Names and meditation or reflection. The benefits of this repetition and meditation are too many to count. Apart from the benefits for one's afterlife and for the attainment of human perfections, just one of their benefits concerning this tumultuous worldly life is as follows:

Every person seeks some consolation or pleasure for relief amidst the turbulence and burdensome responsibilities of life; seeks some intimacy to relieve the solitude and gloom around him. Modern social gatherings can give to one or two out of ten persons the means of relief and satisfy the need for a friendly atmosphere, but only in a heedless and intoxicating way.

Eighty per cent of people lack true consolation and relief;

they are also devoid of the relief possible through the sort of social gatherings mentioned, either because of modern attitudes and life-style or because of the struggle to make a living or because of other factors such as illness, afflictions and old age which lead them to turn their thoughts more to the other world than to this one.

Those people can find a true consolation and contentment, and a faithful friendship, by making their hearts work through meditation and remembrance of God, by repeating His Names and, turning to their inner selves for intimacy, by coming to understand that everywhere is full of God's creatures, visible or invisible, so that they are not alone wherever they may be. Belief in, and remembrance of, God lead them to make friends with every creature and to live a pleasant, contented life. Besides, the feeling that they are always in the company of God, their Creator and Provider, gives them the greatest of pleasures and removes all the gloom and solitude, leading them to be thankful to God.

The third clarification

Sainthood is a proof for Divine Messengership and the way or spiritual order *(tariqa)* is evidence for the Shari'a. For a saint experiences with certainty of seeing the truths of belief communicated by the Messenger and confirms them through the witnessing of his heart and the spiritual pleasure he derives. Such confirmation is a decisive proof for the truth of Divine Messengership.

A member of a spiritual order is convinced through the pleasure and enlightenment he gets and the ability of spiritual discovery he acquires, that the commandments and principles of the Shari'a which he is instructed in and follows in his daily life are of wholly Divine origin and undeniably true. As sainthood and *tariqa* are thus proofs for the truth of Messengership

273

and the Shari'a, they are also an expression of the perfection of Islam and a source of its light, and a means for mankind to make progress and a source to get enlightenment by virtue of attachment to Islam.

Despite the considerable significance of this great truth, some deviant sects have gone so far as to deny it. Being themselves deprived of the lights of *tariqa,* they have also led some others to be deprived of them also. It is most unfortunate that certain scholars of superficial knowledge among the *Ahl al-Sunnah wa'l-Jama'ah,* and some heedless of politicians, using as an excuse some abuses and mistakes witnessed in the conduct of some members of *tariqas,* are trying to close down or even destroy this great treasury, to dry up this pure source of the water of life. It is, however, a fact that there can hardly be found in the world any way, order or system without faults, so that if incompetent and unqualified people are admitted into a job or an order, they will certainly be the cause of some abuses. But God Almighty will show in the Hereafter the justice of His Lordship in calling people to account for their deeds by weighing the good and evil deeds against each other. That is, if one's good deeds weigh more, God Almighty will reward him; if otherwise, He will punish him. Further, the balancing of the good and evil deeds will be not according to their number but according to their quality. It may happen that a single good deed will outweigh a thousand evil ones and cause them to be forgiven. Since Divine Justice decides this way and truth judges so, then a *tariqa* should not be condemned because of some abuses by some few of its members. For the good of *tariqa* or following a spiritual way according to the *Sunnah* of the Prophet, upon him be peace and blessings, is always greater than its evils. A most decisive proof of this is that the people of *tariqa* preserve their faith at the most critical times when the people of misguidance attack all the religious values. A sincere ordinary member of *tariqa* preserves, through the spiritual pleasure he gets in *tariqa* and his love for saints, his faith more than a man of superficial scientific knowledge. He may be a transgressor on account of committing some major sins, yet he never deviates to unbelief, nor does he join the heretics. No power in the world can cause him to refute a chain of spiritual guides whom he accepts with a strong love and firm conviction as the spiritual poles of the world. Since he cannot made to refute them, he does not lose his trust in them; and since he does not lose his trust in them, he does not join the party of heresy. It is, however, difficult for a man, however great a truth-seeking scholar he may be, to save himself against the intrigues of the modern people of heresy, if he has no connection with *tariqa* and his heart is inoperative.

There is another point to mention, namely that the *tariqa* is not to be condemned because of the evils of some orders which wrongly call themselves a *tariqa*, or of some schools which have broken with the circle of piety and even of Islam. Apart from its very significant fruits, religious and spiritual and pertaining to the Hereafter, *tariqa* has always exerted a foremost influence for the development and flourishing of brotherhood, the sacred bond in the Muslim world, as well as being one of the three most important and firm strongholds of Islam against the formidable attacks of the world of unbelief and Christian politics aimed to extinguish its light. The power which protected Istanbul, the centre of Caliphate, for five hundred years against a large world of Christianity, lies in the lights of monotheism which diffused from five hundred places in Istanbul and, as a point of support for believers in that centre of Islam, in the strength of belief of those invoking 'God, God!', in the dervish lodges behind mosques, and their going into raptures with the spiritual pleasure coming from knowledge of God.

So, O senseless ones who claim national zeal,who pretend to Turkish nationalism! Tell me what evils *tariqa* has that you can ignore all of its benefits for the social life of this nation!

The fourth clarification

The way of sainthood is both very easy and, paradoxically, very difficult; is very short and, at the same time, very long; very precious and desirable, yet quite risky; it is a broad way, but also, sometimes, very narrow.

It is on account of such paradoxical aspects of it that those who follow this road sometimes drown and are sometimes lost. Times even come when some turn back and cause others to deviate.

To summarize, there are two ways of travelling in *tariqa*, one is *travelling in the inner world*, the other, *travelling in the outer world*.

The traveller in the inner world begins from the carnal self and, without ever stretching towards the outer world, heads straight for the heart. He penetrates through egotism and self-conceit and, by making a way through the heart, reaches the truth. After the completion of his travel in the inner world, he sets off in the outer world, where he finishes his travel in a short period. He witnesses also in this world the truth he has seen in the inner.

Most of the spiritual orders that have adopted loud invocation of God's Names follow this way of spiritual travel. What is demanded of travellers in this way is breaking egotism and self-conceit, abandoning whims and fancies, and destroying the carnal self.

The traveller in the other way starts from the outer world and, after having observed the reflections of God's Names and Attributes in all the objects of this vast world, enters the inner world. In his heart, he witnesses to some extent the same lights that he has observed in the outer world and makes his quickest way into the heart. When he finally perceives that the heart is the mirror of God, the Eternally-Besought-of-All, he has attained his goal.

Thus, if those who go in the first way do not succeed in destroying their carnal selves, in abandoning whims and fancies and breaking egotism and self-conceit, they fall from the rank of thanksgiving to the point of self-pride, and therefrom to vanity. If, besides, they are in ecstasy because of Divine love, and in a spiritually intoxicated state because of feeling attracted by God, they make very excessive, exaggerated claims called *shathiyat*, like disregarding God's threats and chastisement or belittling Paradise, or seeing their own rank as above everybody else's, thus bringing harm both to themselves and others.

For example, a lieutenant who is boastful of his rank of command, and enraptured with the pleasure it gives, may see himself as if a marshal. He confuses his small sphere of command with the larger one of the marshal. Likewise, the reflection of the sun in a little mirror may, on account of its being a reflection of the sun, sometimes be regarded as the same as the magnificent reflection of the sun on the surface of a sea. So, there are many people of sainthood who, though like a fly in comparison with a peacock, regard and even see themselves as superior to those much greater than themselves. I once even witnessed that an initiate who was awakened to some truths and felt the mystery of sainthood obtained by himself to a slight degree, considered himself as, and assumed the attitude of, the greatest spiritual pole of the world. I said to him:

'Brother! As a king has, through laws and on account of rulership, relations with, and authority over, all the members of the state from the prime minister down to a strict governor, because of which every officer feels connected to him, so the rank of a spiritual pole has different manifestations or reflections in countless ranks of sainthood. Each rank has also many forms of manifestations. You see the greatest rank of a spiritual pole, which may be likened to that of a prime minister in a state, reflected in your rank, like that of a strict governor, and are thereby deceived. What you see may be true, but your judgement is wrong. For a fly, a bowl of water is like a small sea.'

That person came, by God's Will, to his senses and escaped a great danger.

I have also encountered several persons who know themselves as of the kind of the Mahdi, and claim that they will be the greatest Mahdi promised for the period near the end of time. They are not liars, nor deceivers, but are deluded in so far as they regard their vision as the ultimate truth. As there are as many degrees of the manifestation of the Divine Names as the number of the objects in the universe, material or immaterial, from the Greatest Throne of God down to a minute particle on earth, and the objects receiving this manifestation are in as different degrees as their number, so the ranks of sainthood are of the same variety. What causes deception or confusion in this matter is this:

Some ranks of sainthood have a particular connection with the function of the Mahdi and are somehow related to the greatest Spiritual Pole and even to Khadr. Likewise, there are some other ranks related to some famous saints and thereby called, for example, the rank of Khadr, the rank of Uways, and the rank of the Mahdi.

It is for this reason that those who receive a few manifestations of any of those ranks think themselves to be the owner of that rank, regarding themselves as Khadr himself, or the Mahdi or the greatest Spiritual Pole of the time. If those persons have broken their egotism and do not pursue any spiritual position, they are not to be condemned for such assertions, and their excessive claims are to be counted as *shathiyat*. If, by contrast, they seek a spiritual position to satisfy their self-conceit and therefore turn from being thankful to God to self-pride, they will ultimately lapse into vanity and deviate from the truth. For they begin to regard the greater saints as of the same degree and character as themselves and, since a soul, however self-conceited it may be, is aware of its faults, their good opinion of those saints turns into imagining them to be faulty like themselves. They may even go so far that their respect for the Prophets may diminish.

Those who are captivated by such state should judge according to the rules of the Shari'a, and follow the guiding principles laid down by the scholars of religious methodology and the instructions of the saints of meticulous research and truth-seeking such as Imam Ghazali and Imam Rabbani. Also, they should always reproach their carnal selves, ascribing to them nothing but defects, helplessness and poverty. The excessive and exaggerated claims of those in such a state originate from self-love. For love prevents the lover from discerning the defects of the beloved. Therefore, because of self-love, they imagine their carnal souls or selfhood – as valueless and insignificant as glass – to be as precious and brilliant as diamond.

A most grievous mistake likely to be made by those in this state is that they imagine the meanings inspired to them to be 'words of God' and therefore call them revealed verses. However, this causes them to belittle the most sacred and exalted rank of Divine Revelation. Indeed, all the inspirations from those of the honey-bee and other animals to those of human beings, including the common and the distinguished among them, are each a word of God. However, the Speech of God comes through seventy thousand veils according to the capacity of each receiver, and therefore has innumerable kinds of manifestation and degrees of reception. Because of this, it is absolutely wrong to call those inspirations 'revealed verses', as the revealed verse is the proper name given to each light-diffusing sentence of the Qur'an, which is the most evident and illustrious embodiment, and the proper name of the Divine Word and Revelation. As explained and proved in the *Twelfth*, *Twenty-fifth* and *Thirty-first Words*, what occurs in the hearts of those people are, compared to the sun of the Qur'an, which is the direct Word of God, like the shadowy and obscure reflections of the sun in the coloured mirror in your hand, when compared to the sun itself. Al-though the reflections in each mirror are rightly attributed to the sun and do have some relation with it, the earth will never gravitate to those mirrors nor revolve around them.

The fifth clarification

Among the important schools of *tariqa*, the school of 'the Unity of Being', which almost denies the essential existence of the universe in the name of the Necessarily-Existent Being, goes so far as to regard the apparently existing creatures as imagined mirrors reflecting the manifestations of the Divine Names.

There is, however, an important truth which provides a basis for this school, that the existence of contingent beings becomes, due to the strength of his belief in, and the firmness of his conviction of, the existence of the Necessarily-Existent Being, so insignificant in the sight of a saint of a very high rank and ecstasies, that he denies in the name of God, the existence of all creatures, which seem to him as no more than mere illusions.

Nevertheless, there are risks in this school, the foremost of which is this:

The fundamentals of belief are six. Belief in God is only one of these fundamentals; a Muslim also believes in the Day of Judgement, the Angels, the Prophets, the Divine Scriptures and Divine Destiny, each of which requires the actual existence of contingencies. These fundamentals of faith are substantial and therefore cannot be based on illusions or imaginations. For this reason, a saint belonging to this school should not act according to the requirements of his school when he turns back to the world of realities from the state of spiritual intoxication. Being based on the experiences of the heart and on spiritual pleasures and ecstasies, this school should not be regarded as rational or scientific, and those experiences and pleasures should not be put into words in this world of realities. For this school is not in accordance with the intellectual principles, the scientific laws and theological rules coming from the Qur'an and the *Sunnah*. Because of this, neither the Four Rightly-Guided Caliphs, nor the greatest jurists, nor the righteous scholars of the first centuries of Islam are reported to have made any reference to, or suggestion of, this school. So, this is not the most exalted of the schools of *tariqa*; although considerably exalted, it has defects: important but risky; difficult but very pleasant. Those who enter it on account of the pleasures it gives, do not like to leave it but, because of haughtiness, they suppose it to be of the highest rank. Referring the reader, concerning its real nature and essentials, to certain other *Words* and *Letters*, I would like to explain here an important risk of this school, namely:

The way of this school (the Unity of Being it envisions) is sound, based on direct experience in the state of absolute spiritual intoxication by the most distinguished of saints who, going beyond the sphere of causality, renounce all else besides God and have nothing left to do with contingencies. But to offer it as a way to those who are immersed in causality and fond of this world, and cling to the material and natural philosophy, would be to drown them in the swamp of matter and nature and deviate them from the truth of Islam. For the one who loves the world and is enveloped within causality, wishes to give a kind of permanence to this world of transience. Unwilling to renounce his beloved (the world), he fancies for it, by way of the Unity of Being, unimagined eternity, going so far as – God forbid! – to deny God in the name of the world.

Materialism is so widespread in this century that some people ascribe everything to matter. Now the people of belief may assert, in such a century, the Unity of Being in order to deny matter and material existence because of its insignificance. It is, therefore, highly probable that materialists may adopt the concept, on behalf of matter, in the form of monism or naturalism or pantheism – though the school furthest removed from materialism, naturalism, monism and pantheism is the school of the Unity of Being. Whereas, the followers of this school are so deeply absorbed in the Divine Existence through strength of belief, that on Its behalf, they deny the essential existence of the universe, materialists attribute existence exclusively to matter and deny God in the name of the universe. How far, then, are the latter from the former!

The sixth clarification

There are three points to be made here.

The first point

The most beautiful, the straightest and brightest of the ways of sainthood is following the Example – the *Sunnah*– of the Prophet, upon him be peace and blessings, in all one's deeds and transactions, and obeying the commandments of the Shari'a.

It is because of this following and obeying that even one's ordinary deeds and actions and natural movements become a form of worship, and, reminds him of the *Sunnah* and Shari'a. The remembrance of the *Sunnah* and Shari'a causes one to think of the Prophet, which calls, in turn, God Almighty to mind. This remembrance gives a kind of peace and contentment. The minutes of life can thus be counted as being spent in continuous worship. Being the broadest highway, this way is the way of the Companions and their righteous followers, who truly represented the succession to the Prophetic mission, which is the greatest sainthood.

The second point

The most important basis of the ways of sainthood and the schools of *tariqa* is sincerity or purity of intention. For one is saved through sincerity from the implicit forms of associating partners with God. Whoever has not been able to acquire sincerity cannot travel in those ways. And, the most direct means, the most effective and penetrating power in those ways is love.

A lover does not try to find faults with his beloved and becomes blind to his or her defects; rather, even the weak indications of his beloved's perfection are decisive proofs in the sight of the lover. He always sides with his beloved.

That is why those who have directed themselves to knowledge of God through love, do not give ear to objections and doubts. Even if thousands of devils come together, they cannot invalidate in their sight even the least indication to the perfection of their True Beloved (God). But for this love, they would have to strive against the resistance of their carnal selves, against their personal and external devils. In order to save themselves, they must resist heroically, with firmness, strong faith, and careful vision and discernment.

Because of this, love of God originating in knowledge of God is the most important 'ferment' in all the steps to sainthood, which changes an initiate and elevates him to higher ranks, and the remedy that cures all spiritual illnesses. There is, however, a risk in the way of love, namely that the lover may turn from complete modesty, from being a supplicant before God, to putting on airs and graces and behaving affectedly to show himself as valued and worthy of God's love, and he therein transgresses the measure. When he is inclined in love to another being than God, he may love him on his account, that is, for his personal perfections and spiritual grace, not on account of God or his being a mirror of God's Names. This sort of love becomes, for the lover, a poison not a remedy to cure his spiritual illnesses. The love for other beings than God, however perfect and great they may be, which is not in the name of God and His Prophet, will become a veil before love of God, not a means for it. If, by contrast, that love is cherished on account of, or in the name of, God, then it leads the lover to the love of God, and his love becomes a manifestation of Divine love.

The third point

This world is the abode of wisdom and service, not the abode of wages and reward. Everything in this world happens in accordance with God's Wisdom, and people will be rewarded in the Hereafter in return for the good deeds they do and the services they render in this world. That being so, the fruits of good deeds done for the good pleasure of God should not be sought in this world; if they are given, they should be accepted not with delight, but with sorrow. For it is not reasonable to use up here in this world the fruits which will be replaced in Paradise immediately with new ones each time they are eaten. It is like exchanging a lamp giving permanent light for one which is extinguished in a minute.

It is for this reason that men of sainthood warmly welcome hardships, misfortunes, troubles and services, not complainingly. They always say: 'Praise be to God in all circumstances and conditions.'

If they are endowed with the capacity of spiritual discovery and working wonders, and given spiritual pleasures and lights, they accept them as Divine favours and try to conceal them. Never proud of them, they increase their thanksgiving and worship in return for them. Many saints have even requested God to take those favours back so that their sincerity and purity of intention will not be adulterated. Indeed, a most significant Divine kindness or favour for a man approved by God is that God does not make him feel His favours for him, so that he should not turn from being in the state of supplication and thankfulness to God to self-pride and putting on airs and graces and behaving affectedly.

Because of this, if those who seek sainthood by *tariqa* pursue spiritual pleasures and the capacity of working wonders, which are among the insignificant fruits of sainthood, and, when given, welcome these with pleasure, it will lead them – besides eating up here in this world the permanent fruits of Paradise – to lose purity of intention and finally sainthood itself.

The seventh clarification

Four subtleties are reflected upon here:

The first subtlety

The Shari'a, that is, the collection of Divine religious principles, commandments and prohibitions, is the result of the Divine address directly to man through the Prophet, from the point of His absolute Oneness and Lordship. Therefore, even the most important rules of *tariqa* are included in the Shari'a, and the ranks attained through *tariqa*, however high they may be, can never be counted as having been attained outside the Shari'a. All the types of *tariqa* being means and steps to reach the truths of the Shari'a, the results obtained through *tariqa* are included in the confirmations of the Shari'a. Unlike the misconceptions of some people of Sufism, the Shari'a is not a mere outer covering, and *tariqa* the inner part and *haqiqa* (the truth) the kernel or essence. The Shari'a flourishes in different degrees according to the different levels of people; that is, for every level there is a corresponding degree of understanding and practising the Shari'a. The higher or deeper, the better or more developed a man is in understanding, practising and tasting the Shari'a, the better and deeper, the more high-ranking a Muslim he is. For this reason, it is wrong to think of the understanding and practise of the common people as the Shari'a, and to name the level of the Shari'a practised by men of sainthood *tariqa* and *haqiqa*. *Tariqa* is, in essence, the name of a discipline or technique to practise the Shari'a in a better way, and the Shari'a has numerous different degrees of understanding and practise according to the different levels of people.

It is for this reason that the more advanced in *tariqa* the Sufis are, the more devoted, attached and obedient to the Shari'a they are. They regard even a most insignificant commandment of the Prophet as something absolutely to be obeyed, and perform it with utmost care. For the rules of the Shari'a concerning good manners, which are the fruits of Divine Revelation, are higher in rank and more important than the good manners taught in *tariqa*, which are the products of inspiration, as Revelation is higher in comparison with inspiration. For this reason, the most important fundamental of *tariqa* is to follow the exalted *Sunnah* of the Prophet, upon him be peace and blessings.

The second subtlety

Tariqa should always be regarded as a means and never be accorded more attention or importance than is accorded to a means. If *tariqa* is taken as the aim or end in itself, then the commandments of the Shari'a and principles of the *Sunnah* are reduced to mere ceremonies for outward performance, with the heart turned directly toward *tariqa*. That is, a man of *tariqa* attaches more importance to recitation of God's Names in the circle of dervishes than to performing the daily prescribed prayers; he concentrates more on his daily supererogatory recitations than on his religious obligations, he refrains more from any opposition to the good manners taught by *tariqa* than he does from the major sins. Whereas the truth is that not even one of the religious obligations, which are among the established commandments of the Shari'a, can be compensated for by all of the the daily supererogatory recitations of *tariqa*. Therefore, those recitations and the good manners required by *tariqa* should be taken as a means of consolation for not being able to derive the true pleasure from the religious obligations, not as the real source of that pleasure. In other words, his recitations and his observance of manners in his lodge should be a means for the pleasure and exact performance of his prescribed prayer in mosque. If one who, by contrast, performs the prescribed prayer in mosque in the manner of carrying out a formality in order, thereafter, to run to his lodge as soon as possible to get the true pleasure and attain spiritual perfection, is in a grave loss and deviates from the truth.

The third subtlety

Is *tariqa* possible outside the sphere of the *Sunnah* and the commandments of the Shari'a?

Answer

It is both possible and impossible. It is possible, for some perfect saints have been executed with the sword of the Shari'a. It is impossible, for the truth-seeking scholars of sainthood are all agreed on the principle, as expressed by Sa'di al-Shir'azi:

> *Sa'di, it is inconceivable for one who does not follow the way of Muhammad to find the lights of the truth.*

This is true because God's noble Messenger, upon him be peace and blessings, is the Seal of the Prophets and the addressee of God on behalf of all mankind: therefore, mankind cannot follow another path than the broad highway of his and therefore should come under his flag. On the other hand, since people in trance or ecstasy or spiritual absorption are not counted as responsible for any acts of theirs contrary to the Shari'a, and since a man is not asked to account for his opposition to the religious commandments when he is under the influence of senses or faculties which can neither be controlled by will-power and reason nor be made to take on any responsibility, then when an ecstatic saint is under the influence of such circumstances or such spiritual or mental states, he does not lose sainthood. Of course, such a man should not openly deny, condemn or debase the rules of belief and the truths of the Shari'a. Even if he does not do the prescribed acts, he should admit their truth. Otherwise, if, overcome by that state of trance, he acts in a way to suggest – God forbid! – any denial or contradiction of the established truths of belief and the Shari'a, this is a sign of falling off and deviation.

In short: The people of *tariqa* outside the sphere of the Shari'a fall into two categories.

The first category consists of those who, overcome, as mentioned before, by trance or ecstasy, or spiritual absorption and intoxication, or under the influence of senses or faculties uncontrollable by reason and will-power, leave the sphere of the Shari'a. This leaving occurs unintentionally, not because they do not approve the commandments of the Shari'a. There have been, among that group, men of sainthood, even some significant saints, whom the truth-seeking scholars of sainthood, having been with them temporarily, have judged to be outside the sphere not only of the Shari'a but also of Islam. The condition for the preservation of their sainthood is that they do not intentionally deny or contradict any of the commandments conveyed by the Prophet Muhammad, upon him be peace and blessings, and any neglect of such commandments comes from their ignorance or spiritual intoxication, trance and ecstasy.

The second category comprises those who, fascinated by the splendid pleasures of *tariqa*, esteem the truths of the Shari'a as tasteless, as mere ceremonies, since they are unable to perceive their taste, and become indifferent to them. They go so far as to think of the Shari'a as only a superficial covering and are content with what they have found in *tariqa* considering that as the real object of their efforts, and they act in contradiction to the commandments of the Shari'a. Those who are 'sober' among this group are held responsible for their un-Islamic actions; they are reduced to the lowest rank and even become the object of ridicule by Satan.

The fourth subtlety

Some persons among the people, or belonging to the sects, of deviation are approved by the *Ummah*, while some others who are apparently of the same standing are rejected. For example, so radical a Mu'tazili as Zamakhshari is not judged to be a heretic or unbeliever by the meticulous scholars of the *Ahl al-Sunnah*, while the Mu'tazili leaders such as Abu 'Ali Jubba'i are rejected and refuted although they are much less severe in their opposition to the *Ahl al-Sunnah wa'l-Jama'ah*. This perplexed me for a long time. Finally, I came to understand, by God's grace, that the objections of Zamakhshari to *Ahl al-Sunnah* were due to his love of and, devotion to, truth. That is, he sided with the views of the Mu'tazili School since he, for example, thought that God could be held free from all defects by attributing to animate beings themselves the function of creating or giving external existence to their acts. Because of the importance he attached to, and the efforts he expended to affirm, the exemption of God from every defect, he did not accept the principle of the *Ahl al-Sunnah* concerning the creation of the acts of animate beings. As for the other Mu'tazili leaders rejected by the *Ahl al-Sunnah*, they opposed the *Ahl al-Sunnah*, not because they sought the truth sincerely, but because they were unable to perceive the exalted principles of the *Ahl al-Sunnah* and were too narrow-minded to understand the comprehensive rules they follow in establishing those principles.

The opposition of some people of *tariqa* outside the exalted *Sunnah* of the Prophet, to some secondary commandments of the Shari'a comes, as with that of the Mu'tazili School to the *Ahl al-Sunnah* in theological matters, from two different groups:

The first group become, as with Zamakshari, indifferent to the secondary commandments of the Shari'a, the taste of which they are unable to perceive, because they are attached to their way with a pure intention and are overcome by the pleasures they derive in following that way.

The other group consider those commandments inferior to the principles of *tariqa* because they are unable to comprehend them or to experience the profound pleasure they give.

The eighth clarification

Herein are explained eight dangers which an initiate may face in following *tariqa*.

The first danger

Some initiates who do not strictly follow the *Sunnah* of the Prophet, upon him be peace and blessings, may court danger by preferring sainthood over Prophethood. It has been proved in the *Twenty-fourth* and *Thirty-first Words* how much higher in rank Prophethood is in comparison with sainthood and how dim sainthood is when compared to Prophethood.

The second danger

They court danger by regarding some saints of excessive views as superior to the Companions of the Prophet and even of the same rank as Prophets. It has been decisively proved in the *Twelfth* and *Twenty-seventh Words,* and in the 'Addendum' to the *Twenty-seventh Word* concerning the Companions, that they had a very high rank on account of being the Companions of the Prophet, upon him be peace and blessings. Also, it is absolutely impossible for a saint, however great, to attain the rank of a Prophet.

The third danger

Some fanatical followers of *tariqa* prefer the daily recitations and the secondary principles of *tariqa* to the exalted *Sunnah* of the Prophet and go so far as to abandon the *Sunnah* in favour of the recitations of their *tariqa*. By becoming, in consequence, indifferent to the supererogatory commandments of the Shari'a of the secondary degree, they risk danger.

As proved in several *Words,* and proclaimed by the truth-seeking scholars of sainthood like Imam Ghazali and Imam Rabbani, the reward or degree acquired by carrying out a single religious obligation is more rewarding than a thousand commandments of the *Sunnah,* so also a single principle of the *Sunnah* is preferable to a thousand secondary acts of *tariqa*.

The fourth danger

Some followers of *tariqa* who go to excess risk danger by regarding inspiration as of the same kind as Divine Revelation. It has been decisively proved in some treatises including, primarily, the *Twelfth Word* and the *Twenty-fifth Word*, concerning the miraculousness of the Qur'an, that Divine Revelation is incomparably higher in rank and more comprehensive and sacred than inspiration, and that inspiration is very dim and narrow when compared to Divine Revelation.

The fifth danger

Some who pretend to Sufism but are, in reality, unaware of the truth of *tariqa*, become engrossed by the spiritual pleasures, enlightenment and wonder-working – granted (without being desired) to some followers of *tariqa* in order to reinforce the weak-willed, to encourage those lacking in zeal, and to lighten the tedium and troubles coming from service in the way of God – and come to prefer these over acts of worship, daily recitations and services, thus going into danger. However, as stated briefly in the 'Third Point' of the 'Sixth Clarification' above, and proved in several *Words*, this world is the realm of rendering service, not the realm of wages. Those who demand their wages here in this world for their religious acts and services will reduce the ever-lasting fruits of Paradise to the dying, transient fruits of this life, and, attracted by a manifestation of the Hereafter in this world in the form of a limited permanence, cannot look forward to the intermediate life or to the Hereafter with desire and longing.

The sixth danger

Some initiates who are not people of verification and truth run into danger by confusing the real and universal ranks of sainthood with their particular examples and shadows. As proved in the 'Second Branch' of the *Twenty-fourth Word* and in some other *Words*, the sun is multiplied through its reflections, which, despite having light and heat like the sun itself, are very faint in comparison with their origin. Likewise, the ranks of the

291

Prophets and the greatest saints have some shadows and reflections. When initiates enter those shadows, or receive some of those reflections, they see themselves as greater than the greatest saints and even the Prophets, and thereby fall into danger.

In order to escape all the dangers mentioned, including this last one, one should always take as guiding principles the essentials of belief and fundamentals of the Shari'a, and condemn any visions or experiences in opposition to them.

The seventh danger

Some people of enthusiasm and spiritual pleasures court danger by preferring vanity, airs and graces, exaggerated claims, and gaining the love of people and being a resort for them, to thankfulness and being in a state of entreaty and supplication to God, and indifference to people's love, attention and wealth. It should, however, be known that he greatest of the spiritual ranks is the servanthood of Muhammad, upon him be peace and blessings, which is exalted with the title or rank of being the Beloved of God. The foundation of such servanthood is thankfulness, entreaty, supplication, pious reverence, perception of human poverty and helplessness and indifference to people's belongings, love and attention. Although some great saints have sometimes displayed vanity, and airs and graces, and acted in an affected way before God, but unintentionally and for a temporary period, they are not, however, to be followed intentionally in this matter, for they are not guides in this respect, even though they themselves were guided.

The eight danger

Some selfish and impatient initiates desire to 'eat' in the world the fruits of sainthood which will be obtained in the Hereafter, and thereby fall into danger. Whereas, as proved in many of the *Words* and proclaimed in Qur'anic verses such as, *The life of this world is but comfort of illusion,*[37] a single fruit of the Permanent

---

37. *A. Imran,* 3.185.

World is preferable to a thousand orchards of this temporary one. So, those blessed fruits should not be eaten up here. If they are granted without our desiring them, we should be thankful to God and regard them not as a reward, but as a Divine grace to encourage us.

The ninth clarification

Out of numerous fruits and benefits of *tariqa*, I will cite here only nine briefly.

The first benefit

Through straightforward *tariqa*, one can attain, to the degree of certainty of seeing, full perception of the truths of faith which are the keys to, and means of, obtaining the eternal treasures in the Eternal World of happiness.

The second benefit

By setting, through *tariqa*, the heart to work, which is the centre and spring of the human factory, and thereby directing the other human faculties to their creative functions, one can attain true humanity.

The third benefit

By following *tariqa*, the believer joins a chain or caravan of saints in the journeying to the Intermediate World and the Hereafter, and he makes those saints friends in that way to eternity, thus being relieved of solitude and benefiting from their noble company in both this and the intermediate worlds. He also regards each of his spiritual masters as a support and strong proof against the attacks of doubts and, relying on their concern for him, he saves himself from falling into misguidance.

The fourth benefit

By experiencing the pleasure of knowing God through belief and of love of God coming from the knowledge of Him, he is relieved of utter solitude in the world and loneliness in the universe. As explained in many of the *Words*, the happiness in both worlds, and the pleasure without sorrow, as well as communion without loneliness, lie in the truth of beliefs and the Islamic way of life. As was stated in the *Second Word*, faith bears the seed of what is in effect a Tuba tree of Paradise.

It is through the training of *tariqa* that that seed germinates and grows.

The fifth benefit

By inwardly feeling, through *tariqa*, the truths contained in the religious duties, through spiritual alertness and the remembrance of God, he performs those duties willingly and enthusiastically, not like a slave compelled to a task.

The sixth benefit

He attains the station of reliance on, and absolute submission to, God, and the rank of being approved and loved by Him, which are the means for a true pleasure and consolation without grief, and familiarity and communion without loneliness and separation.

The seventh benefit

He saves himself, by means of sincerity and purity of intention achieved through *tariqa*, from disguised association of partners with God and degrading attitudes like show and pretence. He is also delivered, by purifying himself through the spiritual operations particular to *tariqa*, from the dangers caused by egotism and the carnal self.

The eighth benefit

Through turning in heart and mind toward God, and spiritual peace and sound intentions acquired through silent recitation of God's Names and reflection, in *tariqa*, he transforms his everyday acts into acts of worship and his ordinary dealings and transactions into deeds related to the Hereafter, thus making good use of the capital of his life-span in a way to make its minutes like innumerable seeds to multiply into seed-pods for his eternal life.

The ninth benefit

Through the journeying by heart and the unceasing struggle against the temptations of Satan and his carnal self, and the spiritual progress attained, he tries to be a perfect man. That is, by becoming a true believer and perfect Muslim, in other words, by attaining the truth or the essence of faith and Islam, and therefore reaching, as a representative of the universe, the rank of being a true servant of God, as well as being His addressee and friend, and a mirror reflecting His Names and Attributes, and by demonstrating his being the best pattern of creation, he proves the superiority of humankind to the angels and, by flying through the highest ranks of humanity with the Islamic wings of belief and practices, he gains, or even experiences, the eternal happiness while in this world.

> *Glory be to You, we have no knowledge save what You have taught us. Surely You are the All-Knowing, the All-Wise.*

> *O God, bestow blessings and peace on the Greatest Saint of Helping for all ages, and the Mightiest Pole of Sainthood for all times - our master Muhammad, the magnificence of whose sainthood and the degree of whose being beloved by God were manifested in his Ascension, and in the shadow of whose Ascension are all forms and degrees of sainthood contained, and on all of his family and Companions! Amen. And all praise be to God, the Lord of all the Worlds.*

***

ADDENDUM

In the name of God, the Merciful, the Compassionate

[This short addendum is of great importance, and is beneficial to everyone.]

There are many ways leading to Almighty God; all of these ways have been derived from the Qur'an, but some of them are safer and more comprehensive, and lead to the destination more directly than the others. The way I have derived from the Qur'an by my own defective understanding, depends upon a man's perception and confession of his *helplessness* and *poverty* before God's Might and Riches, and upon *affection* and *meditation.*

Man's perception and confession of his helplessness is a way as sure as the way of love of God, or even safer than that, since it elevates a man so as to be loved by God on account of sincere devotion to Him. Man's perception and confession of his poverty or inadequacy leads to the Divine Name, the All-Merciful. Affection is more effective than love and leads to the Name, the All-Compassionate. Meditation is more bright and comprehensive than love and leads to the Name, the All-Wise.

This way of ours is unlike some Sufi orders which have conceived ten steps to purify and sharpen ten outer and inner senses or faculties of man, and whose members prefer silent recitation of God's Names. It is equally unlike others which have adopted public recitation and seek to enable man to purify himself from all the defects contained in the seven stations of the carnal self.

Our way consists of four steps and, rather than being a *tariqa*, it is *Shari'a*, or the truth itself. The fundamental principles of this way consist in following the *Sunnah*, performing the religious obligations, avoiding the heinous, major sins, and in performing the five prescribed prayers properly, and in reciting litanies of praise and glorification of God after every prayer.

The first step of this way finds its expression in the verse, *Do not justify and hold yourselves as sinless.*[38]

The second step is indicated by the verse, *Be not like those who forget God, and He therefore makes them forget their own selves.*[39]

The verse, *Whatever good visits you is from God, but whatever evil befalls you is from yourself,*[40] points to the third step.

The final step is shown by the verse, *All things perish except His Face and His good pleasure.*[41]

The following is a brief explanation of these four steps:

The first step

As the verse, *Do not justify and hold yourselves as sinless,* suggests, man must never regard himself as infallible and sinless, since he loves his self, first, on account of his nature and innate disposition, in a way to sacrifice everything other than himself to satisfy it. He praises himself as though he were one worthy of worship, and holds himself to be free from every defect. He endeavors to prove himself free from guilt and defends himself passionately as though worshipping himself. Furthermore, he appropriates for his own self the faculties entrusted to him to praise and glorify God, the True Object of Worship, and thus becomes a referent of the verse, *who takes as his god his own desires and fancies.*[42]

The second step

As the verse, *Be not like those who forget God, and He therefore*

---

38. *al-Najm*, 53.32.
39. *al-Hashr*, 59.19.
40. *al-Nisa'*, 4.79.
41. *al-Qasas*, 28.88.
42. *al-Furqan*, 25.43.

makes them forget their own selves, teaches, man is oblivious of himself and is not aware of himself. When he thinks of death, he thinks of it in relation to others, and never attributes to himself decline and mortality. He holds back at the time of bearing hardships and rendering services, but considers he should be the first to receive the reward at the time of collecting fruits and enjoying benefits. A man can train and purify himself at this step by discharging his responsibilities, and being prepared for death, and by renouncing the reward he might obtain and the benefits he might enjoy.

The third step

As the verse, *Whatever good visits you is from God, but whatever evil befalls you is from yourself,* teaches, the evil-commanding self always ascribes good to himself and feels conceited, whereas in reality he should perceive his defects and insufficiency and give thanks to God and praise Him for whatever good he is able to do and whatever perfection he has. According to the meaning of the verse, *Prosperous is he who purifies it,*[43] his purification at this step is possible by knowing his perfection to lie in confession of his imperfection, his power in perception of his helplessness, and his wealth in acceptance of his essential poverty and inadequacy.

The fourth step

As the verse, All things perish except His Face and good pleasure, teaches, man, under the influence of his evil-commanding self, considers himself to be completely free and independent and existent of itself. Because of this, he goes so far as to claim some sort of Lordship for himself and rebels against his Creator, Who alone deserves to be worshipped. He can save himself from this perilous situation only by perceiving the following truth:

---

43. *al-Shams*, 91.19.

According to what each thing signifies by itself, and on account of its very nature, everything is essentially non-existent, contingent, ephemeral and mortal. But according to what it signifies with respect to something other than itself and on account of being a mirror reflecting the Names of the Majestic Maker and charged with various duties, each is a witness, it is witnessed, it gives existence and is existent.

A man can purify himself in this stage by perceiving that his existence lies in confession of his essential non-existence. He must know that when he considers himself to be self-existent, he falls into a darkness of non-existence as great as the universe. In other words, if he relies upon his individual existence and is unmindful of the Real Giver of Existence, he has an individual light of existence like that of a fire-fly and is drowned in the infinite darkness of non-existence and separation. If, on the contrary, he abandons pride and egotism and recognizes that he is nothing but a mirror in which the Real Giver of Existence manifests Himself, then he establishes a relation with all other beings and gains an infinite existence. For he who finds the Necessarily-Existent Being, the manifestations of Whose Names cause all things to come into existence, finds everything.

Conclusion

The four steps in this way of affection and meditation, and the individual's recognition of his own impotence and insufficiency, have been explained in *The Words*, which are concerned with knowledge of truth, the truth of the Shari'a, and the wisdom of the Qur'an.

Indeed, this path is shorter, because it consists of only four steps. A man's recognition of his impotence leads him to rely upon God alone, once he has succeeded in freeing himself from the influence of his evil-commanding self. Whereas, love, the sharpest way, can lead to the True Beloved only after a man perceives that the false beloved he is attached to after he is freed from evil-commanding self, is ephemeral.

Also, this way is safer, because instead of leading a man, under the influence of ecstatic love, to utter boastful words and make false claims such as being of a highest spiritual rank, it obliges him to recognize his impotence, poverty and essential imperfection.

Also, this way is a main 'highway', much broader and universal. For, in order to attain a constant awareness of God's presence, it requires neither the denial nor the ignoring of the actual existence of the universe, as is demanded by those who assert the 'Unity of Being' *(Wahdat al-Wujud)* or 'Unity of the Witnessed' *(Wahdat al-Shuhud)*. Instead, it admits the actual existence of the universe as proclaimed in the Qur'an, by ascribing it directly to the Majestic Creator. Considering the creation as things that signify something other than themselves, not as self-existent and working on their own behalf, and employing them on behalf of the Majestic Creator, and in the duty of manifesting His Beautiful Names and being mirrors reflecting them, it saves man from absolute heedlessness to make him always aware of Almighty God's presence, and opens up a way to Him through everything.

In short: This way considers beings as neither self-existent nor working on their own behalf, rather, beings function, according to this way, as signs showing not themselves, but something other than themselves.

***

Epigrams
SEEDS OF TRUTHS

In the name of God, the Merciful, the Compassionate
All praise be to God, and all blessing and peace be upon our master
Muhammad and on all his family and Companions.

1   The prescription for a diseased age, for crippled limbs, for disabled organs, is: follow the Qur'an.

2   For a great, greatly afflicted continent, for a once glorious, now humbled and wretched state, for an invaluable, now undefended people, the prescription is: unity under the guidance of Islam.

3   If you cannot turn between your fingers the earth and the other planets and all the stars as easily as you turn the beads in your rosary, you have no right to claim any part in creation: for all things are intertwined with all things.

4   It is as easy for the Power of God to raise all the dead on Judgement Day as to rouse, from its winter sleep, a single fly in springtime. Such Power is of the Essence of the Divine – it does not change, neither decaying nor diminishing, nor can it be impeded in any way. Being absolute, the Power of God admits no degrees – everything, vast or slight, is equal before it.

5   He who created the gnat's eye also created the sun.

6   He who arranged the flea's stomach also arranged the solar system.

7   Seeing the miraculous harmony in the universe, all material causes (supposing that they have any sort of independent agency) bow down, nor can they help but say: *Glory be to You! We have no power. Surely, You are the All-Mighty, the All-Wise!*

8   As befits the Oneness and Majesty of God, causes have

no reality or effect in the inner dimensions of the creation and functioning of the universe; as for its manifest, outward forms, they serve as a veil before the operation of Divine Power so that certain entities and events, seemingly disagreeable or banal, might not be attributed directly to It.

9   Where the Divine Power operates directly, in the inner dimension of everything, is pure transparency.

10   The visible, corporeal world is a lace curtain before the worlds of the Unseen.

11   The creation of even a dot in just the right place requires infinite power, the same that created the universe in its entirety. For every letter of this great book of the universe, especially every 'living' letter, has a face turned toward, and an eye staring at, one of its sentences.

12   As commonly happens at the end of Ramadan, people were scanning the horizon to catch sight of the new crescent indicating 'Id (the religious festival). No one saw anything. However, one old man claimed to have seen the new crescent. What he had seen was in reality the curve of a white one of his own eyelashes. Now, how could an eye-lash have any equivalence with the crescent? Then again, how could the motion of minute particles be taken in the place of the One Who manages the formation of whole species?

13   Nature may be likened to something printed, but not to the printer. It is a design, not the designer; a recipient, not the agent; a composition, not the composer; an order, not the orderer; and it is a collection of laws established by the Divine Will, laws [which our minds can grasp but] which in themselves have no power or material reality.

14   Attraction and being attracted are felt in human conscience (which is innate in man) because of the attractive power of truth.

15   The innate drive in things is not contradictory to their nature. For example, the urge of a seed to grow says: 'I will grow into such and such plant and produce fruit!' Then, it does what it says. An egg has an urge to life which says: 'I will be a chick.' Then, by God's leave, it becomes a chick. A quantity of water says, from an urge to freeze, 'I will spread myself more thinly on the ground.' Then, so as to avoid contradicting the water, hard, solid iron (pipes) make a way for it. Such drives and urges are manifestations of the Divine commands of creation, issuing from the Divine Will.

16   The Eternal Power provides ants with a leader and bees with a queen; the same Power would not deprive human beings of the leadership of a Prophet. The splitting of the moon is a miracle of the Prophet Muhammad demonstrated in the visible, corporeal world. His Ascension (to the Presence of God through the heavens) is a miracle demonstrated to the angels and other spirit beings in the world of inner dimensions: it proves and makes manifest the sainthood contained within his Prophethood. Also through that miracle, that most illustrious of beings extended and diffused his radiance, like a flash of lightning or a bright moon, into the world of inner dimensions.

17   The two halves of the proclamation of belief – *I testify that there is no deity except God, and I testify that Muhammad is His servant and Messenger* – mutually attest each other's truth. The first is the argument *a priori* for the second, and the second is the argument *a posteriori* for the first.

18   Life is a manifestation of individuality in the sphere of multiplicity; therefore, it leads to unity which can enable a single thing to come into the ownership of everything.

19   The spirit is a law with consciousness and a real, sensible existence: Divine Power has clothed it in an energetic envelope within a body of sensory organs. This spirit which exists in man is a counterpart to the laws of nature, which have merely

theoretical existence. Both are unchanging and permanent, and both have issued from the world of the Divine Commands. If the Eternal Power had clothed the laws with material existence, each would have been a spirit; and if the human spirit were stripped of consciousness, it would become an immaterial law.

20 Existents are seen by the agency of light, and their existence is known through life. Light and life are each discoverers.

21 Christianity will either become extinct or be purified [of its pagan elements] and abandon its struggle against Islam. It split several times and produced Protestantism which, in turn, split [into diverse sects and groupings] and [some of these] drew near to monotheism. Christianity will split further. Then, it will either die out or, finding before it the truths of Islam which include the essentials of the original religion of Jesus, will submit itself to Islam.

This very important truth is indicated in this saying of the noble Prophet, upon him be peace and blessings: *The Prophet Jesus will come back to the world and, joining my community, practise according to my Shari'a.*[44]

22 The majority of ordinary people are not drawn so much by [the strength of] proofs as by the sacredness of the origin or source of authority.

23 Ninety out of a hundred parts of the Shari'a – the indispensable, indisputable points or principles of Islam – may each be likened to a diamond pillar. What remains to be determined by the judgements of the authorities on Islamic law – the remaining ten percent of the Shari'a – may be likened to pieces of gold. Ninety diamond pillars are not to be left under the protection of ten gold pieces. Rather, the books, and arguments and judgements, of jurisprudents should serve as binoculars to see the Qur'an better, or as mirrors to reflect its meanings; they should not serve to veil or replace it.

---

44. Bukhari, *Mazalim*, 31; Muslim, *Iman*, 242; I. Maja, *Fitan*, 33.

24   Every individual qualified to practise *ijtihad* – the deri-
vation, from established principles of the Qur'an and *Sunnah*, of
legal judgements for new circumstances – can proclaim a new
law for himself, but he cannot generalize for others, nor for the
whole Muslim community.

25   Extending an idea to others must await its acceptance,
first, by the majority of scholars; otherwise, it will be regarded
as an 'innovation' contrary to the principles of Islamic jurispru-
dence, and therefore rejected.

26   Since man is created of a noble disposition, he pursues
truth. Sometimes falsehood finds him and he embraces it warmly. While searching for the truth, he is, in spite of his intentions,
captivated by misguidance and, thinking it to be the truth [he
was seeking], mistakes it for the truth.

27   There are numerous mirrors to reflect Divine Power,
each more subtle than the other. They range from water to air,
from air to the ether, and thence to the world of ideal forms,
and higher still to the world of spirits and even to time and ideas. A word multiplies a million times in the mirror of air. The
Pen of the Divine Power does this multiplying in a quite amazing way. Things are reflected in those mirrors with their apparent identities or both identities and characters (nature). The reflections of solid entities are each a moving lifeless form, but
the reflections of luminous, spiritual entities are each a living
form connected to the original. Even if the reflection (of a lumi-
nou entity) is not exactly identical to the original, it is not something other than the original.

28   Since the sun turns in convulsive movements around its
own axis, its fruits – the planets – do not fall. If it stopped moving, its fruits would scatter.

29   An idea is dark and spreads darkness unless it is illumined with light of the heart. As the cornea or white portion of
the eye, which can be likened to day, is not sufficient to enable

vision until it is combined with the iris and pupil [the dark portion of the eye], which can be likened to night, so the 'cornea' of an idea does not suffice for one to see the truth of it unless it is combined with the 'iris and pupil' of the heart.

30   Knowledge of something without conviction is little better than ignorance. Taking sides with or 'adopting' something is quite different from conviction in regard to it and attachment.

31   A fanciful, elaborate account of something bad can cause immature minds to stray.

32   A scholar should give guidance in the way a sheep feeds its young, not in the way a bird does. A sheep feeds its lambs on its milk, a fully-digested and processed substance, whereas a bird feeds its chicks on what it has half-chewed and then regurgitated.

33   The existence of a thing is dependent upon the existence of all its parts. Since the non-existence of a thing is, by contrast, possible through the non-existence of only some of its parts, a man of weak character tends to be destructive and act negatively as a way of proving his power.

34   Principles of wisdom and laws of truth cannot have the desired effect on the ordinary people unless the former are combined with the laws of the state and the latter with the bonds of power.

35   Injustice has placed on its head the conical fez of justice; treason has put on the cloak of patriotic zeal; *Jihad*, that is, Islamic struggle in the way of God and for the good of humanity is called aggression and violation of human rights, and enslavement is presented as emancipation. In short: opposites have exchanged forms.

36   Politics engaged in for personal interests is bestial.

37   A show of mildness to a hungry wild animal excites not

its pity but its appetite. Moreover, it then demands a further payment, after it has fed upon you, for feeding upon you.

38 Time has demonstrated that Paradise is not cheap, nor is Hell altogether futile.

39 The merits of the people regarded in the world as the elite lead them to haughtiness and oppression, whereas they should be inspired by those merits to be modest and self-effacing. Instead of arousing in mankind feelings of compassion and benevolence, the helpless destitution of the poor leads to their deeper captivity and subjection.

40 Honours and fineries are made presents of for the elite; shortages and defects and evil consequences are shared out among the common people.

41 The absence or the forgetting of an ideal leads minds to turn into themselves in self-interest.

42 The cause of all revolutions and societal corruption, and the root of all moral failings, are these two attitudes:

First: I don't care if others die of hunger so long as my own stomach is full.

Second: You must bear the costs of my ease – you must work so that I may eat.

The cure for the first attitude is the obligation of *zakat*, the alms-tax prescribed by the Qur'an. The cure for the second attitude is the prohibition of all interest-bearing transactions. The justice of the Qur'an stands at the door of the world and turns away interest, proclaiming – 'No! you have no right to enter!' Mankind did not heed this prohibition and have suffered terrible blows in consequence. Let them heed it now to avoid still greater suffering.

43 Wars between nations and states are being replaced by wars between social classes. For human beings no more wish to be wage-earners than they wish to be slaves.

44   One who takes an [Islamically] unlawful route to a lawful objective is often made to attain, by way of punishment, what is opposite to his goal. The reward for an un-Islamic love, like the love of Europe, is the pitiless enmity of the beloved.

45   Whatever is past as well as [present] misfortunes should be considered in the light of Destiny, and what is to come, and sins and questions of responsibility, should be referred to human free will. In this way, the extremes of fatalism (*jabr*) and the denial of a role for Destiny in human actions (*i'tizal*, the view of the *Mu'tazila*) may be reconciled.

46   One should seek solace neither in lamentations over one's failure in regard to what one cannot do, nor in demonstrations of impotence in regard to what one can do.

47   The wounds of an individual life can be healed. But the wounds that have been struck against the dignity of Islam and the honour of the nation are too deep to heal.

48   It sometimes happens that a single utterance may drive an army to defeat, as a single bullet may lead to the deaths of thirty million people. (A bullet fired by a Serbian private at the heir to the Austrian throne became the final pretext for the outbreak of the First World War, which resulted in thirty million deaths.) Under the appropriate conditions a [seemingly] insignificant act may cause its doer to be elevated to the highest of the high, as it may cause him to be reduced to the lowest of the low, according to the circumstances and conditions in which it is done.

49   A single truth can bring down a whole heap of lies. Again, a single reality is to be preferred to a whole heap of fancies.

50   He who attends to the good side of everything contemplates the good, and one who contemplates the good enjoys his life.

51   What energizes people is ambition and hope; it is the absence of hope that demoralizes them.

52   This exalted State collapsed. It had carried through centuries of self-sacrifice the banner and burden of Islamic Caliphate, the collective duty to fight for the protection and independence of the Muslim peoples, for the exaltation of the Word of God. Its collapse will be compensated in the future with the general happiness and full independence of the whole Muslim world – for its collapse is a calamity that urges us to develop brotherhood, which is the essence of our life as Muslims.

53   A demonstration of how the wheel of time can rotate backwards: the beauties of civilization are ascribed to Christianity which has no share in them; Islam is accused of encouraging barbarism and regressiveness of which it is an enemy.

54   A fine diamond though tarnished is always preferable to a piece of glass no matter how it has been polished up.

55   Those who regard matter as the origin of everything have limited their intellectual capacity to what their eyes can see. But eyes cannot see the domain of the spirit.

56   When a metaphor is appropriated by the ignorant, they take it literally as the reality, which opens a door for them to superstitions.

57   To represent someone as better than the virtues with which God endowed him does him no favour at all. Better describe everything as it really is.

58   Fame gathers to the famous what they do not truly own.

59   The sayings of the Prophet, upon him be peace and the blessings of God, are the authority and source for Islamic life, and the inspiration of truths.

60   The revival of the religion means the revival of the nation. The being of the religion is the light of life.

61   The Qur'an is a mercy for mankind; therefore it urges a civilization which really secures the greatest happiness of the greatest number.

Western civilization in its present phase is founded upon five negative principles:

1   It is founded and rests upon power; power tends to oppression.

2   It aims at the realization of individual self-interests; pursuit of their self-interests causes people to rush madly upon things in order to possess them.

3   Its understanding or philosophy of the nature of life is struggle; struggle causes internal and external conflicts.

4   It unifies the mass of its people on the basis of national and/or racial separatism, fed by swallowing up the resources and territories of 'others'; and racism leads to terrible collisions between peoples.

5   The service it offers to people is satisfaction of the novel caprices or desires it arouses in them; (whether the satisfaction is real or not) this service brutalizes people.

As for the civilization founded upon and sustained by Islam:

1   It rests upon right, not upon power; and right requires justice and balance.

2   It aims to encourage people to virtue, which is a spur to mutual affection and love.

3   Its understanding or philosophy of the nature of life is not struggle but mutual help, which leads to unity and solidarity.

4   It unifies people on the basis of a common religion in a common state, which leads to internal peace and brotherhood and a willing self-defence against external enemies.

5   Islam guides people to the truth. Therefore, besides en-

couraging them to scientific progress, it elevates them, through moral perfection, to the higher ranks of humanity.

Never break with Islam, for it is the guarantee of our survival; stick to it, heart and soul, or we shall perish utterly.

62   A general misfortune is the consequence of a failing in which the majority of the people have a part. While every misfortune is the consequence of a failing, it is also a door opening to a means of reward.

63   A martyr knows that he is still living. Since he does not experience the event of his death as death, he sees the life that he sacrificed for the sake of God as permanent and uninterrupted, indeed he finds it more refined.

64   The perfect justice of the Qur'an does not permit the taking of an innocent life, not even as a sacrifice for the whole of the rest of mankind. In the sight of Divine Power and Justice, a single life is equal in value to the life of the whole of mankind. Yet, there are people whose selfishness is such that they would, if they could, if the realization of their ambitions is frustrated, destroy everything, including the whole of mankind.

65   Timidity and weakness give encouragement to the agents of external enemies.

66   A benefit certain to come should not be renounced for fear of a harm that is only suppositional.

67   Politics at the present time is a disease like 'the Spanish disease' so-called, syphilis.

68   It is not uncommon for the sanity of a lunatic to be restored by telling him repeatedly that he is sane; and a good man can become bad after hearing repeatedly that he is bad.

69   As long as an enemy persists in his enmity, his enemy is a friend. As long as a friend maintains his friendship, his enemy's friend is an enemy.

70   Obstinacy in one's cause can lead one to regard a devil-ish person as angelic because he assists and supports the same cause, and then to call God's mercy on him. Equally, it can lead one to regard an angelic person as devilish because he opposes that cause, and then to call God's curse upon him.

71   What is a cure for one condition may be a poison for an-other. Excessive doses of a medicine can create new illnesses.

72   A community among whose members there is solidarity is a means created to get moving those who lack movement; one among whose members there is jealousy is a means created to bring to a halt those who are moving.

73   The sort of superficial unity which lacks substance, depth and sincerity, in fact breaks up a community making it slighter and weaker, just as a fraction multiplied by a fraction makes the resulting sum smaller. (As everyone knows, a whole number multiplied by a whole number leads to a sum which is greater than the two numbers: for example, three times two is six; but a fraction multiplied by a fraction leads to a sum which is smaller: for example, a third times a third is a ninth.) Thus, a community that lacks a sound and sincere unity will grow weaker by mere multiplication of numbers, by mere growth of population.

74   Not affirming that something exists is often confounded with affirming that something does not exist. The absence of a sign or evidence that a thing exists may justify someone not af-firming its existence if he is disinclined to accept its existence. But affirming the non-existence of something requires clear evi-dence that proves its non-existence. For not-affirming its exis-tence is doubt; whereas affirming its non-existence is denial.

75   Even if doubt upon a point of belief were to bring to nothing a hundred proofs for it, the truth of that point of belief would yet remain intact since the number of proofs for it abound in their thousands.

76   One should follow the consensus of the majority of the Muslim *ummah*. Following such a consensus, the partisans of the Ummayyads finally joined the *Ahl al-Sunnah wa l-Jama'ah*, though they had used to be, at the beginning, neglectful of the principles of Islam. But the Shi'a, who had been strict in following the principles of religion, became in the end Rafizites in part, since they preferred to remain a small minority.

77   When the pursuit of what is better or truer leads to dissensions, consensus on what is good and true should be sought. Consensus on what is good and true is always preferable to dissension on anything more than that. Thus, what is good and true sometimes turns out to be better and truer than what, in the abstract, appears to be better and truer. So, let a man declare by all means that 'My way is good and true'; but let him never claim that 'My way is the only way, the truest and best'.

78   But for Paradise, the torment of Hell could not be perceived or known as such.

79   As time grows older, the Qur'an becomes younger, its secrets and signs clearer and better understood. As light may be mistaken sometimes for fire, so force of eloquence may lead some to find excess in it.

80   Gradations of heat are measurable because of their present contrast with cold; likewise degrees of beauty are known by the admixture of ugliness. The Eternal Power of God is an essential attribute of Divine Being, necessary to His Essence. Since impotence cannot dilute it, there are no degrees of the Power of God, everything is equal before It.

81   Consider: the reflection of the sun in both the whole expanse of the sea and in the smallest wave or bubble of it has the same identity.

82   Life is a manifestation of the Oneness of God and brings the multiplicity to unity.

83   Among the people, who the saints are; on Friday, the hour when prayers are most acceptable; among the nights of Ramadan, which the Night of Power *(Qadr)* is; among the Beautiful Names of God, the Greatest Name; in a life, the time appointed for its death – these are not known to mankind. And because they are not known, the rest are also esteemed and given importance. A life of twenty years with an unknown end is preferable to a life of a thousand years whose end is known.

84   The outcome in the world of the evils done in it are a demonstration that their punishment is to come in the Hereafter.

85   In the sight of Divine Power, the provisioning of a life is as important as the life. Provision is produced by Power, apportioned by Destiny, and given out by Grace (Favour). Life is the sure, certain outcome of particular circumstances and events, and so it is witnessed. But provision is not sure and certain, it is not something obtained within a certain time. Rather, it comes by uncertain degrees, leading man to contemplation. Those who appear to die of hunger die before the sustenance stored in the body (as fat, for example) is wholly consumed; thus, what they die of is the diseases caused by alteration or abandonment of the routine form of nourishment.

86   The carcasses of animals constitute the lawful sustenance of many wild carnivores. By consuming those carcasses they both feed themselves and cleanse the surface of the earth.

87   Two morsels of food, one priced at ten cents, the other at ten dollars, which, usually, do not differ in nutritional value. For the sake of the few seconds of pleasure it may give to the sense of taste (which is, as it were, the inspector and doorkeeper of the factory of the stomach), is it not the meanest form of waste to prefer the morsel priced at ten dollars?

88   When a pleasures draws you, you should say, 'Enjoyed

it already'. A man who adopted this principle did not spend the money which he used to build a mosque, now called the Mosque of 'Enjoyed it Already'.

89 Where the majority of Muslims are not hungry, a life of ease may appeal to the imagination. But where the majority of Muslims are hungry, no Muslim can choose to live such a life.

90 Rather than welcoming with a smile transient pleasures, one should so welcome transient ailments. Pleasures past lead one to sigh with regret, the cry 'alas!' being a sign of a hidden ailment. Ailments past lead one to sigh with relief, which is news of a hidden joy and a favour to come.

91 Forgetting is a blessing in some ways. It leads one to suffer the hardships of the present day, and forget the accumulated store of the hardships past.

92 There are degrees of Divine Favour in every misfortune. Be mindful of the greater misfortune so as to be thankful for the favour of the lesser misfortune. Concentrating on the latter and so exaggerating it only doubles it, making it greater. Its exaggerated reflection in the heart or its imagination makes it real and that gives serious trouble to the heart.

93 In social life each man has a window called status through which he looks out to see others and be seen. If the window is built higher than his real stature, he tries, through vanity and giving himself airs, to stretch himself up to be seen taller than he really is. If the window is set lower than his real stature, he must bow in humility in order to look out, to see and be seen. Humility is the measure of a man's greatness; just as vanity or conceit is the measure of a low character.

94 The self-respect which a weak man should wear before a powerful man becomes, if the powerful man assumes it, self-conceit. The humility which a powerful man should wear before a weak man becomes, if assumed by a weak man, self-abase-

ment. The solemnity of an administrator in his office is dignity, while his humility in the same place is self-abasement. The same solemnity in his house is self-conceit, but his humility there is humility. Forbearance and sacrifice (of one's rights) on one's own account is good and a virtue; but when done on behalf of others, it is bad and a treason. An individual may bear patiently with whatever is done to him personally; but it is impermissible for him to, on behalf of the nation, bear patiently what is being done to the nation. Whereas pride and indignation on behalf of the nation are commendable, on one's own behalf they are not.

95 Entrusting an affair to God without, at the outset, taking all the necessary precautions, and making the necessary arrangements with regard to it, is laziness. To leave to God achievement of the desired outcome, having first done all that one can, to God, is to put one's trust in God. Contentment with what one has obtained as a result of all one's efforts is a laudable virtue which encourages further efforts and reinvigorates one's energy and industry. Contentment with what one already has is to lack endeavour.

96 A man is free to obey or disobey the commandments of the Religious Law. He is likewise free to obey or disobey the Divine Laws of creation and life. While the return for one's obedience or disobedience to the former is usually deferred to the Hereafter, the return for obedience or disobedience to the latter usually comes in this life. For example, the reward for patience is success, while the punishment for indolence is privation. Industry brings wealth, and steadfastness victory. Any claim to justice which has not observed equality is a false claim.

97 Likeness and identity cause rivalry and conflict. Complementarity is the basis of solidarity. An inferiority complex provokes arrogance. Weakness of character provokes haughtiness. The origin of hostility and finding fault is impotence. Curiosity about something leads one to learn it.

98   The Power which has created everything with a disposition singular to it has restrained mankind and all the animals, first of all, by means of their neediness (especially hunger), and ranked them in a certain hierarchy. It has also saved the world from disorder and confusion and, by making neediness a motive for civilization, secured progress in every field.

99   Boredom schools a person in (fantasies of) indulgence. Despair leads him into intellectual deviations. Spiritual ignorance, the darkness of the heart, brings him to distress and depression.

100   When men become womanish through over-cherishing worldly whims and fancies, women become mannish through crudity and authoritarianism.

If an attractive woman enters a company of men, sentiments of display, rivalry and envy are aroused among them. The unveiling of women, that is, their mixing freely among strange men, has led to the encouragement in people of bad morals.

101   Pictures and statues, especially obscene ones, have a significant part in the present sinfulness and ill-temper of mankind.

102   Statues – which are prohibited by religion – are either an injustice fixed in stone, or a fantasy personified, or ostentatious pride monumentally exaggerated.

103   If a man follows the injunctions of Islam, strictly and with firm belief and complete sincerity, his desire and efforts to find Islamic solutions to new problems are a tendency toward perfection. Such desire or efforts on the part of one who is so indifferent to the Islamic injunctions as to place himself outside the circle of Islam are a tendency toward ruin. The right course of action in a time of 'tempests and earthquakes' is not to throw open the doors to far-fetched efforts to derive 'new' laws from the Qur'an and *Sunnah;* rather to close the doors and even shut-

ter the windows against innovations. Those who are already indifferent to religious duties, free and easy about whether they do them or not, must not be rewarded with special dispensations to release them altogether from those duties. Rather, they should be urged with severe warnings to do them as best they can.

104   The sphere of being to which we belong bears some resemblance to a living organism. If it were compressed to the size of an egg, would it then be a kind of animal? Or if the sphere of a microbe were to be enlarged to the dimensions of our sphere, would one be like the other? If the sphere is living, it has a soul. If the universe were compressed to the size of a man with its stars forming the elements of that man's constitution, would it not be a conscious, animate being? God has created so many kinds of living organisms like this.

106   There are two kinds of Shari'a or Divine Laws. One: the kind issuing from the Divine Attribute of Speech, which regulate the deeds and states of man who constitutes the normo-universe. Two: the kind which, greater in number, govern the creation and operation of the universe. They issue from the Divine Attribute of Will and regulate the movement of the universe which is a macro-human. This second group of laws is wrongly called nature.

Angels constitute a mighty community and convey, represent and embody the Divine commandments of creation and order, issuing from Divine Will and called the Laws of Creation and Order.

107   When you compare the senses of a microscopic creature and those of a man, you will confront an astounding, mysterious truth. Man is in the form of the *sura Ya Sin*; in him is inscribed the *sura Ya Sin*.

108   Materialism is a spiritual plague that has infected man-

kind, as a Divine punishment, with a sort of terrible fever. So long as false propaganda and cynicism spread among people, so too will that plague.

109   The unhappiest of men, who suffers the greatest distress, is the one with nothing to do. For doing nothing is a close relative of non-existence, whereas working hard is the vigour of the body and the awakening of life.

110   The benefits that come from banks, which are houses of usury and open the doors for usury, go to the unbelievers, especially to the most unjust and the most dissolute among them. The harm they bring to the Muslim world can hardly be denied. They cannot be left alone just because they happen to benefit a portion of mankind. The unbelievers, especially those of them who are aggressive and on a war footing with the Muslims, do not deserve to be respected or defended.

111   The sermons in the Friday prayers are to remind the congregation about the essentials of Islam, not to expound to them its abstract, theoretical points. Therefore, the Arabic phrases in which those essentials are expressed are the best fitted for this reminding.

When the Qur'anic verses are compared with the sayings of the Prophet, upon him be peace and the blessings of God, it will be noticed that even the most eloquent of human beings cannot compete with the eloquence of the Qur'an.

Said Nursi

***

Indexes

Index of names of persons, places, peoples and books

Index of words